AMI PEDAHZUR **THE ISRAELI SECRET SERVICES
AND THE STRUGGLE AGAINST TERRORISM**

COLUMBIA UNIVERSITY PRESS   NEW YORK

COLUMBIA UNIVERSITY PRESS
Publishers Since 1893

NEW YORK   CHICHESTER, WEST SUSSEX

Library of Congress Cataloging-in-Publication Data

Pedahzur, Ami.

The Israeli secret services and the struggle against terrorism / Ami Pedahzur.

p. cm.

Includes bibliographical references and index.

ISBN 978-0-231-14042-3 (cloth : alk. paper) — ISBN 978-0-231-51161-2 (e-book)

1. Terrorism—Israel—Prevention. 2. Intelligence service—Israel. 3. Secret service—Israel. I. Title.

HV6433.I75P47 2009

363.325'156095694—dc22

2008025949

BOOK DESIGN BY MARTIN N. HINZE

CONTENTS

LIST OF FIGURES VII

ACKNOWLEDGMENTS IX

INTRODUCTION 1

ONE THE EMERGENCE OF ISRAEL'S
COUNTERTERRORISM DOCTRINE 14

TWO THE PATH TO THE DEFENSIVE MODEL AND BACK 30

THREE RESCUING HOSTAGES 47

FOUR THE LEBANESE PUZZLE 66

FIVE NEW CHALLENGES FROM
THE WEST BANK AND GAZA 75

SIX THE GLOBAL CHALLENGE
OF IRAN AND HEZBOLLAH 83

SEVEN NEW RIVALS, OLD RESPONSES 94

EIGHT A WAR AGAINST AN ELUSIVE ENEMY 111

NINE THE SECOND LEBANON WAR AND BEYOND 128

TEN FIGHTING THE TERRORISM PLAGUE 135

NOTES 151

GLOSSARY 187

INDEX 201

FIGURES

1.1 The Israeli Intelligence Community 4

1.2 Israeli Thwarting Forces 5

1.3 Palestinian Terrorist Groups, 1957–2007 6

1.4 Summary of the Argument 11

1.1 Fedayeen Attacks, 1952–1957 24

1.2 Palestinian Terrorists Attacks, 1952–1956 26

2.1 Operation Wrath of God
and Palestinian Retaliation Operations 41

8.1 Suicide Attacks and Targeted Killings
During the Al-Aqsa Intifada 122

10.1 Palestinian Terrorist Attacks
on Israeli Targets, 1948–2006 136

10.2 Palestinian Terrorist Attacks
on Israeli Targets by Tactic, 1993–2007 139

ACKNOWLEDGMENTS

WHILE WORKING ON THIS book, I traveled a long and fascinating road. A number of dear friends and colleagues made my work possible. Arie Perliger, who put his own work aside in order to help me accomplish this mission, conducted interviews in Israel, oversaw the work of research assistants, gathered material himself, and read, commented, and corrected the various chapters over and over again. This book could not have been completed without his constant support, and I owe him so much for that. Special thanks to Alex Bialsky, my research assistant, who spent many days interviewing policy-makers, former members of the intelligence community, and senior military officials. He also worked tirelessly in gathering information and meticulously checking and corroborating facts. I owe profound thanks to the interviewees as well, some of whom require the protection of anonymity in the pages that follow.

I owe great thanks, too, to Anne Routon of Columbia University Press, who was my partner in this journey and has always been there to support me with her reassuring words and wise advice. Bruce Hoffman, a dear friend, helped this project from its very first days. I greatly value his advice and support and appreciate his pushing me to write the best book that I could. Gregory McNamee did a wonderful job of editing the manuscript and furthering that goal.

Gary Freeman, Zoltan Barany, Martha Crenshaw, and Leonard Weinberg generously offered friendship and support, comments, and ideas that helped shape my analysis. I was lucky to spend many hours in discussions with Yoav Gelber, a retired lieutenant colonel in the Israeli Special Forces and diligent historian. He encouraged me to look into the arguments and facts repeatedly and make sure that everything added up. Equally important, he shared with me his experiences as a young officer during the years in which Israel shaped its counterterrorism doctrine.

I am also grateful to the National Security Studies Center at the University of Haifa and to its directors, Gabi Ben-Dor and Dan Schueftan, who helped me in a time of need.

I am lucky to have Galit, Rotem, Shahar, Doron, and Nissim, who were always there to help me with good advice, as well as love and patience. In closing, a word of gratitude and love to my parents, Max and Ruth Pedahzur. My father first instilled in me an interest in politics in general and intelligence affairs in particular. I dedicate this book to him.

THE LITERATURE OF COUNTERTERRORISM makes an analytical distinction between the war model, the criminal-justice model, and the reconciliatory model of terrorism. Terrorism, from the perspective of the war model, is regarded as an act of revolutionary warfare. The criminal-justice model considers it a criminal act, and the reconciliatory model sees it as a political problem. In line with these respective views are their different responses to terrorism. The war model places the responsibility for response on the military, which can marshal all the means at its disposal to quash terrorist activities. The criminal-justice model places accountability for contending with the phenomenon on the police, whose actions are restrained by the state legal system.[1] The reconciliatory model leaves the problem in the hands of politicians and diplomats, who deal with its root causes through negotiations and compromise (see table I.1). Standing in the background is the defensive model, which does not deal directly with the terrorists or their grievances but rather protects the targets of terrorism.

These models are not mutually exclusive, and democratic regimes tend to apply one or more of them at the same time. However, when democracies sense impending threat, they tend to minimize the use of the reconciliatory model and extend the use of defensive measures. If the struggle against terrorism takes place beyond the borders of the democratic state, policymakers are apt to worry less about limiting their methods to constitutionally approved ones and tend to favor the war model.

Thus far, most of the literature devoted to these models has dealt with the "democratic dilemma," a predicament presented by Paul Wilkinson in his seminal work *Terrorism and the Liberal State* (1986):

> The primary objective of counter-terrorist strategy must be the protection and maintenance of liberal democracy and the rule of law. It cannot be sufficiently stressed that this aim overrides in importance even the objective of eliminating terrorism and political violence as such. Any bloody tyrant

even after 9/11 would you say it this way?

TABLE 1.1 **COUNTERTERRORISM MODELS: A TYPOLOGY**

MODEL	DEFENSIVE	RECONCILIATORY	CRIMINAL-JUSTICE	WAR
GENERAL FEATURES	Terrorism is regarded as a physical and psychological threat	Terrorism is regarded as a political problem	Terrorism is regarded as a crime	Terrorism is regarded as an act of war
STATE AIMS AND MEANS	Protecting potential targets and victims of terrorist attacks	Addressing the root causes of terrorism	Arrest and punishment of terrorists while adhering to the rule of law	Elimination of terrorism
CONSTITUTIONAL AND LEGAL ASPECTS	In most cases, corresponds with elements of liberal democracy; exceptions can be found when practices undermine civil liberties	Corresponds with the law	The state responds to terrorist incidents in compliance with state criminal law and is subject to constant judiciary regulation	Laws of war dictate counterterrorist measures, and consequently, any constitutional or legal considerations are secondary
AGENTS	Police, private security companies, firefighters, and medical first responders, as well as other state and municipal agencies	Policymakers, brokers, diplomats	Police and the criminal-justice system	Intelligence and military units

Sources: Ronald D. Crelinsten and Alex Schmid, "Western Responses to Terrorism: A Twenty-five Year Balance Sheet," *Terrorism and Political Violence* 4, no. 4 (1992): 332–333; Peter Chalk, "The Liberal Democratic Response to Terrorism," *Terrorism and Political Violence* 7, no. 4 (1995): 10–44; Peter Chalk, *West European Terrorism and Counter-Terrorism: The Evolving Dynamic* (London: Macmillan, 1996).

can "solve" the problem of political violence if he is prepared to sacrifice all considerations of humanity, and to trample down all constitutional and judicial rights.[2]

Over the two decades following the publication of *Terrorism and the Liberal State,* many scholars have devoted attention to the tension between the adherence to democratic values and the ways and means employed by democracies in the struggle against terrorism.[3] While most scholars emphasized the question of democratic acceptability, little attention has been given to the other side of the coin—the relative effectiveness of each model in coping with security challenges posed by terrorism. I will address this issue using the Israeli case study. Furthermore, I will look into the various causes for selecting and maintaining particular models and assess the consequences of such decisions for national security. Throughout, I will consider the evolution of these models in light of the evolution of the Israeli intelligence community and counterterrorist military forces, as well as of Palestinian terrorist groups (see figures I.1, I.2, and I.3).

THE SHAPING OF A COUNTERTERRORISM DOCTRINE

Israel has never developed an unambiguous and official doctrine for countering terrorism, as Boaz Ganor clearly shows through his interviews with policymakers and heads of the security establishment.[4] Each of them, when asked about the goals that should be defined in the struggle against terrorism, had a somewhat different objective in mind and suggested a different response. On one end of the spectrum is Binyamin Netanyahu, who believes that terrorism can be eliminated all together and thus adheres to the war model. The former head of Mossad, Shabtai Shavit, agrees with Netanyahu that terrorism can be eliminated. However, he contends that this policy cannot be executed because of constraints imposed by the international community. Others, including the present head of Mossad, Meir Dagan, and the former chief of staff of the Israeli Defense Forces, Amnon Lipkin-Shahak, set the bar lower. They argue that terrorism can be contained only to the extent that it does not affect policymakers.

A survey of over six decades of counterterrorism policies indicates that the hard-liners have the upper hand. In the vast majority of cases, Israel's struggle against terrorism fits the war model. Although this finding is not surprising, the preference for the more military model is not self-evident. The immense intelligence efforts and thwarting operations carried out by Israel have brought about short-term accomplishments. However, a retrospective analysis of the evolution

FIGURE I.1 **THE ISRAELI INTELLIGENCE COMMUNITY**

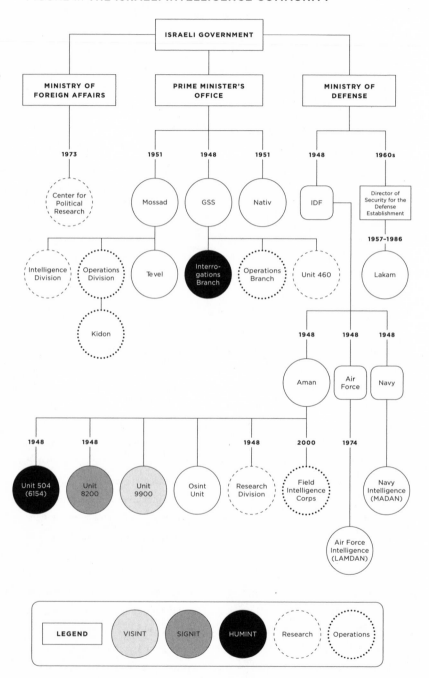

FIGURE I.2 **ISRAELI THWARTING FORCES**

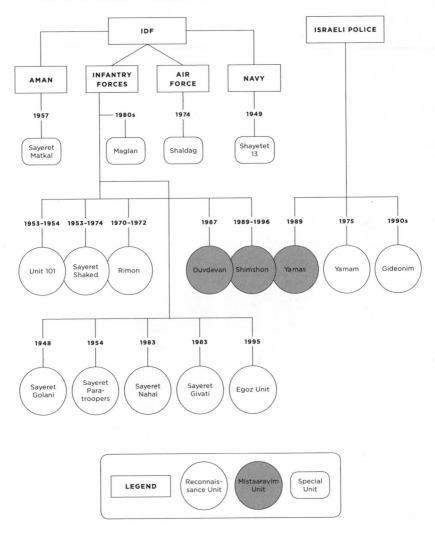

of terrorism committed against Israel demonstrates that the long-term aims of stamping out terrorism or even containing it have not been achieved. Organizations that suffered setbacks did not dissolve; they simply changed form. Terrorist tactics that Israel was able to suppress were replaced by other, often much more devastating modes of operation.[5] In terms of psychological and preventive or deterrent warfare, success was only partial. While state leaders and heads of the

FIGURE I.3 PALESTINIAN TERRORIST GROUPS, 1957-2007

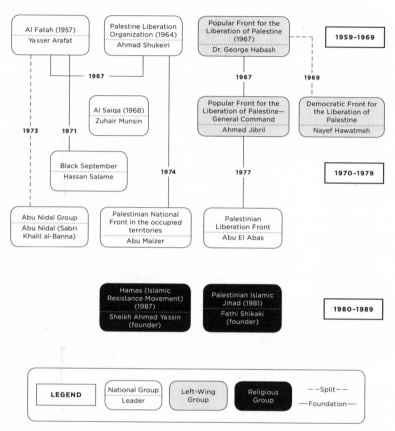

security establishment basked in the glorified status accorded to Israel as a major power in the field of counterterrorism, the psychological effect on Palestinian and Lebanese fighters was of no great consequence.[6] Not only were they not deterred from continuing to strike at Israel, but their efforts also intensified over the years, and support for the militants among their respective publics only swelled.

Why isn't the war model more effective? The well-known benefits of superior technology and troop size, which are featured in military literature as significant components in deciding wars, do not constitute an advantage in the struggle against terrorism. Unlike military struggles, the lack of symmetry between the state and the terrorists often works in favor of the latter. Many of the groups that employ terrorism are not institutions, and they tend to splinter or change

form frequently. They likewise lack a systematic war doctrine or organizational memory, which prompts them to seek constantly means that will help them realize the goals they have set for themselves. They usually do this by copying the tactics of other terrorists who have proven themselves "successful." If a certain tactic does not meet expectations, it is abandoned, and the quest for alternatives begins again. Intelligence and military security organizations tend to exhibit high levels of institutionalization, a fact that is usually considered an asset. In the struggle against terrorism, however, this is not the case. Institutionalization means cumbersome bureaucracy and lengthy response time. By the time an intelligence organization may have identified the changes in a terrorist group and the armed forces have subsequently made adjustments to cope with them, the terrorists are already in the midst of the next transformation. Furthermore, intelligence and military forces rely on a long-term organizational memory encoded in thick tomes of procedures and written with a substantial investment of deliberation and calculation. Hence, their natural tendency is to rely on accumulated experience and thus to respond to the terrorists' innovativeness modifying methods drawn from an existing repertoire, which are not necessarily relevant to the challenges immediately facing them.[7]

A great deal of scholarly attention has been given to the reasons for and obstacles to successful innovations in security organizations, mostly notably the armed forces. Yet few scholars addressed innovations that were considered or adopted in the face of challenges posed by substate actors. This could be because such innovations are less visible and have a lesser impact on the security establishment as a whole. In most cases, an innovation in the counterterrorism or insurgency realms would include the introduction of new technologies and tactics of small-scale warfare, an expansion of the roles of elite forces, and the establishment of new designated units.

Despite its dominance in the literature, not all the scholars use the term *innovation*. In her research of the American intelligence community and its counterterrorism efforts, Amy Zegart uses the term *adaptation* instead. She sees adaptation as an organizational change of a substantial scale that leads to improved fit between the organization and its environment.[8] These two terms are not synonymous, but in this context they refer to very similar phenomena.

The lack of consensus regarding the definition of a military innovation leads to some theoretical difficulties that become crucial in the area of counterterrorism. Adam Grissom sees military innovation as a "change in operational praxis that produces a significant increase in military effectiveness as measured by battlefield results." The problem with this definition is that it does not make a distinction between the very adoption of an innovation and its outcomes. In contrast, Michael Horowitz emphasizes the need to separate the change from the outcome to avoid tautology. I concur with this contention. Innovation precedes its outcome. The degree of success of an innovation should be measured against the stated goals of those who introduced it as well as its ability to mitigate the phenomenon for which it was introduced and its effect on the broader national-security interest.[9]

THE ARGUMENT

Barry Posen suggests that in order to implement a military innovation, the intervention of policymakers, preferably with the assistance of maverick officers, is necessary. A failure of cooperation between civil policymakers and service personnel may end up in the stagnation of the organization. Yet with regard to counterterrorism policies, unlike other situations that require innovations, the higher ranks of the political system operate under a complicated set of pressures. Terrorism is a psychological tactic that is aimed at civilians. A terrorized public that is not satisfied with the government's response to terrorism can cut short the careers of elected leaders. Thus, policymakers feel pressured to counter the *psychological* impact of terrorism. The "defensive model" has proven to be successful in offering physical protection to civilian centers. Yet applying it is usually a long process, sometimes much longer than the tenure of an elected policymaker. Hence, it does not have the same instant impact of the war model. Political enemies and, more important, constituents can portray politicians who opt for the defensive model as "hesitant." Successful offensive operations, which take place immediately after a terrorist attack, reassure the terrorized public, boost morale, and carry political perks that are very appealing for elected officials. Their directives to the military to acquire new technologies, expand the counterterrorism capabilities of existing units, and establish new ones results in no mean measure from these pressures. In the case of intelligence organizations, pressures applied to the heads of the organizations to deliver the goods trickle down to all divisions and are particularly felt by agents working in intelligence gathering and interrogations. The perpetual race against the clock in the attempt to get hold of information forces operatives and interrogators to seek new effective measures in obtaining information. These may include experimenting with new methods for applying physical and mental pressure on informants and detainees. During the first intifada, for instance, there was great pressure on Israeli General Security Service (GSS) investigators in the Gaza Strip to provide counterterrorism intelligence. The large amount of interrogates and the demands and pressure placed by the heads of the GSS on interrogators led to several cases where attempts to extract information from detainees were accompanied by brutal violence. In some cases, it led to several incidents of death. If these new methods are successful, however, heads of state are then inclined to glorify the armed forces and intelligence agencies. On the other hand, failure is an orphan, and when there is failure, members of the security establishment are often required to pay the price.[10]

Another explanation for military innovations, according to Adam Grissom, relates to the struggle among the various organizations and units over scarce resources. New security challenges force branches of the armed services to compete and innovate in order to remain relevant and protect their resources. Terrorism is no different. However, since policymakers are eager to find a response that will reassure their constituents, they upgrade the struggle against terrorism to the top of their agendas. This opens a window of opportunity for different security branches that aspire to contribute to this struggle. The more importance that policymakers attribute to the campaign against terrorism, the more eager the heads of the organizations are to increase the potential role of their respective organizations in this campaign. Successfully persuading policymakers carries the potential of enhancing the reputation of the organization and securing resources. However, the immediate outcome of such competition among intelligence organizations is the unwillingness to cooperate and share knowledge and information. This can have a devastating impact on the struggle against terrorism. In operational units that place emphasis on status symbols and esprit de corps, the problem is by no means less complicated. Unlike most security branches, elite units whose goal is to undertake complicated scenarios take pride in their ability to think and operate outside the box. Hence, as military analyst John Nagl suggests, while the commanders of other units serve as gatekeepers who are usually reluctant to approach new challenges, the commanders of special units are eager to engage and thus prove their superiority over other units, as well as enjoy glory and secure resources. On certain occasions, this enthusiasm may affect the presence of mind required by the officers who lead these units. Consequently, commanders may insist on taking on operations that do not entirely conform to the training or particular skills of its members. A prominent example in this regard is the conduct of the heads of the security system in Nachshon Wachsman's case in 1994. While Sayeret

Matkal was selected to carry out this rescue operation (and hostage rescue is not its main designation), the Yamam unit, whose specific designation is hostage rescue, did not take part in the operation.[11]

This fits into Stephen Rosen's explanation regarding the structure of military innovations.[12] He contends that an innovation requires an alignment of senior and mid-level officers who will introduce and promote it as well as the supportive institutional arrangements necessary to protect it. The senior officers who present and advocate a new paradigm gather around them successful young officers who are enthusiastic about the novel approach and opportunities that may be associated with it. Such a process is very likely to happen among intelligence and special-operations officers. Through their highly specialized training and clandestine operations, such officers are more open to creative ideas and at the same time are less visible to the higher echelons of the security establishment, which lessens their prospects for promotion to commanding roles beyond their own units. The nature of terrorism and its perpetrators opens a window of opportunity for such officers. As intimated earlier, highly technological minor tactical warfare is considered more suitable for counterterrorist operations than the use of traditional military doctrines and troops. The adoption of the tactics that these officers advocate is liable to create a self-fulfilling prophecy. The heads of their organizations as well as policymakers will embrace these officers for their counterterrorism expertise. This is likely to result in the promotion to key roles in the security establishment. From this position, they are likely to reject alternatives to their doctrine and at the same time act to increase the importance of counterterrorism operations within the army, subsequently creating more functions and filling them with their peers.

The main arguments that I will raise in this book are as follows (see figure I.4). Terrorism, in most cases, should not be considered a major threat to the national security of a country. Yet it has a much stronger impact on the public in comparison with other threats. When adopting a counterterrorism policy, elected officials are highly aware of this fact. Public officials are very much interested in mitigating the psychological effect of terrorism and in reassuring their terrorized constituents that they are taking action in order to solve the problem. This leads them to put more emphasis on the war model, which has been proven to be effective in offering immediate relief to the psychological impact of terrorism, rather than the defensive model, which offers better results in the long run. Leaders of security organizations, which traditionally have been in charge of other duties in the state's national security framework, see the struggle against terrorism as

FIGURE I.4 **SUMMARY OF THE ARGUMENT**

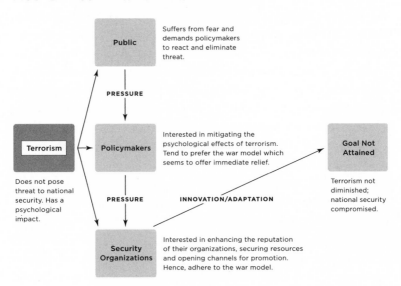

a window of opportunity for enhancing the reputation of their organizations, obtaining resources, and gaining promotion. Thus, even if the options advocated by policymakers do not seem to be highly effective in responding to the problem, they will be hesitant to seek alternative routes. Rather, they will introduce innovations within their own frameworks. Moreover, for the reasons mentioned earlier, organizations will compete with one another rather than cooperate. While the continuous attempts to find offensive responses to terrorism serve the interests of both the policymakers and the organizations, they offer only a partial solution to the problem itself. At the same time, these attempts distract security organizations from their original roles in the state's national security framework and thus undermine strategic interests.

SOURCES OF INFORMATION

My purpose in writing this book is twofold. First, I want to assess the Israeli counterterrorism policy in terms of its effectiveness and test the ability of the aforementioned hypotheses to assess the outcomes of intelligence and military innovations in the realm of the struggle against terrorism. Second, I am interested in telling the story of Israel's counterterrorism endeavor. My aim is to reach both academics who are interested in conceptual issues related to counterterrorism and readers from different walks of life who simply have an interest in the Israeli story. To do so, I highlighted the main theoretical issues in this introduction as well as in the conclusion, while the rest of the chapters will focus upon offering a detailed account of this interesting and challenging effort.

Writing a book on Israeli counterterrorism, especially from the perspective of the war model, is not an easy undertaking. We are speaking of intelligence and military organizations in which secrecy is a fundamental element of their very existence. These institutions will do everything possible to prevent the disclosure of their various modi operandi. I was aware of this fact from the very beginning of my research for the book. Hence, the book does not purport to provide a full chronology of Israel's struggle against terrorism by describing each case. Its aim is to assess the counterterrorism models that Israel has chosen to employ. To do so, I included only those case studies that were documented with enough credible and accessible information.

My research method involved several levels. The bulk of the research material was collected from unrestricted, public-domain sources that any citizen of Israel and abroad has access to without much difficulty. These are academic sources, memoirs by members of the intelligence community, books by journalists and re-searchers, journalistic investigations, and articles published in newspapers and on the Internet.[13] A major challenge was to verify the authenticity of the informa-tion. To this end, every item that eventually made its way into the book had to rely on two independent sources. If incongruities were found, additional sources were brought in. At a later stage, one-on-one interviews were conducted with former members of the intelligence community and the army, as well as with policymak-ers. The aim of the interviews was to inquire into disputed items and to obtain a personal and unmediated perspective on issues discussed in the book. The inter-viewees were not asked to divulge and did not divulge classified details.

The reality that some of the facts found in the media and in secondary sources were proven wrong forced me to omit a large number of case studies whose inclusion would have been beneficial for this book. Based on the interviews, I concluded that certain cases have yet to be explored by either journalists or the academia. It will probably take many more years before the files become accessible for research outside the intelligence community. Therefore, I chose to present a sample of case studies.

The team of researchers and I, who worked long and hard on the collection and verification of the materials, did our best to present the reader with a por-trayal that was as close as possible to the sometimes-elusive reality. Nevertheless, despite repeated processes of gathering and double-checking our facts, I cannot certify beyond the shadow of a doubt that there were no inaccuracies or over- sights. Research for this book made me realize—if only to a small degree—the feelings and fears that members of the covert agencies have to contend with on a daily basis. While I can step forward and apologize to my readers for mistakes that might have occurred in my research, members of the counterterrorism com- munity do not enjoy this privilege. At the end of the day, after submitting the information they gathered and the assessments they made on the basis of this information, they must return home cognizant that a mistake on their part, no matter how small, might very well be paid for in human lives.

Finally, it is worth noting what this book is not about. Although most of the text revolves around violence and counterviolence between Palestinians and Israelis, it does not deal directly with the Arab-Israeli conflict. I am not looking into the root causes of the violence, and I have no intention of putting the blame on someone. The subject is complicated and contentious, and such a discussion is way beyond the scope of this book. Yet I cannot hide the fact that besides my training as a political scientist I am also an Israeli, who, incidentally, never served in any of the intelligence branches. I served in the Medical Corps and became acquainted with the world of intelligence only during my years as a student and then as a lecturer at the National Defense College. My background as an Israeli helped me a lot in completing the research for the book; however, it can also be seen as a cause for bias. This has always been on my mind, and I have tried to control this bias. I truly hope that the book reflects more of my academic side than my national origins.

A last point: Like most people who follow conflicts in general and the Israeli- Arab one in particular, I also have political views. I think that moral debates about violence are essential. Both Israelis and Palestinians are constantly criti- cized for using excessive violence and causing harm to innocent civilians. Like so many others, I have opinions and emotions regarding this issue. However, in this volume, in order to focus on the aforementioned research questions and the following debates, I had to leave the moral aspect aside. This does not mean that I find it of lesser importance.

CHAPTER ONE THE EMERGENCE OF ISRAEL'S COUNTERTERRORISM DOCTRINE

THE COUNCIL OF DELEGATES (Vaad Hatzirim), led by Chaim Weizmann, was the board in charge of the daily affairs of the Jewish Yishuv before the establishment of Israel. As far back as 1918, thirty years before the State of Israel came into being, the Council of Delegates founded the Intelligence Bureau, the first Jewish Palestine-based information service. In charge of the Intelligence Bureau was Levi Yitzhak Schneorson, a former member of Nili, the Jewish underground movement that operated in Palestine and assisted the British military forces during World War I, mainly by providing intelligence on the status of the Ottoman Army. The organization first operated out of an office in Jaffa and later relocated to Jerusalem. Intelligence Bureau agents recruited Palestinian informants who, for a certain price, would disclose information on prominent Arab figures, Palestinian nationalist groups, and even plots of land that Arabs had put up for sale. One of the critical subjects was the collection of intelligence regarding groups whose members planned on harming Jews. The information was then passed on to the Council of Delegates and in certain cases to the secret police of the British Mandate authorities.

A short while after the Haganah was conceived in 1920, its commanders began to create an intelligence department that in due course formed the basis for the Shai (from the Hebrew acronym for Sherut Yediot, "information service"), which was officially established in 1933. The head of the organization was Shaul Avigur, who established a human-intelligence (HUMINT) infrastructure throughout the country. Shai intelligence handlers were appointed in charge of regional districts, and in each district, agents were planted who provided handlers with information. Avigur was responsible for collecting information items and disseminating them to Haganah commanders. However, despite the efforts of Avigur and his people, the Great Arab Revolt, which broke out in 1936, took the Shai and the Yishuv leadership by surprise.[1]

THE RESPONSE TO THE 1936 REVOLT

The revolt began with attacks against Jews in mixed cities, but violence quickly spread to agricultural settlements and transportation routes throughout the country. Unlike previous violence waged against the Yishuv, this time the attacks were well planned. Up until the outbreak of the events, Shai officials assumed that the Arabs in Palestine lacked a central leadership and operated mainly on a regional and familial or clan (*hamula*) basis. The foremost reason for the failure to identify the development of a new kind of central leadership was that Shai local operatives gathered intelligence only on regional *hamulas* without crosschecking their items with each other, and they vehemently guarded their own information-collection areas. There was no main intelligence-processing center within the Shai organization, so local operatives worked almost independently. In 1921, Haj Amin al-Husseini was appointed mufti of Jerusalem, the highest-ranking religious ruler in Palestine, and in 1922 he became the head of the Muslim High Council of Palestine, which managed Muslim life there. Al-Husseini brought together the heads of the biggest and most important *hamulas* in Palestine, as well as intellectuals and political leaders, under the control of a new organization called the Supreme Arab Committee. The mufti's ability to form and coordinate this committee, which was established in 1936 in order to manage the Great Arab Revolt, was a task unprecedented and hence overlooked.[2]

The committee led the events from the second day of the revolt and controlled the uprising for a period of three years. Eventually it forced the Shai to alter its basic assessments and improve its HUMINT network in Palestinian society. One of the lessons drawn from the intelligence failure of 1936 was the need to expand intelligence-gathering efforts among the Palestinian population by installing Shai intelligence handlers in Palestinian communities. This type of agent would have a good command of the nuances and codes of the Arabic language and a deep familiarity with the inner workings of Palestinian society. Ezra Danin, a citrus grower, founded the Shai Arab Department. Most of the handlers he was in charge of did not have a background in intelligence work; they were essentially watchmen and cattle dealers who knew the local language and culture of the residents. The Haganah also rebuilt its Nodedet detachment, a roving field-intelligence corps founded as a special unit of the Haganah during 1933–1935, which spread out into the countryside to locate pockets of organized Arab resistance and neutralize them before they could develop operational capabilities. Even so, the extensive efforts of the Jewish forces did not bear the anticipated results.[3]

The British Mandate authorities finally suppressed the revolt. The British forces were experienced in anticolonialist activity and imposed collective punishments on Arab neighborhoods and villages that sheltered the rebels. The British additionally conducted mass arrests and executed more than 150 men found guilty of illegal arms possession or of participating in or aiding violent activities. By the end of the revolt, in 1939, the Arab population was in a state of collapse. More than six thousand people had been killed during the uprising, and another six thousand were incarcerated. More than two thousand homes had been destroyed, and the agricultural infrastructure of most Arab villages had been critically damaged. In addition, commerce with the Yishuv was paralyzed, resulting in extensive unemployment. The mufti of Jerusalem fled in fear of the Mandate authorities; after a long period of wandering, he found refuge in Nazi Germany.[4]

In 1940, Shai underwent additional reforms, which included the establishment of a national headquarters whose function was to centralize the activities of the local branches as well as to initiate a counterespionage department. The purpose of this department, called Ran, was to track down Jews who were collaborating with the British Mandate authorities. Some two years later, under the leadership of Yisrael Zblodovsky (Amir), the Shai began to take shape as a bona fide intelligence organization. Its headquarters started out in an apartment on Melchett Street and later relocated to an ordinary-looking building at 85 Ben Yehuda Street in Tel Aviv. Above the entrance to the building hung a sign reading "Consulting Offices." In practice, the apartment served as the nerve center of the regional and designated departments of the organization. The General Department functioned as the Yishuv's secret police, its main job was the surveillance of Jewish offenders. The task of the other designated departments—the Jewish and the Communist—was to gather information on political factions from both right and left that refused to accept the Haganah's authority. The Arab Department, which would later serve as the foundation for the Arab arm of the Shin Bet (the first letters of "security service" in Hebrew), was in charge of intelligence activities among Palestinian populations all over the country.[5]

In 1945, the Shai special forces broadened their range of activities. The organization began to gather intelligence from "open" (unrestricted) sources. At the top of its list were the media. It began conducting basic research on demographic and economic trends as well as the customs and conventions of the Palestinian populace. Equal importance was devoted to laying down the infrastructure for the development of signal intelligence (SIGINT) departments. Although Shai activities were still relatively limited, its technical department and the Haganah signal services engaged in the wiretapping of British and Palestinian communication networks. With the assistance of cryptographic experts, they intercepted British Army communications and decrypted its codes.[6]

THE UN PARTITION RESOLUTION

On November 30, 1947, one day after the United Nations General Assembly voted to approve the partition of Palestine between the Jews and the Arabs, three Palestinians ambushed a Jewish bus traveling from Netanya to Jerusalem. When the bus passed by the airport near Lod, it came under a hail of bullets, and five passengers were killed. During the following weeks, the attacks spread to Jewish neighborhoods in mixed towns and cities such as Jerusalem, Jaffa, and Haifa. The most notable attack in the port city of Haifa took place on December 30, 1947, when thirty-nine Jewish laborers were massacred at the city's oil refineries. In Jerusalem the most prominent attack occurred four and a half months later, on April 13, 1948, when a medical convoy consisting of a military armored truck, ambulances, and several cars was attacked on its way to Mount Scopus in Jerusalem. As the convoy drove near the Sheikh Jarrah neighborhood, militants lying in ambush detonated electric mines that had been planted on the road. Some of the cars flipped over from the explosions, and immediately after, shots were fired and grenades were thrown at the convoy. Seven hours after the battle initially broke out, the gunfire finally ceased. Seventy-eight of the convoy passengers, including doctors, nurses, and employees of the Hebrew University were killed, many of them burned alive inside the cars.[7]

These larger-scale operations demonstrated to the Shai that while the Yishuv was improving its intelligence and operational faculties, the military capabilities of the Palestinians had also advanced dramatically. Even though local cells executed many of the attacks, once again there was evidence of an external guiding hand. This was in effect the Supreme Arab Committee, which was reorganizing under the leadership of the mufti who had returned from exile. The Supreme Committee opposed the UN decision on the partition and sought to undermine it by activating militias composed of local paramilitary units and led by the mufti's cousin, Abdel-Kader al-Husseini. Another important organization was the Arab Salvation Army, which numbered more than three thousand volunteers from various Arab countries who were deployed to Palestine under the leadership of Fawzi Al-Qawuqji, a Lebanese-born Arab nationalist who had received his military training at the Military College in Istanbul. He participated in the Syrian rebellion against the French in 1932 and in 1948 was appointed commander of the Arab Salvation Army. The army was established by the Arab League in order to seize control of Palestine after the withdrawal of the British and thus prevent the Jews or the Supreme Arab Committee from taking command of the area.[8]

Despite severe attacks, the Yishuv intelligence units were much more prepared than they had been a decade earlier. Informant networks recruited by Shai from the various echelons of Palestinian society provided the intelligence agency with vital strategic information. For example, Shai recruited one of the senior clerks from the Supreme Arab Committee, who, when learning of the military actions planned by the committee in response to the UN partition decision, passed them on to his operators. In another example, a Shai agent relayed information about Arabs in Tsefat who were planning to dig a tunnel into the Jewish market center. This information was one of the leading factors in the state leadership's decision to conquer the city. The Shai technical department exhibited impressive capabilities in intercepting transmissions between Palestinian forces and those of other Arab countries, as well as among the different arms of the Palestinians forces inside Palestine. Members of the unit discovered that Husseini's people were using a telephone cable from Palestine to Cairo that was laid near the fields of the Jewish agriculture school Mikveh Israel. In a secret operation, they connected eavesdropping devices to the cable, enabling Shai to listen in on the talks between Husseini's commanders and the Egyptian military command. In another case, Shai officer Tuvia Lishansky attached an eavesdropping device to the telephone cable that ran between Al-Qawuqji's headquarters in Jaba village and his forces in northern Palestine. With this device, they discovered that an attack was planned for February 1948 on Kibbutz Tirat-Zvi. This information helped the Haganah repel the Palestinian attack.

Senior Shai officials who received information on the tension between the Supreme Arab Committee and the Salvation Army also engaged in attempts to divide and conquer. They negotiated with the heads of both organizations and took advantage of the rift to further the Yishuv's interests. In a meeting on April 1, 1948, in the village of Nur A-Shams near Tulkarm, Yehoshua (Josh) Palmon, a senior Shai officer, met with Fawzi Al-Qawuqji and convinced him not to take part in the fighting that had broken out between the Haganah and Husseini's army. The Shai also kept channels of communication open with the Mandate authorities. In February 27, 1948, the Shai received information that Abdel-Kader Husseini's men had prepared huge explosive devices in Bir Zeit that were to be installed on two stolen military trucks and blown up on King George Street in Jerusalem. Chaim Herzog, the Shai liaison officer to the British forces in Jerusalem, communicated this information to the Mandate authorities. Two days later, Mandate intelligence agents returned his favor by informing him of the Palestinian intention to blow up a building at the Hebrew University of Jerusalem on Mount Scopus.[9]

Along with the intelligence-gathering divisions that they developed, the heads of Shai also took advantage of the Shahar Unit from the Palmach. Fighters from this elite undercover unit were trained to infiltrate and blend in completely with the Arab population—a process called *histaarevut,* a neologism made up of two Hebrew words meaning "to disguise oneself" and "to become Arab"—in order to collect information and engage in special clandestine operations. The members of this unit, known as *mistaarvim,* were the sons of families that had immigrated to Israel from North African or Middle Eastern countries and who had grown up near Arab neighborhoods and had a good command of the Palestinian dialect. Before seeing action, the recruits underwent a demanding preparation course. They were trained as commando fighters and were proficient in sabotage, sharpshooting, and communications. In addition, they would learn Islamic cultural codes, the lifestyles of Palestinians in the cities and villages, and the customs that set apart various Arab communities all over the country.

From their base, nestled in Kibbutz Alonim in the Jezreel Valley, small teams of fighters dressed up as Arabs would set out on missions in Jewish-Arab mixed cities such as Haifa and Jaffa, as well as remote villages and Palestinian cities in the West Bank, including Nablus and Hebron. The reputation gained by the Shahar troops among the Haganah and Palmach led the higher command of these organizations to dispatch them on special missions in neighboring Arab countries. Although most of these missions were devoted to gathering intelligence, in some cases they were also asked to carry out attacks on Arab leaders.

Sheikh Nimer Al-Hatib of Haifa was the target of one of these operations. In February 1948, a cell from the Shahar Unit was sent to execute this charismatic preacher. However, the protective shield around the sheikh called for a change of plans. One week later, members of the unit sat in a car waiting for the sheikh's entourage, which was just returning from a visit in Damascus. In the neighborhood of Kiryat Motzkin, the convoy was identified, and a vehicle whose function was to slow down the preacher's car shot after him. A few minutes later, another car joined the chase. The sheikh was able to observe the second car only when it pulled alongside his own car. Several seconds later, shots rang out from the same car, and four bullets struck his body, severely injuring the sheikh and putting him out of political action.[10]

THE FORMATION OF THE ISRAELI INTELLIGENCE ORGANIZATIONS

Immediately after Israel's declaration as an independent state on May 14, 1948, Shai faced a new challenge. The combined attack of the Arab armies on the fledgling state made quality military intelligence an essential priority and sidelined the preoccupation with Palestinian attacks.[11] The fighting between the Israel Defense Forces and the Arab armies continued for almost a year, concluding in the Rhodes Armistice of 1949. Israel and Jordan, Syria, Lebanon, Egypt, and Iraq signed this agreement, which established the borders of Israel.

On the basis of consultations in June 1948 with Reuven Shiloah, the prime minister's advisor for intelligence affairs, who later also founded Mossad, and Chaim Herzog, former head of intelligence for the Haganah, Prime Minister David Ben-Gurion decided to create three intelligence institutions. Isser Beeri, who had been the chief of Shai, was assigned to head the military intelligence branch, known as Aman. The functions of this organization were to compile intelligence on the armies of Arab countries and maintain internal military security. Isser Harel, head of the Tel Aviv district of Shai, was appointed in charge of the Internal Security Services (later to become known as the Shin Bet), which dealt with gathering information within the sovereign territory of the State of Israel and counterespionage. These two institutions, with lieutenant colonels as their commanders, were subordinated to the IDF. Then, at the end of the 1948 war, the Political Department of the Ministry of Foreign Affairs was established. Its aim was to collect information outside Israel. Boris Guriel, the head of the political department of the Haganah, was appointed as head of the new Political Department, but he also continued to report to Shiloah.[12]

Toward the end of 1949, Ben-Gurion decided to institute the first structural reform of the Israeli intelligence community. One of the main reasons for this decision was the ongoing struggle for authority among its various arms. Reuven Shiloah understood that these tensions were detrimental to the effective functioning of the intelligence community and proposed that there be an overriding institution to coordinate intelligence services and security. In April 1949, the Varash—Committee of the Heads of Services—was formed. For its first convention on April 8, the heads of the various intelligence arms and the commissioner of the

Israeli police force, Yehezkel Sahar, were all summoned. Varash had no clear mandate, though, and its activities soon tapered off. In July 1949, Shiloah suggested to Ben-Gurion that an institution should be created and called the Central Agency for Intelligence and Security Problems, whose chief would also be advisor to the prime minister on intelligence affairs. The principal aim of the planned organization was to avert jurisdictional rivalry among the intelligence departments, in particular between Aman and the Political Department. However, the very debate over its proposed establishment was cause for discontent, as Chaim Herzog from Aman and Isser Harel from the Shin Bet made clear to all.[13]

On December 13, 1949, Ben-Gurion took the matter into his own hands. He assigned Shiloah to establish and head the organization. Shiloah and his people were consequently attached to the Ministry of Foreign Affairs. One of their critical functions was to set up a unit for collecting intelligence beyond Israel's borders. Until that point, the activities of the various intelligence organizations were not geographically limited, so that all of them—and particularly Aman— maintained independent information-gathering networks outside of Israel. The small unit, whose very creation provoked strong objections from both Aman and the Political Department, provided the infrastructure for the future founding of the Central Institute for Intelligence and Security—the full name of the initial version of Mossad. The unit's activities gained momentum between 1952 and 1963, when Isser Harel, who also headed Shin Bet, was appointed to command the organization. Harel received full support from Ben-Gurion to fashion the structure of the services in accordance with his activist vision and was placed in charge of the Security Services.[14]

MECHANISMS OF CONTROL OVER PALESTINIAN CITIZENS OF ISRAEL

In its first few years, the State of Israel embarked on a rapid process of establishing sovereignty. At the same time the Palestinians underwent a severe battering politically, economically, and militarily. About half of the Palestinians—over 700,000 men and women who had lived in the territory now declared part of the sovereign State of Israel—were exiled or fled, becoming refugees in the countries bordering Israel. The local political elites found haven in Arab countries, while the Supreme Arab Committee foundered once more. Palestinian refugees on both sides of the border had family ties to one another and were united in their frustration over the results of the war. Still, despite their outrage, the disintegration of their political leadership and the urgent need to cope with the new reality prevented any immediate formation of an organized opposition movement, much to the relief of the Israeli intelligence. A Palestinian Shai informant summed up the situation in these words: "The refugees are in a terrible state and living in dire poverty; [they are] paying no attention to politics and do not care whether they are ruled by King Abdullah or have their own government."[15]

It was not only their dismal economic situation and the deterioration of their political leadership that prevented the Palestinians from pursuing their political struggle. In 1949 the Israeli government announced the institution of martial law in three major areas of the state: the Galilee, the "Little Triangle" in the eastern Sharon plain, and the Negev. The military administration served as a means of monitoring Palestinian Israeli citizens, whom the defense establishment perceived as a potential fifth column. For the Shin Bet, which adopted the operating methods of its predecessor, the Shai, the evolving situation was almost ideal. Thanks to the strict dictates of the military administration, the local Shin Bet handler could virtually control the everyday lives of the region's residents, who were subject to his authority. If he so desired, he could assist them by granting work permits and travel and business licenses; if not, he could withhold these "kindnesses." In exchange, the residents were required to provide information. The names of those who refused to collaborate were added to the list of Palestinians classified as subversive and anti-Israeli. This was a highly effective tool for recruiting informants, mainly among Arab civil servants, who knew that if their names were included in the list, they risked the loss of their livelihoods.

This supervisory mechanism of the military administration and the Shin Bet also served to drive a wedge among the different factions of Palestinian Israeli citizens. A few religious and ethnic groups, such as the Druze and the Circassians, enjoyed preferential treatment, while others, and mainly the large Muslim minority, were relegated to the margins of the public sphere. Furthermore, the security establishment's tight control over Arab politics was instrumental in the formation of Arab Zionist parties whose lists of candidates for the Knesset were determined by the Shin Bet and dominant Mapai party in consultation with the heads of the extended family clans. The alternative for those Palestinians who declined to be a part of these institutions, which were devoid of political content and at best represented clan interests, was to join the Communist Party, which was associated with the Soviet Union and subject to the close supervision of the Shin Bet. The Shin Bet's policy toward Palestinian Israeli citizens, which to a large extent was reminiscent of operational methods used by internal intelligence services in authoritarian countries, yielded results. Israeli intelligence succeeded in uncovering a number of local organized initiatives in the early formation stages and prevented them from developing into any type of threat.[16]

FIRST INDICATIONS OF THE ISRAELI COUNTERTERRORISM DOCTRINE

Unlike the Palestinians who remained in Israel and who maintained the clan structure so familiar to the Shin Bet, the scattered refugees had to build their social frameworks anew. The forced uprooting from their homes and the refugee state in which they found themselves laid the ground for political turmoil. Palestinian political structures that began to develop outside of Israel's borders compelled intelligence organizations to invest much greater efforts abroad than locally. The biggest challenge was posed by groups of fedayeen organized and run by the intelligence services of supportive Arab countries, most notably Egypt. In the 1950s they infiltrated Israeli borders in order to attack isolated settlements and ambush vehicles on the roads. The Israeli leadership was forced to formulate a counterterrorism doctrine and instructed military intelligence to find ways for coping with the challenge.[17]

Toward the end of July 1953, as the initial signs of the escalation of fedayeen terrorist attacks appeared (see figure 1.1), the IDF created its first counterterrorism force—Unit 101. The decision to form this unit was essentially unplanned. Mishael Shacham, commander of the IDF Jerusalem Division, wished to settle a score with Mustafa Samueli, a resident of the village of Nabi Samuel who was alleged to be one of the most active fedayeen in the region. Shacham appealed to the commanders of the Paratroopers and Givati infantry brigades to take on the assignment of infiltrating the village and striking Samueli; however, both commanders rejected his request. On the other hand, Shacham's subordinate, Major Ariel Sharon, who at the time was studying Middle Eastern history at the Hebrew University in Jerusalem, reacted more favorably. The twenty-five-year-old Sharon collected seven of his friends, all of them highly experienced infantry combatants, and in the dark of night led them to Samueli's house and planted an explosive device. Although the blast caused minimal damage to Samueli's house and obliged the force to withdraw quickly from the waking village, Shacham realized the significant potential of dispatching a small commando unit to perform such raids. The idea he proposed to Chief of Staff Mordechai Maklef was to form an elite unit whose fighters would raid concentrations of civilians and military personnel in the areas where infiltrators came from. They would quickly cross the border into Jordan or Egypt, strike the targets, and disappear as if they

FIGURE 1.1 **FEDAYEEN ATTACKS, 1952–1957**

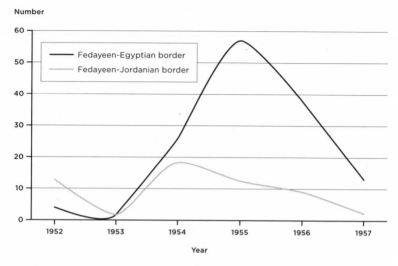

Number

Source: NSSC Dataset on Palestinian Terrorism, www.nssc.haifa.ac.il

never had been there. Maklef gave his approval to the establishment of such a unit, much to the dismay of the head of the IDF Operations Division, Moshe Dayan, who objected to the general idea that the IDF activate commando units whose goal was retaliatory attacks. Regardless, on August 5, 1953, the directive to establish the unit was issued.

In Camp Sataf in the hills of Jerusalem, Sharon and his deputy Shlomo Baum started shaping the Israeli counterterrorism doctrine. They trained their soldiers in land navigation, survival, and close-quarters combat. Sharon led the unit, which had been recruited by means of the friend-brings-a-friend method, with an informal atmosphere that was very similar to the Palmach units and later became the trademark of IDF elite units. While during the course of training great demands were made on the soldiers, back on base they enjoyed a number of rewarding perks. They were allowed to walk about with an unkempt appearance and were not required to adhere to the prevailing military discipline. Sharon and his men would also spice up the typical drab IDF menu with meals cooked from the wild animals they hunted in their leisure hours. The decision to introduce behavioral precedents that were different from the conventional IDF ones was not arbitrary. The militia nature of Unit 101 also enabled the political echelons to deny the fact that commando operations were in fact carried out by IDF soldiers.

Despite the highly qualified military capabilities displayed by soldiers of Unit 101, the inaugural special force was in fact incorporated into the Paratroopers Brigade a little while after its establishment. This was mainly due to the criticism leveled at Prime Minister David Ben-Gurion and Ariel Sharon, commander of the unit, in the wake of the operation at the Qibya village in Samaria on October 14. The raid on Qibya was carried out in retaliation for the murder of members of the Kanias family—a mother and her two children—by infiltrators. The Israeli public demanded a fitting act of retribution; however, this time as well, the Paratroopers Brigade was reluctant to lead the operation. Sharon, on the other hand, showed full readiness to carry out the action. Ultimately, the strike team consisted of a platoon of Unit 101 and two and a half Paratroopers platoons. Sharon led the forces, which overpowered the village after four hours of heavy fighting. At that point, the act of retribution was executed. Sharon first selected a number of buildings in the center of the town, including the school, the police building, a coffeehouse, and residential homes. Next, a Unit 101 cell commanded by Shlomo Gruber cleared out the buildings and sabotaged them. Hurrying, the soldiers did not check to see that the buildings had been vacated. At 3:20 in the morning, when the forces began their march back to Israeli territory, the ruins of forty-two buildings remained behind them in Qibya. The next day, it became evident that during the course of the operation sixty-nine Palestinians had been killed, half of them elderly people, women, and children. Many of the victims had been inside the buildings while they were blown up. There was an outcry of world public opinion, and ten days after the operation, the United Nations Security Council condemned Israel.

To the world, Ben-Gurion argued that Israeli civilians, refugees from Arab countries, or Holocaust survivors had taken the law into their own hands and carried out the operation. Domestically, his tone was quite different. Sharon was summoned to a meeting with Ben-Gurion and was required to provide explanations. Despite the overall positive impression that Prime Minister Ben-Gurion had of the young officer, the first IDF commando unit was disbanded. From an operational point of view, the unit had not succeeded in reducing the level of fedayeen terrorism (see figure 1.2), and after it was dismantled Palestinian violence continued in full force. This was demonstrated most notably in the infamous attack at the Maale Akrabim road in March 1954, when a bus commuting from Tel-Aviv to the southern city of Eilat was ambushed and attacked by Palestinians who breached the Jordanian border. The terrorists killed twelve passengers, while a child and a woman who had played dead were the only ones to survive.[18]

FIGURE 1.2 **PALESTINIAN TERRORIST ATTACKS, 1952–1956**

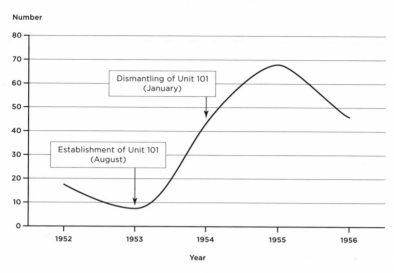

Source: NSSC Dataset on Palestinian Terrorism, www.nssc.haifa.ac.il

At any rate, the dismantling of the unit did not hurt Sharon's military career—quite the opposite. Unit 101 was not fully disbanded, and Sharon was appointed as the commander of the 890 Battalion of the Paratroopers. His soldiers from the unit joined him, and together they turned the conservative Paratroopers Battalion into a unit that specialized in retaliatory attacks against fedayeen strongholds.

The raids undertaken by Unit 101 were not the only manifestation of the Israeli inclination toward the war model. By the mid-1950s, Israel performed the first counterterrorism-related assassination. The target was Colonel Mustafa Hafez, who held one of the most sensitive positions in Egyptian intelligence, namely commander of the Palestine unit. His position included mounting espionage missions in Israeli territories and thwarting Israeli intelligence efforts at recruiting and activating agents in the Gaza Strip. In the spring of 1955, Hafez's range of authorities was extended. The commander of the Egyptian army, General Amar, put him in charge of six hundred fedayeen fighters who had been assembled into a battalion and trained for action by Egypt. Under his brazen leadership, Hafez's soldiers were transformed from a nuisance into a genuine security risk. At its worst, during the week of April 1–7, 1956, dozens of cells numbering some two hundred soldiers were able to penetrate Israeli borders. They attacked civilians and soldiers in Lod, Kfar Habad, and the moshavim of Shafrir and Stariya and even reached the main road from Tel Aviv to Ramla. The terrorized citizens of Israel were afraid to leave their houses.

The intense activities of the young Egyptian intelligence officer were a source of great concern for Moshe Dayan, who by then was the chief of staff. He saw Hafez as directly responsible for the fedayeen battalion's successes and applied pressure on the chief of Aman, Colonel Yehoshafat Harkabi, to deal with the problem. Harkabi did not waste time. He approached Rehaviah Vardi, commander of the 154th Unit of the Intelligence Corps, and asked him for ideas on how to eliminate Hafez. Avraham Dar, a Mossad operative who was sent to Egypt in 1951 to establish a network of informants in the Jewish community there, was designated to help Vardi plan the operation. He had a personal incentive to take part in this operation. His Egyptian network was exposed in July 1954 in an attempt to plant a bomb in a movie theater in Alexandria. Two of its members were executed, while the others were put in prison for life.

The main obstacle was the tight circle of security that surrounded Hafez after an earlier assassination attempt by Unit 101 had failed. The two officers rolled up their sleeves and produced a series of plots that were designed to get around Hafez's bodyguards. Among other ideas, they proposed that a letter bomb or a poisoned fruit basket be delivered by post to Hafez. These schemes were rejected for fear of harming other innocent persons. Then Dar had an inspired idea. One of the operatives engaged by the southern unit of the 154th, twenty-five-year-old Suleiman Al-Talalka, turned out to be a double agent who was also in the service of the Egyptian intelligence. Israeli intelligence did not inform him that his cover was blown; instead, they decided to exploit the young Bedouin's loyalty to Egyptian intelligence to their own benefit. Early in the summer of 1956, Al-Talalka was summoned to the 154th Unit's headquarters in Be'er Sheva. The officers awaiting him appeared troubled, a fact that clearly piqued his curiosity. After much pleading, the Israeli intelligence people were finally "kind" enough to inform him that they were planning a top-priority operation in the Gaza area and that they were debating whether to saddle him with the grave responsibility of carrying it out. The double agent could hardly contain himself in his efforts to persuade his superiors that he was worthy of executing the operation, and, after much deliberation, they seemed satisfied. Al-Talalka became even more excited when he learned of the goal of the operation—consigning a new code to the most senior Israeli agent in the Gaza Strip. Al-Talalka was simply stunned when he heard the identity of the "agent"—Lutfi Al-Akawi, the chief of the Gaza Police. In fact, Al-Akawi never colluded with Israeli intelligence, and the story was a pure fabrication.

In the late afternoon hours of Wednesday, July 11, 1956, two agents of the 154th accompanied Al-Talalka on his way from Be'er Sheva to the Gaza Strip. Among his belongings, he carried the autobiography of the renowned German Field Marshal Gerd von Rundstedt. As far as Al-Talalka was aware of, the book contained the codes that were being sent to Al-Akawi. His dispatchers even showed him a copy of this book before wrapping it up in order to satisfy his curiosity. One detail not made known to Al-Talalka was that the copy of the book he saw with his own eyes was not the item he carried. The package among his effects contained a copy whose inner pages had been carefully removed; in their place was an explosive device.

The double agent did not disappoint his Israeli dispatchers. After parting and wishing him good luck, they continued to follow him closely for a long while. Instead of making his way to Al-Akawi's house, he set off for an Egyptian army outpost. There Al-Talalka demanded that its commander, Lieutenant Faraj Ismail, contact his intermediary in Egyptian intelligence. The telephone line at the outpost was out of order, so Al-Talalka was rushed to the Egyptian intelligence offices in Gaza. While Al-Talalka waited for his direct handler, who was busy at the time, word that he was carrying highly valuable information reached Colonel Hafez. Although he had heard rumors about Al-Akawi being complicit with Israel, Hafez found it difficult to believe and therefore asked to see the package that Al-Talalka carried. The two began to argue. Al-Talalka was afraid that if Hafez opened the package, it would not be possible to return it to its original state. But Hafez demanded to see concrete evidence of the betrayal by the senior police officer.

At six in the evening, they peeled the wrappings from the book. Hafez and Al-Talalka had time enough for one last glance at a small slip of paper that fell from the pages of the book. Then there was a tremendous explosion. Eleven hours later, Hafez died at the hospital in Gaza. His deputy, Amro Al-Haridi, was severely wounded but survived the explosion, while Al-Talalka was blinded for life. It was the first state-mandated assassination in Israeli history. In the absence of Hafez's leadership, the organizational backbone of the fedayeen battalion and its activities were significantly hampered and its capabilities diminished. Three and a half months later, Israel initiated the Sinai War, which to some degree came as a response to the attacks by the fedayeen squads.[19]

The war brought the fedayeen saga to an end, but soon afterward terrorism began to crop up in other locations. Israel had no explicit counterterrorism doctrine, but its actions in the first decade after the state's establishment, which included military offensives as well as assassinations in retaliation to terrorism, indicated a clear tendency toward the war model. While some policymakers, including the first prime minister, doubted the effectiveness of this policy, Israeli counterterrorism architect Ariel Sharon and his followers were the ones to set the tone.

ON JANUARY 13, 1965, four Palestinian men approached the water pumps of the National Water Carrier in the Netofa Valley and rigged an explosive device up to one of them. On their way back they encountered an IDF patrol, and a gunfight broke out, injuring one of the Palestinians. Although the device did not explode, Fatah hastened to release a memorandum from its office in Beirut announcing the success of the operation. The failed attack was just a small sign of bigger things to come. On May 25, three Fatah members penetrated the Israeli border from Jordan and attached explosives to the walls of four houses on the eastern side of Kibbutz Ramat Hakovesh. In the dead of the night, several sharp reports shook up the peaceful community, and four residents of the kibbutz were slightly injured in the explosion.[1]

On October 7, 1966, it became clear that not just settlements on the periphery of Israel were vulnerable to attacks; the Israeli capital was also at risk. On that night, Fatah members hid explosives at the entrances to several buildings on Gadera Street in the Romema neighborhood of Jerusalem. Seven residents were injured, and many apartments were severely damaged. It was now quite clear to the Israeli political leadership that these Palestinian forays demanded a serious response. Prime Minister Eshkol declared, "The notebook is open and the hand is writing," meaning the offenders would pay for their deeds. Indeed, a week after the attack in Jerusalem, an IDF force crossed the Jordanian border and infiltrated the village of Samoah, a known Fatah base. The force blew up many of the buildings on the base, killing dozens of Fatah operatives and Jordanian soldiers.[2]

Despite the growing number of terrorist attacks in those days, the Israeli leadership could never imagine that the troubles would mushroom into one of the major concerns of the Israeli security establishment.

THE 1967 WAR AND NEW SECURITY CHALLENGES

In May 1967, the tension between Israel and Egypt mounted to new heights. Egypt imposed a blockade on the Tiran Straits, preventing Israeli ships from passing between the port of Eilat and the Red Sea, and deployed its army in the Sinai Peninsula, violating the bilateral cease-fire agreements between the two countries. Israel decided to strike first. On June 5, in a surprise attack, the Israeli air force wiped out the Syrian and Egyptian aerial forces while most of the planes were still parked at their air bases. Enjoying complete aerial superiority, the IDF conquered the Sinai Peninsula, the Gaza Strip, the West Bank, and the Golan Heights in less than six days. Having ended its military control just two years earlier over the 150,000 Palestinians who remained inside its borders after the 1948 war, Israel now ruled over a much larger area and a Palestinian population that was then three times the size of the Israeli-Palestinian one. As a result, the need to prevent the emergence of terrorism from this new, hostile population became a major objective on the agenda of the Israeli security establishment.

The Israeli government's decision to maintain its rule in the areas conquered in June 1967 required the GSS to deepen its familiarity with Palestinian society beyond sovereign Israeli territory and to lay out a HUMINT network in the occupied towns and villages. In order to accomplish this task, the GSS adapted the same model it had applied to Israeli Palestinian citizens, making the most of the advantages of the military administration. The occupied territories were divided into subdistricts controlled by three or four intelligence handlers who would pick out potential recruits, mainly Palestinians who needed assistance or special permits. In addition to the assistance they required, collaborators received various benefits, including permits for travel and hospitalization in Israel when necessary. However, their favorite form of remuneration was periodical cash payments. These informants monitored Palestinian neighborhoods and villages for the GSS and immediately reported any irregularities in people's daily lives that might indicate preparations for hostile action. In order to contend with its new tasks, the GSS had to initiate a vast recruiting operation that included the reenlistment of retired GSS personnel, the "borrowing" of Mossad men, and the grooming of new young operatives. Naturally, its budget also increased, and the organization rebuilt its status within the security establishment.

The GSS was not the only organization to conduct recruitment in the occupied West Bank. The Fatah also gained major momentum in the summer of 1967. About a month after the cessation of fighting, Yasser Arafat was able to infiltrate the West Bank and began to take on volunteers for Fatah's ranks. The GSS received information on Arafat's arrival, but he managed to fool Israeli intelligence, which had not yet been able to build an effective network in the region. In one instance, Arafat traveled by bus from Nablus to Ramallah disguised as a shepherd.

Israeli policemen received information that he was on the bus and even checked the papers of its passengers, but they were still unsuccessful at singling out the Fatah leader, who carried a forged identity card.

Several weeks later, GSS headquarters received information that Arafat was hiding out in a single-story house in Ramallah. Israeli intelligence handlers, led by Jerusalem Regional Commander Yehuda Arbel, arrived with military reinforcements, but much to their disappointment, all they found in the building was a mattress with rumpled sheets and a radio that was still on. It turned out that Arafat, who realized he was being hunted down, had managed to escape from the house just in time. While military forces were conducting the search, he hid in a Volkswagen parked beside the road leading to the house. At the end of his recruitment campaign in the West Bank, during which he ignited the fire of the struggle among many young Palestinians, Arafat returned to Jordan, this time crossing the border disguised as a pregnant woman.[3]

In the meantime, Fatah did not remain leader of the Palestinian struggle for long. Shortly after its establishment, competing organizations arrived on the scene, which would affect the Palestinian struggle for decades to come. In January 1964, under Egyptian patronage, the Palestine Liberation Organization (PLO) came into being, headed by Ahmad Shukeiri. Tension between Fatah and the PLO began to surface immediately thereafter. It quieted down only four years later, when Yasser Arafat and his Fatah supporters took control of the PLO and converted it into an umbrella organization for most Palestinian groups that emerged at that time.[4] Some of these groups integrated nationalist ideology with radical left-wing convictions, such as the George Habash–led People's Front for the Liberation of Palestine (PFLP) and Nayef Hawatmeh's Democratic Front for the Liberation of Palestine (DFLP), while countries that sought to increase their influence in the Palestinian arena sponsored other groups, such as the Arab Liberation Front, established by Iraq in 1969, and the Palestinian Liberation Front, which was founded in 1977 and influenced by both Syria and Iraq.

THE PLO AND THE FIRST ISRAELI SEMIDEFENSIVE MODEL

On March 19, 1968, an Israeli school bus, laden with students from the Herzliya Hebrew High School, was the target of a terrorist attack. The bus activated a mine near Bet-Ora. Two children were killed, and twenty-eight suffered wounds. In response, Defense Minister Moshe Dayan ordered the IDF to retaliate. On March 21, 1968, forces from the elite Paratroopers Sayeret (Reconnaissance) unit and the Arava Brigade raided Fatah's main base, located near the Jordanian town of Karameh, about 2.5 miles east of the border. During the battle, which lasted more than ten hours, the two thousand Palestinian fighters who manned the base returned fire and exacted heavy casualties from the Israeli infantry and armored forces. The Karameh battle became a major milestone in the Palestinian national memory, particularly because Arafat successfully constructed a heroic myth according to which a small Palestinian force was able to repel the Israeli army where Arab armies had failed to do so one year earlier. This myth, which took hold among Palestinian refugees, resulted in a new wave of volunteers that swelled the Fatah ranks.[5] The outcome of the battle surprised both the Israeli public and policymakers.

Encouraged by their success, the Palestinians intensified their activities on the Israeli-Jordanian border. Between 1968 and 1970, more than 140 attacks were initiated; small cells that crossed the border, ambushed IDF forces, or infiltrated Jewish settlements, and perpetrated gunfire attacks or planted explosives were responsible for most of them. The Israeli retort was a mixture of retaliatory attacks inside Jordan and the implementation of a defensive model inside Israeli territory. The latter consisted of frequent patrols along the Jordanian border and the mounting of observation posts to prevent terrorists from penetrating the West Bank. The IDF also set up a new unit whose function was to take action against cells that succeeded in crossing the border. When the trackers from this unit (known as Unit 299) detected the terrorist cell, special infantry troops with vehicles and helicopters gave pursuit. When there was resistance, the terrorists were killed.[6]

Fears of the growing power of Palestinian militias and suspicion that the Palestinians were setting up a state within a state led the Jordanian government to engage in secret joint efforts with Israel, and toward the end of the 1960s Jordanian officials conducted mass arrests of PLO activists. The arrests were made possible to a large extent by the detailed lists provided to them by the Israeli intelligence community. In exchange, the Jordanians imparted to Israel information on Fatah activists in the West Bank. Since the two countries did not have diplomatic relations at the time, intermediaries conducted the trade—at first MI6, and then the CIA.[7]

The Palestinians' attempt to eliminate King Hussein on September 1, 1970, and the hijacking of three passenger jets and their forced landing at the Zarqa Airport against his explicit orders six days later, ultimately led the king to respond with great force. Two weeks later, King Hussein dispatched his army on a widespread campaign against Palestinian fighters who had gained control of Amman's streets. Jordanian Legion soldiers raided Fatah bases and Palestinian refugee camps. Two and a half weeks after the fighting began, Syrian ground forces, accompanied by armored vehicles, crossed Jordan's northern border. Syria's goal was to force an immediate halt to the fighting against the Palestinians; however, Israel hastened to the aid of its eastern neighbor, sending fighter jets on warning flights over the presidential palace in Damascus. These signaled to Syrian President Hafez al-Assad that the time had come to withdraw his forces. By the end of that month, which the Palestinians called "Black September," more than three thousand Palestinian fighters had been killed and more than ten thousand had been wounded. Those who had survived unscathed crossed the border into Syria and continued from there into Lebanon, where they eventually rehabilitated their military infrastructure. The Palestinian organizations did not forgive the Jordanians. Not long after these events, the Fatah formed the unofficial terrorist arm Black September. The head of the new group was Ali Hassan Salameh, who directed its members to engage in an assassination campaign against prominent Jordanian politicians. The first victim was Jordanian Prime Minister Wasfi Tel, who was killed on November 28, 1971. However, the group did not target Jordan for long. In early 1972, it turned its sights on Israeli targets.[8]

SHARON AND RIMON

Meanwhile, the Gaza Strip became another major source of concern. In the first three years after the 1967 war, local Palestinians initiated more than sixty terrorist attacks there. This prompted Ariel Sharon, who had been promoted to general and was now in charge of the IDF Southern Command, to propose the idea of setting up local counterterrorism units. Members of these units would integrate their familiarity with the area with their skills in close-range combat. Despite the questionable reputation gained by his earlier venture with Unit 101, Sharon still enjoyed the standing of a leading military expert in counterterrorism and subsequently received approval for his initiative.

In 1970, he gave the order to form the Rimon Unit, with Captain Meir Dagan as commander. (Thirty-five years later, Sharon—who by then was prime minister—appointed the same Dagan to head Mossad.) The Rimon Unit adopted the same *histaaravut* technique that was developed by the Palmach. The soldiers of this unit made use of intelligence that arrived from GSS informant networks in the Gaza Strip, going undercover as fishermen, taxi drivers, and even Palestinian women. In this way, they succeeded in gaining relative freedom of movement in the Gaza Strip and carried out detentions and eliminations of terrorism suspects.

In several cases, they disguised themselves as members of Palestinian cells and roamed the streets carrying AK-47s, the automatic rifles most favored by Palestinian fighters. The principal obstacle for the Rimon soldiers had to do with the Arabic language. Most of them did not have a good command of the language, and they were therefore attached to units of Druze and Bedouin soldiers or even Palestinian combatants who were formerly active in the ranks of Fatah. The presence of these agents and their ability to manage a conversation with Gazan residents reduced the locals' fear of the unfamiliar fighters.

In the year 1972, the unit ceased its operations because the Southern Command headquarters concluded that the terrorist infrastructure in the Gaza Strip had been effectively disabled. However the influence of the Rimon Unit's operations on the declining intensity of terrorism coming from Gaza was minor. As David Maimon, the military governor of the Gaza Strip at that time, admitted, the operations of the regular army units and the reconstruction and renovation of the civil infrastructure led to the gradual decline of Palestinian terrorism originating in the Gaza Strip.[9]

HIJACKINGS AND ISRAELI RESPONSES

While the GSS and the IDF focused on Israeli Palestinian citizens and residents of the West Bank and the Gaza Strip, Mossad was contending with a much more complex challenge—gathering intelligence in areas outside of Israel's control. Western Europe and the Arab countries were among the organization's main arenas of operation, especially following the expulsion of the PLO headquarters from Jordan.

In the late 1960s, the various Palestinian groups realized the potential of the psychological impact of a relatively new medium—television. The Palestinian organization understood the great effect of a well-designed attack and how it was able to attract a mass audience all over the world while not necessarily requiring a high number of victims. Via this medium, they could distribute their political agenda quite effectively. Their attacks made use of what scholars termed the tools of a "theater of terror." While the strategic impact of such attacks was minor, its influence on the public and policymakers was immense.

The most prominent manifestation of this theater of terror was the wave of airplane hijackings, successful and attempted, from 1968 to 1976, sixteen of them in all. This method of operation, which was adopted by terrorists throughout the world, deeply affected Israel's policy in its struggle with terrorism. The first hijacking operation occurred on April 23, 1968. Three members of the PFLP hijacked a Boeing 707 belonging to El Al, Israel's national airline, on its return from Rome to Lod Airport. On board were thirty-eight passengers and ten crew-members. A few hours after the hijacking, the plane landed in Algiers. After four days of negotiations, the hostages were freed. In exchange, Israel released sixteen Palestinian prisoners.

The Palestinians realized that they had found an effective way to get the better of the Israeli government. From 1968 to 1976, Palestinian groups initiated thirty-three attacks against aviation targets, utilizing two methods: the first hijacking airplanes, and the second attacking El Al ground offices. During this period offices were attacked in the international airports of Athens, Brussels, Istanbul, and Rome. Members of Palestinian groups infiltrated these relatively unguarded airports and used grenades and gunfire to attack El Al personnel and passengers.

Israel's immediate response was the introduction of armed sky marshals on board all El Al flights. They were trained by the GSS and disguised as regular passengers. This tactic proved quite effective. In February 1969, five PFLP members tried to take control of an El Al flight en route from Zurich to Tel Aviv. Mordechai Rechamim, a sky marshal who was stationed on the plane, overpowered them. Almost the same scenario occurred in September 1970, when security personnel overpowered two PFLP members who tried to take control of an El Al flight from Amsterdam to New York.

In the long run, Israel responded to these developments in Palestinian terrorism in three ways. First, the government made a decision not to surrender to the demands of terrorists holding hostages or prisoners of war. Second, military units began training for hostage rescue missions. Third, GSS instituted strict security procedures on El Al planes and at airports that dispatched flights to Israel. While the last proved to be the most influential factor in reducing aviation terrorism, the first two received most of the attention, mostly because of operations such as the one carried out in the wake of the Sabena hijacking.[10]

SAYERET MATKAL

On May 8, 1972, four members of Black September hijacked Sabena Airlines Flight 572 en route from Vienna to Tel Aviv. The four hijackers, two men and two women, ordered the pilot to land at Ben-Gurion Airport. This was the first time that Palestinian abductors had dared to land a hijacked plane in the lion's den. Shortly after landing, they threatened to blow up the airplane with its passengers on board unless Israel released hundreds of PLO members who were held in Israeli prisons. Israeli Minister of Defense Moshe Dayan gave the order to negotiate with the kidnappers. He did not intend to surrender to their demands but instead meant to gain time for the IDF, and especially the commanders of the Sayeret Matkal Unit chosen for the mission, to plot a rescue operation. At 4:00 p.m. on May 9, sixteen IDF soldiers from the clandestine Sayeret Matkal approached the aircraft, disguised as fuel technicians. When the signal was given, they stormed the cabin at three different entrances. After a short gunfight they were able to kill the two men terrorists and neutralize the two women; however, one passenger died during the rescue and two others were injured.[11]

Sayeret Matkal was founded in 1957. It was subordinated directly to Aman, the Israeli military intelligence organization. This elite force, which became known to the Israeli public as "The Unit," had originally been created in order to enhance Aman intelligence-gathering capabilities in Arab countries. In its early years, the unit's standing was a far cry from the exalted reputation it later acquired. The idea for its conception came from Avraham Arnan, commander in the Aman 154th Unit. One of the unit's roles was the operation and maintenance of Intelligence Corps listening devices that were attached to telephone wires on the other side of the border. Arnan thought that the time had come to initiate comprehensive reform in the unit, principally due to the low motivation and inadequate technical abilities of its soldiers. Under Arnan's charismatic leadership, Sayeret Matkal, modeled on the British Special Air Service Regiment (SAS), began to take shape. Many of the soldiers who became part of the new unit were kibbutz members and similar to the manner in which soldiers were drafted to the 101, they were recruited by means of the friend-brings-a-friend method. After the recruitment procedure, they would undergo one of the hardest training regimes in the IDF. They learned to work in small teams and to penetrate deep into enemy territory to plant listening and monitoring devices at strategic locations. The reception of these devices was highly developed in comparison to the conventional equipment at the time and proved to be a highly valuable asset for military intelligence. The problem was that they operated on batteries, and every so often these had to be replaced. To maintain these devices, the soldiers of the Sayeret had to be highly capable at land navigation, camouflage, and disguise. They also had to be physically very fit in order to march dozens of kilometers behind enemy lines. Other distinctions of the unit's combatants were—and remain—a creative flair and a capability to find solutions to unforeseen problems. Toward the end of the 1960s, the derring-do and creativity of the Sayeret Matkal's soldiers became their trademark and earned them a place of respect among other IDF elite troops.

These traits captured the attention and imagination of policymakers. When terrorism became a security challenge, they immediately assigned the Sayeret Matkal with the task of responding to this new and elusive problem. Though this decision helped the highly clandestine unit gain a more impressive reputation, while at the same time it opened mobility opportunities for its commanders to the higher echelons of the army as well as the political system, it was not all a blessing. Sayeret Matkal was established as a special force for obtaining intelligence behind enemy lines. Now, it had to assume an additional duty that did not fully correspond with its primary goal and that would have an effect on the training process of the unit's combatants and their ability to focus exclusively on the unit's highly specialized missions.[12]

THE FIRST WAVE OF GLOBAL TERRORISM

At the same time that Palestinian terrorists engaged in the unrelenting wave of hijackings, they also made significant progress in other respects. Most notably, they had begun to take advantage of their ability to move with relative ease from country to country and forge alliances with terrorist groups from other areas in the world. Among these were national-liberation organizations such as the Irish Republican Army and the Basque underground (ETA), as well as radical left-wing groups such as the Red Brigades (Italy), Action Directe (France), Red Army Faction (Germany), and the Japanese Red Army.[13] They knew that these connections would present intelligence organizations with major obstacles in their attempts to foil attacks perpetrated by foreign nationals who did not seem to have anything to do with the Israeli-Palestinian conflict.

On Thursday, May 30, 1972, at approximately 10:00 p.m., three Japanese men walked through the passport control terminal at Lod Airport. Several minutes later they picked up their luggage from the conveyor belt carousels. Opening their bags, they removed Czechoslovakian Kalashnikov rifles and hand grenades and began spraying the passenger terminal with long bursts of automatic fire. The three, Takeshi Okudaira, Kozo Okamoto, and the cell leader, Yasuyuki Yasuda, volunteered for this PFLP operation because they had sworn allegiance to the universal Marxist revolutionary struggle. Before setting out, the three had trained at a facility of the Popular Front in the town of Baalbek in the Bekaa Valley of Lebanon. On May 25, they boarded a flight for Frankfurt. A PFLP operative awaited them in Germany and provided them with forged Japanese passports. From here, they took a train to Rome where they met the leader of the Japanese Red Army and Okudaira's spouse, Fusako Shigenobu, who presented them with flight tickets and the bags that contained the weapons they would need. In the afternoon hours of May 30, the three arrived at Fiumicino Airport, just outside of Rome. Their fake passports did not raise any suspicions, and they boarded an Air France flight to Tokyo, which was scheduled for a stopover at Lod Airport.

During the attack, one of his colleagues shot Okudaira by mistake, and Yasuda died when one of the grenades he was handling exploded. When Okamoto saw his friends weltering in their blood, he left the terminal building and opened fire on a group of travelers who had just disembarked from a plane that arrived from Paris. After he ran out of ammunition, he tried to escape, but an airport employee caught him. In the end, the number of fatalities was twenty-six, and seven more travelers were wounded.[14]

As a result of the attack, increased security measures were enforced at Israel's international airport. Under the supervision of the GSS, new security procedures were introduced, including the use of metal detectors, X-ray machines for baggage and passenger inspection, and surveillance cameras designed to pick up suspicious behavior. Furthermore, after going through check-in, passenger luggage was put in a pressure chamber to trigger any possible explosive devices. Outside the terminal, several security measures were also established: All vehicles entering the airport complex had to go through a preliminary security checkpoint; armed personnel patrolled the area outside the airport buildings; armed security personnel were stationed at the terminal entrances and kept a close watch on those entering the buildings; and security personnel stationed inside the terminal constantly monitored the behavior of passengers, alert for any signs of dangerous or suspicious persons, including bulky clothing or a nervous manner. They looked for "anything out of the ordinary, anything that does not fit," as one reporter put it. Over the years, those measures became standard in most Western airports, reducing aerial terrorism dramatically.[15]

However, Israel did not limit its response solely to defensive measures. Five weeks after the Lod massacre, Israel reintroduced its use of the war model in the form of a retaliation operation. This time, Ghassan Kanafani, a Palestinian writer who served as PFLP spokesman, was the target. He had claimed responsibility for the attack on behalf of the organization, and photographs of him and the three Japanese terrorists were sent to Beirut newspapers. Israeli public opinion was outraged at this display. On July 8, 1972, Kanafani left his house in one of the Beirut suburbs, accompanied by his seventeen-year-old niece, Lamees. When he started the engine of his Austin 1100, a grenade connected to the ignition switch exploded. The grenade acted as a detonator for a bomb containing three kilograms of plastic explosives hidden under the car's front bumper. The car burst into flames, and both its occupants were killed.[16] This would be the first in a long series of assassinations in 1972 and 1973.

MUNICH AND OPERATION WRATH OF GOD

Israel launched Operation Wrath of God, a series of assassinations of PLO officials in Europe (see figure 2.1), shortly after the attack by the Black September group on the Israeli athletic delegation to the Munich Olympics on September 5, 1972. At 4:00 a.m. that day, eight members of the Palestinian organization infiltrated the Olympic Village and broke into the apartments where the Israeli male athletes were staying. In exchange for the release of the hostages, the terrorists demanded the liberation of more than two hundred Palestinians incarcerated in Israeli prisons, as well as two more who were being held by the Germans. The German authorities felt that their first priority was to distance the events from the Olympic Village in order to ensure the resumption of the Olympic competitions. They reached an understanding with the terrorists, according to which they would be transferred to Tunisia with the hostages, and then negotiations would be continued. At the same time, the German police prepared a rescue operation. Their plan was to be executed after the landing of the two helicopters that transferred the terrorists and hostages from the Olympic Village to Fürstenfeldbruck Air Base. However, the operation was an utter failure. In the exchange of gunfire, the athletes were killed, most of them while they were inside the helicopters with their hands still tied. Five of the terrorists were killed and three others were caught alive. The latter three were released on October 30 after two Black September operatives kidnapped a Lufthansa aircraft on its way from Beirut to Frankfurt and demanded that West Germany free their three comrades in return for releasing the hostages.[17] Later West Germany was blamed for collaborating with Black September in staging the hijacking. The German authorities wanted to get rid of the incarcerated terrorists.

The first assassination of Operation Wrath of God was carried out less than two months after the tragic events in Munich. On October 16, 1972, Abdel Zwaiter, a senior operative of the Black September group stationed in Rome, made his way home from visiting a woman friend. He was on his way to the building where his apartment was located, not far from the Piazza Avellino. When he approached the building entrance, around 10:30 p.m., two Mossad operatives shot him at close range. After confirming that Zwaiter was dead, they dashed into a Fiat car waiting for them across the street. A few days after the assassination, the PLO

FIGURE 2.1 **OPERATION WRATH OF GOD AND PALESTINIAN RETALIATION OPERATIONS**

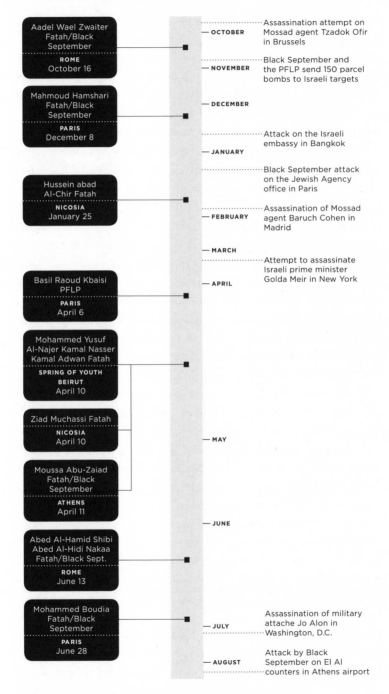

Source: NSSC Dataset on Palestinian Terrorism, www.nssc.haifa.ac.il

announced that Zwaiter had not been involved in any aspect of the attack against the Israeli athletes.[18]

In many respects, most of which have not yet received sufficient attention, the outcomes of the Wrath of God operation could be labeled as problematic. One important example is how the operation undermined Israel's intelligence capabilities. In the late 1960s, in light of the increasing activities of various Palestinian organizations in Western Europe, Mossad was successful in casting a wide network of informants from Palestinian communities in several countries. It also infiltrated the PLO elite in Europe by recruiting and activating key figures from among the organizations' activists and their close associates. Syrian journalist Khader Kano was one of them. He had fled from Syria to Kuwait in 1964 after receiving death threats in the wake of his criticism of the regime in Damascus. A year later he moved to Germany and from there continued on to Paris. There Kano built strong friendships with PLO activists. Mossad recruited him, and he became an important source of information. Despite constant warnings by his operators, Kano did not take strict precautions and maintained a lavish lifestyle. He lived in the prestigious Sixteenth Arrondissement, often hired a chauffeur, and never told his Palestinian friends about the source of his funds. On November 12, 1972, less than a month after the assassination of Zwaiter, three Black September operatives shot him dead at the entrance to his home.[19]

This was not the only case. Palestinian counterintelligence labored tirelessly to locate and strike at European-based Mossad intelligence-gathering officers and their informants. If one of the goals of Operation Wrath of God was indeed an attempt to deter the PLO, Israel fell short of meeting it. The PLO did not submit quietly but in fact repaid Mossad in kind. Baruch Cohen, an intelligence-gathering officer who posed as a businessman by the name of Moshe Hanan Yishai, operated a network of Palestinian informants, many of them students who supplied a steady flow of information on the PLO's political activities in Europe. Toward the end of 1972, with the escalation in the eliminations of PLO people in European capitals, Abu Iyad, head of PLO intelligence, learned about Cohen's network and converted some of his informants into double agents. They provided Cohen with false information, and finally one of them, Samir Ahmad, killed him.[20]

Another illustration of the futility of that operation in its attempt to damage Fatah's operational mechanisms was the series of worldwide reprisal attacks against Israeli targets after almost every one of the assassinations. Just two weeks after the Zwaiter assassination, fourteen letter bombs were sent to Israeli diplomats and Jewish figures in the United Kingdom. In the following weeks another 150 envelopes laden with explosives were sent to Israeli and Jewish figures all over the world. Only the safeguarding procedures which had been enforced by the GSS due to prior attempts to send letter bombs to Israeli embassies, prevented casualties.[21]

The Palestinian response was also quick after the assassination of Mahmud Hamshari, the PLO representative in Paris. On December 8, 1972, he picked up the phone in his apartment. He identified himself by name, answering the question of the man who was on the other side of the phone line. This was a fatal mistake; a few seconds later an explosive attached to the underside of the table exploded. He died of his wounds a few days later. A little more than two weeks later, in the early afternoon hours of December 28, four Palestinians infiltrated the Israeli Embassy in Bangkok and took six Israeli diplomats hostage, including the ambassador. In return for the release of the hostages, they demanded that Israel free thirty-six members of Fatah held in Israeli prisons. After more than twenty-four hours of negotiations, the abductors instead agreed to release the hostages, in return for which they would be flown to Egypt.[22]

In the wake of the attack in Bangkok, security measures at Israeli embassies were greatly intensified, transforming them virtually into fortified strongholds. But Israel also continued to respond with offensive actions, carrying on Operation Wrath of God as Mossad operatives assassinated Hussein Abad Al-Chir, the Fatah representative in Cyprus, on January 25, 1973. The retaliation attack plotted this time by the Black September group could have been very painful. In March 1973, during Prime Minister Golda Meir's visit to New York, Black September operatives succeeded in parking three car bombs along the route where Meir's convoy was scheduled to pass. Simply by chance, the explosives failed to detonate. Israel countered with a series of eight assassinations in April and June 1973, while the Palestinians came back by attacking El Al offices at Athens and Rome airports in June and August, illustrating again the futility of the Wrath of God operations in damaging the Palestinian terrorism infrastructure, as well as its inability to deter its leaders.[23]

The payback motivation is also questionable. Zwaiter was not the only target whose ties to the Munich massacre were not fully established. Basil Al-Kubaysi was a professor of law who had earned degrees from Canadian and American universities and had lectured at the American University in Beirut. Using his standing as a Palestinian intellectual, Kubaysi helped transfer munitions among Fatah cells throughout Europe. Despite these activities, Kubaysi's importance in the Fatah operational network in general and in Black September in particular was quite minimal. He just happened to be an easy target. He had a high public profile and was seen in public almost every day. On April 6, 1973, he was dining at the Café de la Paix, opposite the Opera House in Paris. After finishing his meal, he walked toward the Piper Hotel, at Rue de l'Arcade 6. Two men were waiting for Kubaysi on the corner of Plaza Madeleine, and two others were watching the corner from a car parked nearby. When the men on the corner saw Kubaysi approaching, they readied their weapons. To their surprise, Kubaysi changed his mind, and instead of continuing straight toward the hotel, he decided to enjoy the pleasures of a local prostitute. The Mossad agents watched as Kubaysi bargained with the woman. A few seconds later he entered her car, which disappeared in the bustling traffic. The Mossad team wondered if this unexpected delay was reason enough to call off the operation. The team commander asked them to wait, figuring that the prostitute would return her client to the plaza shortly, to the exact spot where she had picked him up. Sure enough, less than twenty minutes later the car returned, and Kubaysi got out and headed toward the hotel. The two men blocked his path, and when he was very close to them, they opened fire. Silencers apparently muffled the sound of the shots. The surprised Kubaysi managed to shout "*Non, ne faites pas cela!*" ("No, don't do it!") before collapsing to the ground in a pool of his own blood. The two men quickly entered the car, which merged with the traffic and sped away.[24]

The most complicated mission during the course of Operation Wrath of God, in which three senior Fatah members—Kamal Adwan, Kamal Nasser, and Muhammad Yusef Najjar—were killed, seems to have had little connection to Munich. Operation Spring of Youth was a high-risk attack executed on the night of April 9, 1973. Naval commando boats brought Sayeret Matkal and Paratroopers reconnaissance units to the Beirut shore. From there they were taken by Mossad operatives to the city's Verdun neighborhood, where they forced their way into the apartments of three senior Fatah operatives and killed them. The modus operandi in all three instances was the same. The doors of the apartments were blasted open with explosive charges and Sayeret Matkal soldiers entered the apartments and killed the Fatah men after a short exchange of gunfire. The next stage of the operation was meant to include the destruction of one of the other buildings inhabited by PLO members, but the plan was changed after heavy gun battles began to develop. During the evacuation of the Israeli forces, two paratroopers were killed.[25]

In this case, too, the desire to avenge the PLO's actions against Israel seemed to be more imperative than the desire to harm Fatah capabilities. Kamal Nasser, for example, was not even directly involved in terrorist activities against Israel. He was one of the organization's senior spokesmen and in this capacity often appeared in the Arabic and international media. The attacks on the two others, despite their important positions, would have no real impact on the organization's operational capabilities. Even though Yusef Najjar, a lawyer by profession, was number two in Fatah's organizational hierarchy, he was primarily a political figure whose involvement in the direct planning of attacks against Israel was minor. Kamal Adwan was in charge of the organization's mechanisms in the West Bank, which were responsible for launching terrorist attacks on Israel from that area. However, terrorist activities from inside the West Bank during those years were actually in decline, and were less of a problem for Israel.

Operation Wrath of God ended de facto on July 21, 1973, with an event that many still consider one of Mossad's most prominent failures. A team of Mossad agents was conducting a surveillance of a senior PLO operative, who had flown from the organization's headquarters in Geneva to a small Norwegian town, Lillehammer. They discovered that he had met several times there with a suspicious person. The agents rapidly came to the conclusion that this person was actually Ali Hassan Salameh, the head of the Black September Organization. They were not aware that this person was in fact a waiter by the name of Ahmed Bouchiki. He was an Algerian-born Moroccan, but he had no relation to Black September. That morning, as Bouchiki stepped down from a bus escorted by his pregnant wife, two Mossad operatives shot him thirteen times from close range and killed him. The fiasco did not end in a case of mistaken identification. The Mossad agents were caught as they returned the rented car to the airport. They did not even try to change the license numbers of the hired cars or merely abandon them. In addition, one of the arrested agents, Dan Arbel, was claustrophobic. In exchange for being taken out of the small cell where he was put, he revealed many details of the operation. This included Mossad methods of operations, the names of his colleagues—who were arrested as a result—and detailed information about former operations of Mossad in Europe. For the first time, there was clear evidence connecting Israel to the series of assassinations of Palestinians all over Europe.[26]

Ali Hassan Salameh himself did not escape the destiny Mossad had designated for him. In the morning hours of June 22, 1979, a Chevrolet van and a Land Rover made their way slowly down the narrow lane of Verdean Street in Beirut, turning into Marie Curie Street. A few second later, a Volkswagen parked by the side of the road exploded as the two cars passed by. The eight men in the two cars died almost immediately, among them Hassan Salameh. None of the passersby who gathered in the street saw the young woman who was observing the entire event from the window of the upper floor of one of the high buildings bordering the lane. Just few years later it would be revealed that this young woman, Erica Chambers, who pushed the button that triggered the explosives in the car bomb, was part of a Mossad team that operated in Beirut and had targeted Hassan Salameh.

The original goal of Operation Wrath of God was to strike at the heads of Black September, but over the course of time the circle of assassinations widened to include leaders of other Palestinian organizations. There were practical reasons for this. While many Black September members found refuge in Arab countries, senior activists from other organizations traveled among European capitals, making them easy targets. During the seven years of the campaign, twelve Palestinians associated with the PLO were killed. If the heads of the Israeli security establishment had hoped that the assassinations would lead to a renunciation of terrorism by Palestinian organizations, this did not happen. Palestinian terrorism only intensified and became more lethal, as the following decades bear witness.[27]

Although the defensive model had proven to be highly effective and actually forced terrorists to realize that the risk involved in hijacking planes was greater than the chances of success, leading them to abandon that method of operation altogether, this model was still not completely assimilated.[28] The idea of exploring the reconciliatory model by trying to address the grievances of the Palestinians did not even cross the minds of policymakers at the time.

CHAPTER THREE **RESCUING HOSTAGES**

IN THIS CHAPTER I will focus on four case studies of hostage-rescue situations that took place in the years following Operation Wrath of God. The very fact that Palestinian groups persisted in perpetrating such attacks casts further doubt on the deterring effect of the Israeli war model. Here I will look into the causes that led Israeli policymakers to order elite military units, which had little experience with hostage crises, to perform such rescue operations. Furthermore, I will address the paradoxical situation in which the Israeli leadership did not deviate from its original position, despite the tragic consequences of several rescue attempts and a formal commission's clear recommendation to transfer the responsibility for responding to such scenarios from the IDF to the police.

MA'ALOT

On Sunday, May 13, 1974, three members of the Democratic Front for the Liberation of Palestine crossed the border from Lebanon into Israel. When they reached the road connecting the town of Ma'alot with Kibbutz Sasa, they set up an ambush near Moshav Tzuriel. They first attacked a van carrying Arab women home from their jobs in Kiryat Ata. They killed one passenger and wounded two of her friends. Fortunately, the driver kept a cool head and did not stop until the vehicle's motor broke down. After the shootings, the terrorists continued on foot in the direction of Ma'alot. At 3:30 a.m. they broke into the home of the Cohen family and killed a mother and father and one of their children. After that, they left the house and made their way to the Netiv Meir School. At about 4:00 a.m., they ran into Yaakov Kadosh, a fifty-four-year-old man who was on his way to the synagogue for morning prayers. He wished them a good morning. They reciprocated in Hebrew, but a few seconds later the terrorists opened fire, critically wounding him. Three cars were parked in the school parking lot and in one of them sat Yitzhak Vaknin, a teacher chaperoning a group of 102 high-school students. They were from a religious public school in Tsefat and were spending the night at the Ma'alot school while on a field trip in northern Israel. The terrorists threatened Vaknin with their weapons and ordered him to lead them into the school. They quickly took control of the building; two cell members occupied the upper floors and one was left to guard the entrance. The terrorists woke up the children and shouted at them in Arabic and Hebrew to leave the rooms. The bus driver, a number of teachers, and a few students took advantage of the confusion and jumped out through one of the classroom windows into the schoolyard below. From there they ran to the town center and alerted the security forces. In the meanwhile, the abductors herded the rest of the hostages—eighty-five children and four adults—into a classroom.

At 5:30 a.m., the terrorists sent medic Narkiss Mordechai outside the school to announce their demands to the security forces. Twenty of their comrades imprisoned in Israel were to be released and immediately flown to Damascus. The terrorists promised that when the freed prisoners arrived at the Syrian capital, a codeword would be imparted to the French and Romanian ambassadors in Israel. After the ambassadors passed the codeword on to the terrorists, half the hostages would be released. According to the plan, at this stage the abductors and the remaining hostages would be transported to a civilian airport. The second stage of the bargain would then take place in which the hostage-takers would be flown to Damascus and the rest of the hostages would be freed. The plan also included an ultimatum: If the Israeli government did not meet their demands by 6:00 p.m., five explosive devices placed in different corners of the building would be detonated, collapsing the building with all its occupants inside.

Prime Minister Golda Meir had already received initial reports of the incident at 4:45 a.m. Minister of Defense Moshe Dayan, Chief of Staff Motta Gur, and Major General Amiram Levine were all flown to Ma'alot in a military helicopter and landed in the northern town just before 7:00 a.m. Dayan, who took on-site command of the situation, opened two parallel courses of operation. First, he summoned the head of the GSS Interrogations Branch, Victor Cohen, who eighteen months earlier had led negotiations with the Black September terrorist group in Munich, to the site to try and get the terrorists to talk. Cohen was able to make contact with them and engaged in conversation with them by megaphone.

The second course was the devising of a takeover assault. Sikorsky CH-53 helicopters lifted in dozens of Sayeret Matkal soldiers to the location. The terrorists, hearing the noise and seeing the soldiers deployed around the school, began to doubt Cohen's sincerity. Their reaction was not long in coming. Starting at 9:00 a.m., once every half-hour, the cell's commander, Ziad Rahim, stood five hostages in front of a classroom window and fired shots in the air to demonstrate his resolve. As the nervousness of the abductors increased, they began to shoot their guns and throw hand grenades out the windows. One of the shots killed Silvan Zerah, a soldier and resident of Ma'alot, who was observing the whole affair from a distance.

In the late morning hours, Moshe Dayan, whose nephew Uzi served in Sayeret Matkal, flew to Jerusalem for a brief meeting with the prime minister. He used the precedent set by the successful assault on a hijacked Sabena airliner to try to persuade Prime Minister Golda Meir to support a military solution. The prime minister was not convinced and asked that the negotiation option be exhausted before any military steps were taken. Defense Minister Dayan, however, ordered Sayeret Matkal officers to continue to work on devising an assault plan in case the government gave the green light for a takeover operation. During the course of its emergency meeting, the government carefully examined both options from all sides. On one hand, the ministers tried to evaluate the future consequences of giving in to terrorist demands, especially in light of Israel's formal policy not to negotiate with terrorists. On the other, they weighed the chances for the success of a rescue operation. During the 2:00 p.m. newscast, the citizens of Israel learned that the die had been cast. Kol Yisrael ("The Voice of Israel") announced that the government had decided to meet the demands of the hostage takers. The terrorists were exultant when they were informed of the dramatic development and announced that they had defused the bombs in a gesture of good faith.

While the ministers were deliberating, Dayan and Gur continued to proceed with the preparations for a combat operation. Dayan was in constant contact with Sayeret Matkal officers who were compiling information on the school building and the location of the hostages. Several plans were developed that took into account this information. The officers, however, were less convinced than the defense minister regarding the chances of success. They claimed to have warned Dayan that the information they had on the number and location of the explosive devices was incomplete. In addition, the unit's snipers surrounding the building said it was difficult to identify the terrorists clearly and keep them in the sights of their relatively antiquated rifles.

The Sayeret Matkal force was divided into three teams of eleven or twelve soldiers, including officers of the unit who had voluntarily reached the site. The first team, commanded by Zvi Livne, was to breach the building, kill the terrorist leader, climb the staircase leading to the hall on the floor where the hostages were being held, and secure it. The second team, led by Amiram Levine, was to penetrate immediately afterward, slip by the soldiers securing the hall, and reach the room where the children were being held. The third team planned to climb the outside wall of the building and shoot the terrorists through one of the classroom windows.

At 4:15 p.m., the efforts by the Romanian and French ambassadors to broker a compromise ended in failure. The immense pressure of the security establishment, the need to make a decision under tight time constraints, and the general environment of uncertainty had led the government to approve the rescue plan. It authorized the defense minister and chief of staff to decide when to begin.

One hour after the government gave its approval for military action, Motta Gur signaled the go-ahead to the forces. At 5:25 p.m., Sayeret Matkal commanding officer Lieutenant Colonel Giora Zorea ordered one of the snipers to shoot the terrorist leader, who had revealed himself for a moment. The bullet hit Rahim's shoulder and slightly injured him. At that exact moment Livne's team broke into the schoolyard. As his soldiers ran to the staircase, they encountered the wounded Rahim. Livne threw a phosphorus grenade at him, but before it exploded the terrorist had time to fire at the soldiers, wounding three of them, and then run back to the classroom where the students were being held. Livne and Baruch Fein, another soldier who escaped injury, kept to the plan and chased after him. But more blunders followed. Amiram Levine's team, which had entered the building when the shooting began, missed the stairway to the floor where the hostages were being held, and instead climbed to the next one up. It took a few seconds for Levine to understand his mistake and lead his soldiers back down.

The soldiers in Muki Betser's team, who were supposed to shoot at the terrorists through the window, were surprised to hear shots coming from the two other teams, and the confusion slowed them down. Mickey Arditi, the soldier highest on the ladder, jumped down before he reached the window. He later explained that errant bullets from Sayeret Matkal snipers were hitting the wall and prevented him from continuing. Betser ordered another soldier to climb up, but before he could carry out the order, heavy gunfire came from inside the classroom window. The team was forced to find cover behind the wall of the building, thus ending its role.

In the meantime, the other two assault teams were chasing Rahim. He reached the tiny classroom, immediately opened automatic fire on the children, and threw in a grenade. The hostages sitting in the front of the room collapsed and hit the floor, lying in their own blood. Eighteen of them died on the spot, and five more were wounded. The remaining hostages ran to the window and jumped into the yard. By the time the soldiers reached the classroom the sound of shots had ceased. Rahim's weapon had jammed, and he was left standing in the middle of the room. The soldiers shot both him and the second terrorist. The third was killed as soon as the hostages identified him.

On May 20, 1974, a commission of inquiry was appointed to investigate the events at Ma'alot, with Major General Amos Horev appointed as its head. Commission members examined the incident from several perspectives and issued a report listing a long series of mistakes that were the joint responsibility of the political and security echelons. For our purposes, especially important was the conclusion that the Sayeret Matkal soldiers were not sufficiently trained in hostage rescue.[1]

In order to prevent similar mishaps, commission members called for the establishment of a distinctive police antiterrorist response unit specializing in siege and hostage rescue missions. The government adopted the recommendation that could have led Israel to shift toward the criminal justice model, and in February 1975 it established the Yamam as a company within the Border Police. With the appointment of Assaf Hefetz as commander of the unit in 1978, it made a quantum leap in capability and became an independent takeover unit.

Unlike soldiers of Sayeret Matkal, who are conscripts of the regular (mandatory service) army and complete their duty after serving for three and a half years, police officers of the Yamam may remain in the ranks for many years. A significant number of them are recruited in their early twenties after serving in a military combat unit, and they commonly retire from the police only after a ten-year stint and sometimes even longer. The typical training course of a Yamam fighter lasts for twelve months. In the first eight months, all cadets go through basic training in counterterrorism warfare, which includes a familiarity with specialized firearms, land navigation, and structure- and vehicle-takeover exercises. In the next four months, trainees are divided into five fields of specialization: sniping, dynamic entry and use of explosives, negotiation, dog handling, and rappelling. The officers who undertake rope-descent techniques learn how to enter buildings through the windows while hanging from ropes, thus earning themselves the epithet "terror monkeys."[2]

THE SAVOY HOTEL

A little less than a year after the tragedy at Ma'alot, and before the security apparatus implemented the recommendations of the Horev Commission, the PLO mounted another hostage-taking incident, this time in the heart of Tel Aviv. On

May 5, 1975, at 11:15 pm, two Zodiac speedboats landed on the Tel Aviv beach. The eight terrorists on board quickly unloaded their weapons and ammunition and sped toward the city. Police patrolling the area caught sight of them and opened fire, but they were not able to halt the terrorists' progress. The eight reached a wedding hall on Yona Hanavi Street and opened fire inside. From there they continued to a nearby movie theater but failed to breach the doors. Their final target was the Savoy Hotel. The terrorists penetrated the hotel while shooting in all directions, and within a short time had taken control of the building and seized eight hostages. At first they rounded up the terrified hostages in the attic. A short while later, they changed their minds and brought them back down to the third floor of the building. By midnight police and army forces surrounded the building. An IDF officer, Ruby Peled, began to negotiate with the terrorists assisted by Kochava Levi, a hostage fluent in Arabic. Similar to the Ma'alot incident, the terrorists demanded the release of ten prisoners who would be flown from Israel to Damascus, this time together with the ambassadors of Greece and France. Again, as in the past, the terrorists threatened to execute the hostages if their demands were not met by a certain hour—in this case, 7:00 a.m. During the night the terrorists used explosives and trip wire to booby-trap the floor of the room where the hostages were being held, ensuring that any attempt to rescue them would end tragically.[3]

Outside the hotel, the chief officer of the IDF Central Command, Yonah Efrat, supervised the planning for the takeover. Prime Minister Rabin followed the events from the Ministry of Defense high command headquarters in Tel Aviv. The duty officer in Sayeret Matkal's operations room received the order to dispatch the on-call unit to the Savoy site, but the drivers transporting the teams got into two minor accidents on the way, delaying their arrival. When they finally reached the hotel vicinity, they were forced to go from officer to officer before they could discover who was in charge of the operation. They received their first briefing only a short while before their deployment in preparation for the assault. At that stage, there was still no clear intelligence giving an idea how many terrorists there were and where they were located. Because the soldiers were not carrying communication devices, from the time they took their positions until the operation began it was impossible to communicate updated information to them.[4]

At 5:15 a.m., the signal was given. Four teams breached the building at different points. The terrorists expected the assault and activated the explosive devices they had placed during the night, collapsing the stairway leading to the upper floors of the hotel and thus neutralizing the force that had stormed the main entrance to the building. The other teams had more luck. Within twelve minutes after the signal was given they were able to gain control of the building—or so they thought. During their search they found that one of the wounded terrorists was still armed. This man shot and killed Colonel Uzi Ya'iri, who had reached the area on his own initiative. Faulty tactical intelligence led the unit's soldiers to believe that there were seven terrorists, so after seven bodies had been identified they announced that the area was secure. Musa Ibn Jouma Abu Hassan, however, was left uninjured. During the night he had prepared a hiding place on the terrace of a third-floor room and on hearing the first shots took cover there. In the hours after the operation, police took part in a room-to-room search of the hotel. The commander of the Yarkon police region, Moshe Tiomkin, was ordered to search the terrace where Hassan was hiding and was surprised when the terrorist appeared from behind a wooden panel and opened fire. However, the shots were not accurate, and Hassan was caught. In this fashion, another hostage-taking incident ended in only partial success.[5]

Many soldiers of Sayeret Matkal and other elite units have often risked their lives to rescue hostages. The problem is that the counterterrorist training received by the soldiers in these units is minimal, specifically, three weeks to a month at the IDF School for Counterterrorism Training, whereas hostage rescue missions demand an extremely high level of expertise. In any siege situation the terrorists have inherent advantages. They are armed, the hostages are under their complete control, and they can open fire whenever they suspect they are losing control of the situation. In contrast, rescue forces must act quickly and effectively in order to take optimum advantage of the element of surprise. The assault teams are usually not familiar with the environs where they have to rescue the hostages. They may not know how many terrorists they will have to contend with, where they are located, how they are armed, and how determined they are to kill the hostages in the event of a rescue operation.[6] A high level of professional training can partly compensate for the inherently inferior position of the takeover forces, but policymakers have refused to internalize this fact thus preventing the Yamam from using their capabilities to the full.

ENTEBBE

Even in the rescue mission of the hostages at Entebbe, Israel's most illustrious operation in its struggle against terrorism, there was only a very fine line separating triumph from failure. On Saturday, July 3, 1976, the tension inside the air terminal at the Entebbe airport in Uganda had reached new heights. One week after hijacking Air France Flight 139 en route from Tel Aviv to Paris, the abductors nervously awaited the response of the governments of Israel, Kenya, Germany, Switzerland, and France. The hijackers had demanded the release of fifty-three terrorists from the prisons where they were being held, and their ultimatum was to expire the next day. If their demands were not met, they threatened to execute the 104 hostages. The terminal was shrouded in a state of gloom. The hostages who had even considered the idea of being rescued by Israeli forces understood that the chances were very slim. One of them, a former navigator in the Israel Air Force, calculated that approximately 1,870 miles separated Israel from Entebbe. This distance would in all probability make an aerial operation impossible simply because the planes would not be able to carry enough fuel in their tanks.

Dr. Yitzhak Hirsch, as well, felt completely helpless. All he could do was wait until dawn broke and hope that he would not be among the first to be executed. Exactly one week earlier, he had been serving in the reserves as a regimental doctor somewhere in the northern part of Israel. His thoughts at the time were only about the dream vacation that he and his wife, Lily, would soon spend in Sweden and Norway. According to the original plans, both of them were supposed to fly to Paris, rent a car at the airport, and then travel north to Scandinavia. At an early morning hour on Sunday, June 27, 1976, the Hirsch couple arrived at the Ben-Gurion Airport in Lod. After checking their luggage at the Air France counter, they were informed that the plane would make a brief stopover at Athens, but this short delay certainly did not dampen their high spirits.[7]

At 8:57 in the morning, Flight 139 took off as scheduled. After less than three hours, it landed at Athens. During the short stopover, several passengers got off and others took their place. Among the new travelers was twenty-seven-year-old Wilfried Böse, a tall, blue-eyed, light-haired German, accompanied by twenty-five-year-old Brigitte Kuhlmann, also German. Kuhlmann was of medium height, bespectacled, her hair cut in bangs.

Before boarding the plane, the young Germans, both members of the Red Army Faction (RAF), underwent a security check. The fact that they had just arrived on a flight from Bahrain without leaving the terminal enabled them to take the quick-check lane. All they had to do was pass their hand luggage through an X-ray machine. At this point, they had a stroke of luck: The Greek security man who managed the machine was concentrating on a flower he held in his hand and not on the monitor. If he had just been a little more alert, the events of that same day might have taken a completely different turn.

At 12:33 p.m., eight minutes after the plane lifted off from Athens and a short while after the captain had turned off the seatbelt sign, Böse, who sat in first class, asked the stewardess to bring him a glass of champagne. The other passengers, preoccupied with their own affairs, did not notice the young German as he pretended to stretch his limbs. He bent forward and down to where he pulled out a handbag that lay near his feet, then lifted it up in the air. This was the agreed-upon sign for launching the operation. Böse pulled out a gun from his bag and quickly covered the short distance between first class and the cockpit. Kuhlmann, who sat next to him, removed a hand grenade and a gun that were strapped to her thighs. She shouted to the passengers that the plane was being hijacked by the Popular Front for the Liberation of Palestine and ordered them not to move. In those very same seconds, Ali el-Meyari and Haled Haleilah jumped up from their seats in coach. They extracted hand grenades from tin candy boxes and brandished them in the air for all passengers to see.[8]

It was only a matter of seconds until the plane was under their control. Böse broke into the cockpit and forced Captain Michel Bacos to alter the flight plan and turn south. The other hijackers pushed and shoved the rest of the passengers back into the tourist class. Kuhlmann then commanded them all to hand over their passports. On the plane's internal intercom system, Böse announced that the plane was now under the control of members of the Che Guevara Force and Gaza Commando of the Palestine Liberation Forces. At 3:00 p.m., Flight 139—or "Haifa," as Böse called it—touched down at the airport in the city of Benghazi, Libya. Landing in this country was marked by many difficulties. The control tower in Benghazi procrastinated for a long while before giving its permission to land, and when the okay was finally given, the hijackers were coldly received. The six-and-a-half-hour wait at the airport frayed the hijackers' nerves even more. The Libyan junior naval officer who was assigned to be their intermediary at first rejected all their requests. After taxing negotiations his superiors relented, and he gave the order to pump thirty-five tons of fuel into the plane's tanks.[9]

A little after 9:30 p.m., the Air France plane lifted off for the third time on that same day. This time, Bacos was instructed to fly in a southeasterly direction. Six more hours passed until the plane landed at the darkened Entebbe Airport in the heart of Africa. In Uganda, six fellow collaborators from the Popular Front organization waited for the hijackers. Their leader was a former Cuban intelligence officer, Antonio Degas Bouvier, who would become a central figure in the international terrorism network with which Ilich Ramirez Sanchez, known as Carlos the Jackal, was associated. After another nine hours aboard the plane, the hostages were finally allowed to disembark and then herded into a large hall in the old terminal. The Arab hijackers were placed in charge of guarding the hostages. These guards kept their distance and avoided any contact with them. The commanders of the operation, who enjoyed the support of the Ugandan leader, Field Marshal Idi Amin, began to negotiate with the French government. The date they set for the release of their comrades was Thursday, July 1. After locking horns for a while, they finally agreed to postpone the date of the ultimatum by three days, which, in the end, turned out to be critical.

Meanwhile, Ugandan soldiers began to saw off the lower part of the door inside the terminal hall that separated the hostages' room from a neighboring room. Toward evening, the hostages realized the purpose of this effort. Wilfried Böse took the passports out of the bag in his hand and announced that those persons whose names were read aloud were to go to the neighboring, smaller room. All the names he called out were Jewish. Crying and shouting accompanied the entire "selection" process, as the hostages called it. The hostages felt that the young German was in effect condemning them to death.[10]

On the next day, Wednesday, there was a dramatic turn of events. The forty-six passengers who remained behind in the big hall were instructed to board a bus that waited outside the terminal. They were then transported to Kampala, the capital of Uganda, in order to meet with the French ambassador to Uganda. Afterward they were bused back to Entebbe, where an Air France airplane awaited them, and several hours later they were already back in Paris. The Israeli and Jewish passengers, together with members of the plane crew who had refused to board the plane to freedom, all anxiously watched the departure of the liberated hostages.

Thousands of miles northeast of Entebbe, in the Jerusalem and Tel Aviv offices of the prime minister and minister of defense, and in the bureau of the chief of staff, the lights remained on around the clock. From the moment that news of the hijacked plane had reached them on Sunday, 1:30 in the afternoon, the Israeli intelligence community had fervently applied itself to collecting every scrap of information that might shed light on the situation. In this way, they hoped to provide some basis for a possible military rescue operation of the hostages. On Tuesday, while the hostages were undergoing the "selection" process, the intelligence dossier began to take shape.[11]

The release of the non-Jewish hostages was a significant windfall for the intelligence-gathering process of building up a full picture of the situation. Ehud Barak, former chief commander of Sayeret Matkal and, at the time of the hijacking, aide to the Aman head of operations, was assigned the job of consolidating intelligence assessments. When he heard about the release of the hostages, he did not even pause for a moment. He dispatched his former colleague from Sayeret Matkal, Amiram Levine, to Paris in order to question the passengers. Levine was especially interested in details of the building structure where the hostages were being held and in descriptions of the terrorists. To his great fortune, among the freed hostages was also a retired French paratrooper officer who took note of exactly these kinds of particulars. Levine's seven-page report would prove to be a key intelligence document.[12]

While Levine was collecting information in Paris, Israeli military officers who had served in Uganda during the period of cooperation between Israel and Amin's government were being questioned at the IDF intelligence headquarters at the Kirya complex in Tel Aviv. At the same time, interviews were conducted with employees of the Israeli Solel Boneh Company, which had taken part in the construction of the Entebbe terminal in the late 1960s. They provided the officers with photographs and films of the facility from the years when they worked there. Additional intelligence material was collected from public-domain sources, including the *Jeppesen Manual,* which surveys airport structures all over the world, and a French television production that included up-to-date pictures of the terminal. The amassed information made it possible to draw up an exact diagram of the terminal building and provide answers to vital questions, such as the layout of the rooms where the hostages were being held and the location of entrances to the terminal.[13]

In order to corroborate the accuracy of the intelligence profiles taking shape in Tel Aviv, the chief of Mossad, Yitzhak Hofi, sent off two of his people to Africa. These agents carried international pilot licenses and were able to hire a light airplane in Nairobi. They explained to the owners of the airline company that they intended to take photographs for a tourist travel guide. After taking off, they deviated from the flight plan and made straight for the Entebbe Airport. While flying over the airfields they were able to take pictures of the runways and several of the adjacent buildings. The photos reached Tel Aviv several hours later. In those very same hours, officers of the Israel Air Force intelligence squadron were deeply immersed in gathering updated information on the weather forecast and the air forces and anti-aircraft capabilities of the six countries that separated Israel from Uganda. The resultant information was pieced together and used to devise relatively safe flight plans for the Israel Air Force aircrafts.

On the next day, Wednesday, preparations entered high gear. The chief infantry and paratroopers officer, Dan Shomron, was asked to devise a blueprint for the release of the hostages and present it before government ministers. Ehud Barak, who was summoned to Shomron, was asked to expound on the ideas that so far had taken shape. These ideas had been discussed in earlier meetings with Aman officers and representatives of Sayeret Matkal and the naval commando units whose soldiers had training in overcoming terrorists and rescuing hostages. Some of the schemes put forward by Barak seemed to come straight out of a Hollywood action movie. The geographical proximity of the Entebbe Airport to Lake Victoria opened a window of opportunity for a naval commando operation. Among other possible scenarios, he proposed that commandos be parachuted together with their rubber dinghies into the lake or that a yacht set sail from Kenya with special forces on board. However, logistic problems—among them the risk of the lake's dense alligator population or the chance that the boats would not be able to withstand the strong impact of landing on water—led to the shelving of the options of launching an operation from the lake.

The most significant proposal that remained relevant at this stage was the one put forward by Muki Betser, deputy commander of the Sayeret Matkal. When he first heard of the hijacking, he had suggested transporting unit teams by means of Israel Air Force Hercules planes to Kenya. After landing, they would take the terminal by surprise with a convoy of military vehicles and overpower the abductors. Dan Shomron was convinced that despite the great risk involved in carrying out the plan, the chances of success were good enough. Defense Minister Shimon Peres was informed, and the unit received permission to start training.[14]

The preparations made a strong impression on Chief of Staff Mordechai "Motta" Gur, who visited the training facilities of Sayeret Matkal in order to weigh up the plan. In his meeting with Minister of Defense Peres, he said, "There is no reason why we shouldn't carry out the operation. I think that the chances of success are very good. I was present at the training yesterday, and the level of professionalism was just fine." However, the description of Omer Bar-Lev, commander of one of Sayeret Matkal's teams and son of the minister of commerce and industry at the time, was entirely different: "In the evening, there was a dry run. Today, they are making such a big deal out of the dry run, but at that time one of the younger teams approached the runway, and took out a white marking tape. . . . They unwound it and stuck some jute bags on the runway. We still haven't got all the details of the plan down pat and there was a mess of jute bags and we couldn't understand where the openings were, the entrance and the exit. We did the drill: The Hercules landed on the runway and the mock-up was at the far end of the runway. We fired a few shots in the air, and that essentially was the whole dry run."[15]

Two days after the expiration of the deadline of the original ultimatum, on Saturday, July 3, at 2:00 p.m., four Hercules transport aircraft of the Israeli Air Force took off from the airport at Sharm el-Sheikh and set off for Entebbe. The planes carried Sayeret Matkal commandos, whose mission was to rescue the hostages, as well as infantry forces from the Paratroopers and Golani brigades, whose task was to gain control of the airport and provide backup for the assault forces. While at the commanding level there was consensus that the task of freeing the hostages should go to the Sayeret Matkal, the decision to reinforce the latter with two different infantry brigades did not come from entirely straightforward considerations. Dan Shomron, who was well aware of the traditional rivalry between the Paratroopers and Golani, feared that assigning the mission to only one of them would lead to a great dissatisfaction among members of the other. Therefore, he decided to create a joint task force, even though they were not really acquainted with each other and most likely had never even trained together.

At 11:00 p.m., Uganda time, the planes settled down in Entebbe Airport. Within seconds, their huge doors opened. Vehicles and special troops in the tiger-stripe camouflaged fatigues of the Uganda Army quickly descended the ramp into the hot and humid night. Thirty-two soldiers made their way to the terminal mounted on two Land Rovers, escorting an official car, a Mercedes painted in black. This arrangement of the convoy was supposed to mislead the Ugandan soldiers into assuming that the car belonged to Idi Amin.[16]

The occupants of the vehicles sat anxiously as all eyes were fixed on the entrances to the terminal. But suddenly there was an unexpected hitch on the way. Two Ugandan army guards signaled to the drivers to stop. This was standard procedure for checking documents, as Muki Betser knew from his days as an advisor to Amin's army. He urged Yoni Netanyahu, his commander, who sat next to the driver, to pay no heed to the two soldiers, but Yoni fired off several shots in their direction with a silenced gun. The bullets did not hit their target. Seconds later, the machine gunner on one of the Land Rovers sprayed the Ugandans with automatic fire. As a result, the operation lost its element of surprise, and heavy gunfire poured down from the control towers onto the attacking force. The Israeli soldiers abandoned their original plan of action and stormed the terminal entrances in a crowded cluster that bottlenecked the entrance.[17]

Fortunately for the Sayeret soldiers, the terrorists simply could not imagine that Israeli forces were responsible for all the pandemonium outside the terminal.

A soldier by the name of Amir, who stuck to the original plan, spotted the door where they were supposed to storm the hall. Directly across from him, on the other side of a large window, one of the hijackers stood with a Kalashnikov assault rifle. This hijacker detected the commando and pulled the trigger but missed Amir, who immediately returned fire and killed him. Apparently he did not notice another abductor, who crouched off to the left side of the entrance. He and the German woman aimed their weapons at Amir, but his commander, Amnon, who burst into the hall right behind him, was able to gun them down both before they could even pull the trigger. Muki Betser was the third soldier to enter the hall. A soldier named Amos followed him. They identified another kidnapper and were able to shoot him down. Then Amir and Amos announced to the hostages that they were Israeli soldiers who had come to rescue them.[18]

Jean-Jacques Maimoni, a nineteen-year-old from Netanya, jumped up from his place and gave a shout of delight. Two Israeli soldiers who thought he was one of the hijackers shot him. Another hostage, fifty-year-old Pasco Cohen, who ran to the other side of the hall in order to locate his children, was also mistaken for a hijacker. The soldiers of the elite force aimed their guns at him and at one of the abductors who stood next to him. In the end, however, only one hostage, Ida Borowitz, died by hijacker gunfire. Fifteen seconds after the operation had begun, the passenger terminal was under the Sayeret's control.

While the special forces were completing the mission of liberating the hostages, Yoni Netanyahu had been shot outside the terminal. A 7.62 mm rifle bullet, apparently fired by one of the hijackers, penetrated his throat and killed him. In an investigation conducted by Iddo Netanyahu, other theories were raised. One possibility was that the abductor who had shot him in fact stood outside the terminal. Another was that a stray bullet fired by Sayeret fighters, who were also armed with Kalashnikov rifles, might have hit Yoni.

Paratroopers and Golani forces spilled out from the last two Hercules planes and began taking over the airport field. According to the soldiers, utter chaos reigned everywhere. A unit in the command of Omer Bar-Lev blew up eight MiG fighter jets of the Ugandan army without waiting for approval from the operation commander, Dan Shomron. In retrospect, it turned out that if these planes had been armed, the explosion might have reached the hostages and their rescuers. The hostages were led quickly to the Hercules planes. These huge cargo aircraft waited, engines running, for the command to fly back to Lod Airport. The last plane took to the air leaving Entebbe behind approximately one hour and forty minutes since the beginning of the operation.[19]

At the airport in Lod, family members, the highest army echelons, and heads of state were there to receive the occupants of the planes. The feelings of euphoria at the airport had a significant effect on the media in Israel and the Western world in general. The same could not be said for members of Sayeret Matkal. According to Omer Bar-Lev, "On the way back, I really had a lousy feeling. Although we did go, we fought, and it was like in the movies; but war is not fun. Yoni was killed and hostages were killed. There was a feeling of an historical moment, but also of discomfort. We landed in Israel at about nine, and at about six in the morning we began to hear news on the plane. In Israel, there was total hysteria over the happiness of victory, and that made us even more depressed."[20]

One year and seven months later, on Thursday, March 30, 1978, Dr. Wadie Haddad died at an East Berlin hospital at the age of forty-eight. According to his doctors, the cause of death was a severe and unidentified illness. Only some thirty years later were suspicions confirmed that Haddad's death was not a natural one. Israel had made him pay the price for the hijacking of Flight 139. Haddad, who with colleague Dr. George Habash had founded the Popular Front for the Liberation of Palestine, had been one of the most active terrorists in the international arena at the end of the 1960s and in the early 1970s. His people had hijacked the El Al plane that was forced to land in Algeria in June 1968. They were also responsible for "Skyjack Sunday," the hijacking operation of American and European airliners to Zarqa, Jordan, on September 6, 1970.[21]

Two months before the dramatic hijacking of September 1970, Israel made an initial attempt to assassinate Haddad. In the dead of night on Saturday, July 11, a volley of six Soviet-made Katyusha rockets was fired at his apartment on the third floor of the Katerji Building on Muhi a-Din al-Hayat Street in Beirut.[22] To his great fortune, the rockets slammed into the guestroom and bedroom while he himself was in the study at the time. Searches for the gunman led to an apartment in the neighboring building where three rocket launchers were found. A man with an Iranian passport had rented the apartment. In a newspaper interview, the head of Mossad at the time, Zvi Zamir, did not deny that his people had carried out the operation.

The attempt on his life did not stop Haddad from increasing his involvement in international terrorism. However, he became more suspicious and vigilant. The Baath regime in Iraq, which took him under his wing, provided him with breathing space so that he could continue to hatch his plots from his new and highly secure home in Baghdad. However, Mossad did not pass up the chance of "settling the score" with him. Operatives of the Tsomet unit who collected intelligence from agents who were active in Iraq learned about Haddad's weakness for fine chocolate. Procuring this kind of chocolate in the Iraq of those days was no simple feat, so a plan was devised in which Belgian pralines would be delivered to his residence by means of a Palestinian delivery boy who was also a Mossad collaborator. The organization assumed that the gluttonous Haddad would not share his sweet prize with anyone else. Before being wrapped, the pralines were injected with a fatal biological substance that had been developed at the Research Institute of Biology at Nes-Ziona. Several weeks later, the burly Haddad began to shed pounds. Laboratory tests showed that his immune system had collapsed. All attempts to diagnose the source of the problem led to naught. In great agony, Haddad slowly deteriorated. He died a few months later.[23]

The death of Haddad, however, had only a short-term effect on the PFLP. After a year of silence (1980) the organization returned to its campaign of terrorism, initiating attacks against Israeli targets worldwide as well as inside Israel's borders.

MISGAV AM

On the night of April 6, 1980, eight toddlers were asleep in the children's nursery at Kibbutz Misgav Am: four in the Rotem wing and four in the Narkiss wing. That night, kibbutz members Esti Shani and Yehudit Guri were on duty in the Rotem wing, and Meir Peretz in Narkiss. Before Shani went to bed, she asked her husband Sami, the kibbutz secretary, to check out a problem with the electricity. On his way to the nursery he was ambushed and shot. The shooting was carried out by five members of a cell belonging to the Arab Liberation Front, commanded by Kamal Ka'ush. A short while before, the five had crossed the Lebanon-Israel border near the village of Adaisa, on the seam between the territories controlled by the Irish and Nigerian battalions of the UN peacekeeping force. They had cut through an electric fence at the border, but because the electricity was down, no warning had sounded. From there, the walk to the kibbutz, which is very close to the border, was a short distance.[24]

After they reached the nursery the terrorists split into two groups and took control of the two wings of the building. The two women in the Rotem wing heard the shots that killed Sami Shani, and each picked up the infant closest to her and ran to hide in the showers. The terrorists took the remaining two babies with them to the Narkiss wing, where they rejoined their three cohorts, who had already tied up Meir Peretz. The kibbutz members woke to the sounds of gunfire and gathered next to the dining room. They decided to encircle the nursery. The terrorists, noticing the movement, opened with indiscriminate fire. Under cover of the confusion, a member of the kibbutz, Ze'ev Assaf, assisted by three young people, managed to sneak through the back door of the Rotem wing and rescue the women and two babies. While this was happening, the security forces were informed and army units began to fill the kibbutz.[25]

Just before 3:00 a.m., the intervention team of Sayeret Golani, a reconnaissance platoon of the Golani Brigade, which belongs to the Northern Command, arrived from Kiryat Shmona. The force, whose training in hostage rescue missions was limited, prepared to secure the area until takeover forces could arrive. The IDF commanders on site, however, led by Avigdor (Yanush) Ben-Gal of the Northern Command, believed that the situation was deteriorating quickly and that the children were in great danger. He ordered the Sayeret Golani team to storm the building. The commander of the force was the first to get to the door of the nursery. When he tried to breach it, the terrorists opened fire and threw hand grenades. The officer was wounded in the stomach, and one of his men was hit in the limbs. The force of the explosion threw the two into the nursery yard. In the meantime, three more fighters were wounded from another grenade. The team's medic, Eldad Tzafrir, was shot in the head and died on the spot. A number of grenades were thrown toward the backup team as it attempted to break through a side door, and they were forced to take cover. By this stage, the Golani force had one dead and six wounded, three of them critically. Ben-Gal decided to halt the operation. Around 5:00 a.m., Minister of Defense Ezer Weizman arrived with Chief of Staff Rafael Eitan and took command of the situation. Sayeret Matkal teams landed in the area a short time later.[26]

Soon after dawn, an Arabic-speaking soldier equipped with a megaphone was sent to the nursery and asked the terrorists what they wanted. They replied with a list of demands, including one calling for the immediate release of fifty terrorists from Israeli prisons and their transfer to Lebanon, accompanied by a representative of the Red Cross. The terrorists threatened to execute the infants at 7:00 a.m. if these demands were not met. When they were asked to extend the period of the ultimatum, the terrorists agreed to do so and even accepted bottles of milk for the children. Sayeret Matkal took advantage of the negotiations to prepare an assault plan. At the same time, Yamam fighters were making efforts to get to the site with a plan of their own. A few minutes before 10:00 a.m., Rafael Eitan ordered the Sayeret Matkal force to storm the building. In retrospect, Chief of Staff Eitan explained that despite its expertise in takeover situations, Yamam still lacked the necessary experience to carry out such an attack. He also made no effort to hide his lack of sympathy for the unit's commander, Assaf Hefetz.[27]

Two Sayeret teams participated in the assault. Besides enlisted men, several officers also joined in, including Omer Bar-Lev and Shai Avital, future commanders of the unit. The first team breached the entrance door of the building, and the second was to enter through a large glass window. The terrorists were ready for them. They threw a grenade that wounded the commander of the first force and some of his men. After pulling himself together, one soldier from this force penetrated the building, with several others following his lead. They killed three of the terrorists, and the other team, which in the meantime had got through the window, shot two more. During the operation six men were wounded, including the unit commander, Uzi Dayan, and officers Omer Bar-Lev, Amos Ben-Avraham, and Ziv Kolberg. One of the infants, Eyal Gluska, was killed in the exchange of fire. Meir Peretz, who had been held by the terrorists, was also wounded. After the operation, the frustrated Yamam forces assembled, collected their police identity cards in a bag, and threw them away in protest. Misgav Am was the first in a long series of conflicts and disagreements between the two units.[28]

How is it possible to explain the repeated decisions of the heads of the security apparatus to entrust rescue operations to Sayeret Matkal, especially once the Yamam had already been perfectly qualified to carry out such operations? As hypothesized, one of the problems of Sayeret Matkal and other such units is that they mostly participate in operations that take place far from the eyes of the media and the public. In most cases, the operations are secret, technical, and are carried out on enemy territory. In comparison, counterterrorist operations, especially hostage rescues, are prestigious and receive much attention. Such operations help units to enhance their prestige both in the eyes of the public and policymakers. This explains the struggle among infantry regiments, whose role within the armed forces is completely different, to train and take part in such operations. The Entebbe raid was only one example for this rivalry. In addition to the passion for action and glorification of the unit, there is another factor—the culture of improvisation that has developed in elite military units since the period of the Palmach, through the times of the 101st Unit, and until this day. Officers and soldiers in elite units who are required to show resourcefulness in dangerous circumstances relating to their specializations tend also to be confident in their ability to adapt quickly to other unexpected events, especially those involving counterterrorist situations. Policymakers, for their part, tend to buy in to the myths developed by the units and accept the word of their officers without question. Representatives of the security apparatus who supervise these crises are military people who used to be more familiar with Sayeret Matkal than the Yamam. Some served in the unit, and a few even commanded it. Consequently, even though they are aware that the Yamam is the task force most capable of carrying out such operations, time and again they follow their hearts in favor of the Sayeret.

In the early 1980s, the wave of hostage-taking incidents declined. Some analysts attribute this to changes in the nature of world terrorism, while others explain it as a result of the IDF's efforts to drive PLO forces away from Israel's borders during the First Lebanon War. The defensive model, which Israel applied mostly but not exclusively in airplanes and airports, had also contributed considerably. The terrorists slowly realized that in order to execute successful hostage-taking incidents, they would first have to penetrate heavily protected territories, a mission that over the years had become almost impossible.[29]

IN THE EARLY 1970S, the threat from the northern border loomed larger. With the help of the residents of Palestinian refugee camps in southern Lebanon, Arafat and his people had become a significant military force in the region, which became known as Fatahland. They established a paramilitary force consisting of three infantry brigades. The proximity to Israel's northern border enabled the Palestinian fighters to launch a series of attacks inside Israel, some of which have been discussed in the previous chapter. Small cells that invaded Israel by land, lay in wait, and fired at Israeli cars carried out many of these attacks. This was not their only tactic. In several cases, the terrorists broke into frontier settlements and kidnapped or murdered civilians. Fatah seaborne forces breached Israel's beaches, stealing in on rubber dinghies. These terrorists drew on the element of surprise and attacked civilian centers near where they had landed.[1]

One of the methods that proved particularly effective in thwarting terrorist incursions was the introduction of a dense visual-intelligence (VISINT) network that covered Israel's land borders, as well as its air and marine space. To this end, the IDF established new observation outposts aided by advanced optic technologies, keeping a particular eye on Lebanon. Hawkeye spy aircraft and unmanned aerial vehicles (UAVs) were also put into operation at that time. This facilitated the immediate dispatch of forces to locations where suspicious movement was identified. When terrorists still managed to penetrate Israeli territory and reach population centers, military intervention and takeover units were urgently deployed.[2]

Despite all Israeli efforts, the Palestinian attacks on Israeli population centers continued to increase. The most famous attack against Israel that originated in Lebanon at the time was known as the "Blood Bus" attack. On March 11, 1978, eleven Fatah members landed by sea near Highway 2, which connects Haifa and Tel Aviv. They hijacked a bus and two taxis. In the ensuing battle with security forces, thirty-five passengers were killed and seventy-one were injured. Within

the political and the military establishments there was consensus that retaliation was unavoidable after such a bloody attack. Central figures in both circles
concluded that in order to deter the Palestinians from continuing their attacks,
the high cost of such attacks should be made clear to them. Prime Minister Menachem Begin declared in the Knesset: "Gone forever are the days when Jewish
blood could be shed with impunity!" At a meeting with the families bereaved in
the attack, Deputy Prime Minister Yigael Yadin implied that the Israeli response
would be offensive and that revenge was imminent.[3]

Three days later, Israel reaffirmed its commitment to the war model. IDF
forces invaded Lebanon. During the operation, the forces conducted searches
and punitive actions against Palestinians situated in South Lebanon and pushed
Palestinian forces beyond the Litani River. Yet it was not an effective solution
to the attacks on northern Israeli communities. Fatah, which had already struck
Israeli targets with Katyusha missiles in the late 1960s, adjusted to the new situation by returning to this method in the early 1980s. During May–June 1981, Fatah
forces intensified Katyusha missile attacks against Israeli settlements, resulting
in intensive retaliation by the Israeli Air Force. However, the inability of Israeli
aerial forces to reduce the Katyusha attacks led to the signing of cease-fire agreements between the two sides in June 1981. For the first time, Israel had agreed
to negotiate (although through an American arbitrator) with Fatah. While the
cease-fire agreements resulted in some decline in the violence in northern Israel,
Fatah operatives intensified their terrorist campaign against Israeli targets worldwide, conducting no less than nine attacks on Israeli targets between May 1981
and June 1982, mostly against Israeli diplomats and Jewish community centers.
Israeli policymakers, most notably the longtime architect of Israel's counterterrorism doctrine, Ariel Sharon, and military officers awaited the opportunity to
strike again. In the meantime, they devised the Oranim Plan, a detailed scheme
for an Israeli invasion of Lebanon and for the elimination of the entire Palestinian terrorism infrastructure.[4]

THE FIRST LEBANON WAR

On a Thursday afternoon in June 1982, the phone rang on the ground floor at
52 Evelyn Gardens in the Kensington neighborhood of London. The concierge
lifted the receiver, and a man on the other end asked her to call Nawaf al-Rosan,
who lived on the first floor. During a brief conversation, al-Rosan, a member of
the Abu Nidal group, received instructions to set out on his mission. A short time
later he packed his suitcase and walked to the Hilton Hotel on Park Lane. From

the lobby of the hotel he made two phone calls, the first to Marwan al-Banna and the second to Hussein Said, instructing them to meet him at the hotel at 9:30 p.m. When they arrived, al-Rosan revealed their mission—the assassination of the Israeli ambassador to the United Kingdom, who at that moment was dining at the Dorchester Hotel.

Al-Banna brought a brown case from his car containing a Polish WZ63 submachine gun and two magazines. He handed it over to Said in the restroom of the hotel. Said immediately set out for the entrance of the neighboring Dorchester Hotel. A few minutes after 11:00 p.m., the Israeli ambassador, fifty-two-year-old Shlomo Argov, left the hotel lobby with a friend. Colin Simpson, a bodyguard assigned to him by British security, was walking to their car when he heard the blast of gunshots. The ambassador fell to the ground and Simpson began chasing the gunman. When Simpson had narrowed the gap to a few yards, the assassin turned around and opened fire on him. Luckily, Said's aim was off. Simpson drew his gun and shot him in the head before he could get off another round. Ambassador Argov was hospitalized and underwent a number of surgeries, but ultimately, he remained paralyzed for the rest of his life. The three terrorists were caught and sentenced to prison terms of thirty to thirty-five years.[5]

Three days later, on June 6, 1982, Israel responded: Army forces crossed the northern border and penetrated into Lebanese territory. The government of Israel used Argov's assassination attempt to justify a wide-scale invasion of southern Lebanon. The declared objective of the campaign was to eliminate the Palestinian terrorist infrastructure in southern Lebanon, which had made life in the outlying northern regions of Israel intolerable. The armored regiments and infantry, however, did not stop when southern Lebanon fell under IDF control; a week after the outbreak of combat, the Israeli army had massed at the edge of Beirut. The question of why Israeli forces, in fact, advanced that far became the subject of much speculation.[6]

One explanation leads directly to the intelligence community, specifically to Mossad. Mossad agents had operated in Lebanon many years before the military invasion of 1982. Their relationship with the leaders of Maronite Christians began in the 1950s and had developed since the infiltration of Palestinian militias into Lebanon and the outbreak of the Lebanese Civil War. Cooperation with the Christians in Lebanon grew stronger over the course of the 1970s, to a large degree as a result of sharing a common enemy—Syria, which had invaded Lebanon in 1976 in order to help the Maronite camp during the course of the civil war, but soon afterward withdrew its support. With the help of the Maronite elite, Israel had established an intelligence infrastructure in that country. In the months preceding the operation, Mossad had produced assessments asserting that Israeli military involvement would strengthen the political position of the Maronite Christians in the country and would lead to an historic process of reconciliation with Israel. As a result of the assessment, Israeli policymakers, led by Minister of Defense Ariel Sharon, who was eager to uproot the PLO stronghold in Lebanon, visited Phalange leaders in Beirut months before in order to prepare a plan of operation.[7]

In his visits to Lebanon, Sharon was accompanied by Mossad representative in Lebanon Avner Azoulai, deputy head of Mossad Menachem (Nachik) Navot, and David Kimche, who had previously been deputy head of Mossad and was at the time general director of the Ministry of Foreign Affairs. The decisive visit took place on January 12, 1982, when Sharon arrived in Beirut. This time he was accompanied by the deputy head of the general staff, Moshe Levy; the head of Aman, Yehoshua Sagi; and the commanding officer of the Israeli infantry, Lieutenant General Amos Yaron. During the course of the visit, the Israelis presented several alternatives. The Christians pledged their assistance to the IDF forces on the condition that they would not have to openly cooperate with the Israelis. They were concerned that their leader, Bashir Gemayel, would be regarded as a collaborator, and that this would hurt his chances of being elected president of Lebanon. In a follow-up meeting that took place at a villa in the town of Junia, Sharon presented a revised plan to the Gemayel family and representatives of the Maronite elite. Both sides left the meeting satisfied.

The plan went as expected. On August 23, two and a half months after the invasion, and owing to the presence of the Israeli army, Bashir Gemayel was elected president of Lebanon during a lightning parliamentary process. His leadership lasted only four weeks and ended in tragedy. An explosive device planted by the Syrian Social Nationalist Party at the Phalange headquarters in the Ashrafieh neighborhood of Beirut exploded while Gemayel was giving a speech, and the building collapsed on its occupants, including the president. Bashir's brother Amine took over the seat of power, but his relationship with Mossad was much more restrained. Later, he even repudiated his dead brother's commitment to sign a peace treaty with Israel. Indeed, the peace agreement between Israel and Lebanon was never implemented.[8]

The murder of Bashir Gemayel and the retaliatory massacre carried out by Phalange forces in the Palestinian refugee camps of Sabra and Shatilla were a resounding defeat for both Mossad and Sharon, whose role in Lebanon earned mention in the critical report issued by the Kahan Commission. While the committee recommended that Sharon not continue to serve as minister of defense, it also stated that Mossad had failed to provide the government with a decisive warning about the potential hazardous consequences of letting the Phalange enter the refugee camps.[9] During the following two decades, Mossad leaders reduced the agency's involvement in the Lebanese sphere and left it to the GSS and Aman.

THE HEZBOLLAH CHALLENGE

In the late 1970s, while Mossad was strengthening ties with the Maronites, Aman initiated contacts with Shiite leaders in southern Lebanon. These connections facilitated the formation of a network of informers that made Israel's intelligence-gathering efforts in this area easier. The honeymoon with the majority of the Shiites, however, was short-lived. A short time after the Israeli invasion, the Iranian ambassador in Damascus, Ali-Akbar Mohtashamipour, received a direct order from Tehran to assist the Lebanese Sheikh Mohammed Hussein Fadlallah. His mission was to establish Shiite organizations that would spread Khomeini's Islamic revolutionary line and compete with Amal, the Shiite organization that had refused to become an Iranian proxy. Iran had tried to send paramilitary forces to Lebanon as early as 1979, but President Assad refused to let them move through Syrian territory. The Israeli invasion led him to change his mind. Mohtashamipour established the Friendship Family, a union of Islamic movements that gratefully accepted Iranian sponsorship. At this point, the Syrian president allowed Iran to station about three thousand Revolutionary Guards in the Beqaa Valley under Syrian military control. These events did not escape Israeli intelligence, but they rang no warning bells among leaders of the intelligence community.[10]

The seeds sown by the Iranians sprouted and within a few years flourished into a strong organization—Hezbollah, or the Party of Allah. While Israel's intelligence and combat forces were focusing on the struggle against the PLO, strengthening ties with the Christians and paying less attention to the Shiites, the Hezbollah militants and their operators in Tehran were recruiting support in Shiite neighborhoods and villages throughout Lebanon. They kept a very low profile in their military activities, refrained from taking responsibility for attacks they perpetrated and if any responsibility was in fact claimed, names of fictitious organizations were used. The new organization was highly compartmentalized. Young people identified as potential Hezbollah fighters underwent a long process of screening and security checks in order to close breaches through which Israeli intelligence could have penetrated. Even after their recruitment, fighters were not privy to any details of the organization's facilities, the location of its headquarters, or the identity of its leaders. Israel found itself in a paradoxical situation. Contrary to expectations, the expulsion of the PLO forces to Tunis did not diminish the threat of terrorism to the settlements in northern Israel. In place of the PLO, Hezbollah had sprung up right under the noses of the intelligence community. Interagency feuding in the Lebanese arena, especially between Aman and the GSS, impaired Israel's attempts to cope with the threat.[11]

THE ERA OF INTELLIGENCE WARS

One of the first portents of the future was a confrontation played out between IDF supply-line drivers and participants in a procession commemorating the Day of Ashura—the holiest day for Shiites—in the town of Nabatiya on October 16, 1983. One day after the incident, the Shiite leader Mahdi Shams al-Din issued a *fatwa* calling for a public uprising against Israel. Guerilla attacks against IDF soldiers intensified. At the time, it was still not clear that only one organization was behind the attacks. Hezbollah in its more familiar form appeared when Ibrahim al-Amin read an open letter addressed to the "oppressed" Lebanese public at a rally in Beirut on February 16, 1985. In this manifesto, he spelled out the movement's place in the worldwide Islamic nation, following Khomeini's brand of revolutionary ideology. He also pledged armed struggle against Israel.[12]

The invasion of Lebanon had thrown a spanner in the works with regard to the division of jurisdictional sectors among the Israeli intelligence agencies. In principle, the GSS jurisdiction was limited to the State of Israel and the occupied territories; Aman was responsible for Arab countries and the Middle East; and Mossad handled special operations and intelligence in the rest of the world. The problem with this division is that in order to enhance their reputation, prove their importance, and secure resources, intelligence organizations tend to compete with one another. Thus, when they identify a promising lead, they tend to overlook geographical boundaries. Furthermore, when an agency such as Mossad identifies a target operating on foreign soil and has been able to collect human intelligence (HUMINT) regarding its intentions, electronic monitoring is necessary. In many cases, the mission will be assigned to the relatively small signal intelligence (SIGINT) and visual intelligence (VISINT) units of Mossad instead of to Aman, whose specialization lies in monitoring signals and gathering visual intelligence. To make this even more complex, terrorist groups, as well as other targets of the intelligence community, do not necessarily adhere to a similar geographic distribution. Quite often, Palestinian groups, as well as other groups such as Hezbollah, may concurrently operate in the West Bank and the Gaza Strip, or in Arab and other countries. Their various arms may spread to Europe, Africa, and Latin America, and they may also benefit from the collaboration of Palestinian and Arab diasporic communities, other subnational groups, or countries all over the world. The flexibility of these kinds of groups has led to a corresponding distension of Israeli intelligence organization jurisdictions and, in some cases, has led some agencies to step on the toes of other agencies.[13]

A short time after war broke out, Prime Minister Begin decided to have the GSS, by then experienced in gathering HUMINT in the West Bank and the Gaza Strip, assist IDF forces in dealing with the challenges they faced in the unfamiliar and complicated arena of southern Lebanon. In the first stages of the war, Aman operatives accepted the presence of their GSS colleagues and were careful to cooperate with them. As the Israeli presence in Lebanon persisted, however, the relationship cooled. Aman officers who tried to strengthen their ties with the Shiites claimed that the GSS used especially aggressive methods of interrogation on Shiite detainees. On the other hand, GSS operatives complained that Aman officers were young and inexperienced and had no understanding of intelligence work. The two organizations warned of a lack of cooperation, maintaining that concomitant operations were initiated without notification and that agencies were even sabotaging each other's efforts to collect intelligence.[14]

Moshe Arens, who replaced Ariel Sharon as defense minister, felt that the power struggle between the agencies was having a disastrous effect on the intelligence presented to the government. To solve this problem, he appointed Uri Lubrani, former Israeli ambassador in Iran, to coordinate government activities in Lebanon. His involvement did indeed improve the situation for a short while, but the disagreements never really ceased. In June 1985, when Israeli forces were redeployed in the security buffer zone in southern Lebanon, a new effort was made to find a solution to the internal hostilities. The IDF's Lebanese Liaison Unit established a new intelligence body, Gathering and Prevention, that was to concentrate on guerilla forces that were attacking IDF soldiers, enabling the GSS to leave the problematic region. Collecting intelligence on the ever-strengthening Hezbollah, however, was too complicated a challenge for such a young unit, and the GSS was once again called in to give the IDF a hand. The two organizations worked from a common base in the Israeli border town of Metulla. Aman representatives, afraid that GSS handlers were regaining dominance, were not happy about cooperating with them. Confrontations between the organizations occurred on subjects ranging from which techniques to use when operating informants to inconsequential issues, like the allocation of parking spaces. Two years later, Yossi Peled, head of the IDF Northern Command, dismantled the partnership. The quality of the intelligence it had collected was in reverse proportion to the amount of endless bickering that went on between the representatives of the two organizations. With the permission of Minister of Defense Yitzhak Rabin, Peled approached GSS head Yossef Harmelin and asked that his people take over responsibility for all intelligence gathering in the field. To this end, the GSS established a special unit called the Metulla District, which reported directly to the head of the agency.[15]

Not even the transfer of responsibility over southern Lebanon to the GSS could put an end to the territorial struggles between the two intelligence agencies. Hezbollah was extremely active beyond the "red line" of the security zone, in what was called the "gray zone," an area outside of GSS control that was Aman's responsibility. The decision to establish a network of informants within the gray zone aroused resentment in Aman. One of the main factors that finally led to a solution to the disagreement was the warm personal relationship between IDF Lebanese Liaison Unit officers and those of the GSS at the time. Personal relationships, however, can be transient. The appointment of Yitzhak Mordechai as head of the IDF Northern Command in 1991 was a turning point, and relations between representatives of the organizations cooled. Mordechai asked that GSS operations in Lebanon be subject to IDF authority. GSS representative Carmi Gillon opposed the initiative, and it was never approved.[16]

Territorial struggles and personal conflicts were not the only causes of tension between the two intelligence organizations. They also disagreed on how the information in their possession was to be analyzed and which recommendations would be presented to government leaders. In the early 1990s, with financial assistance from Iran, Hezbollah opened a network of social-welfare institutions that provided health and welfare services to the residents of southern Lebanon. To combat this, the GSS recommended that the civilian sphere not be relinquished to the organization and that an effort should be made to compete with Hezbollah in providing such services. One of its recommendations was to strengthen Amal, which at that time still saw itself as an alternative to Hezbollah. The plan was for Amal to support local village leaders who would take social measures similar to those of Hezbollah. Aman and the intelligence unit of the Northern Command rejected the idea out of hand. In their estimation, at that time Hezbollah did not have a real hold on the population, making the initiative unnecessary. Minister of Defense Moshe Arens accepted Aman's position. Over the years, it has been proven that this assessment was far from correct. Hezbollah only grew stronger and mobilized more support. Was this just an incorrect assessment on behalf of Aman's analysts, or did the interagency rivalry encourage them to submit a recommendation that would contradict the one offered by the GSS? I am not convinced that there is a clear-cut answer to the question. At any rate, this conflict of assessments intensified the competition between the two organizations; Aman operatives, who saw the GSS as an organization that should focus solely on thwarting terrorism, rejected its attempts to present assessments relating to the political and social situation in southern Lebanon.[17]

An examination of the relations among the Israeli intelligence agencies at the time shows that often the issues at the root of their disagreements have nothing to do with intelligence or operational matters at all, but are an expression of generic problems in public organizations, which tend to be highly territorial and compete over prestige and resources. These problems are far from being exclusive to Israel. One would expect that organizations experienced in fighting terrorism would be highly capable of accommodating themselves to an ever-changing reality. In reality, they tend to be conservative, close-minded, and apt to engage in struggles over territory, resources, and reputation.[18]

WHILE THE INTELLIGENCE COMMUNITY and the IDF were invested in an attempt to deal with the new threats that emerged from Lebanon, the first signs of unrest became apparent in the Gaza Strip and the West Bank. Despite the tight control of the GSS over these areas, it failed to foresee the increasing turbulence.[1] Moreover, almost ten years after the failed takeover attempt in Ma'alot, the lack of clarity about the division of labor among the various elite units had not been resolved.

THE BUS 300 AFFAIR

This ambiguity of policy was manifested on Thursday, April 12, 1984. Shortly after 6:30 p.m., four Fatah members took control of the number 300 Egged bus en route from Tel Aviv to Ashkelon with thirty-four passengers on board. The abductors, armed with hand grenades, improvised explosive devices, and knives, ordered the driver, Ilan Halevy, to drive toward Gaza. During the course of the trip, the passengers got the impression that the hijackers had no clear plan. Police in cruisers who heard reports of the hijacking began to chase the bus, which broke through the IDF checkpoint at Erez and then through another improvised roadblock. The police were afraid the bus would reach Gaza City, where the chances of a successful rescue were slim, and so they opened fire on the vehicle. Two passengers were wounded, but the bullets punctured the tires, causing the bus to come to a lurching halt near the Dir al-Balah refugee camp in Gaza. Military and police forces were called in. An interrogator from the Intelligence Corps attempted to bargain with the cell's leader, Jamal Qablan, but this led nowhere. The hijackers demanded the immediate release of five hundred prisoners who were to be taken to an Arab country. In the meantime, Yamam forces arrived and prepared for an assault. At some point, the terrorists announced that one of the passengers had been badly wounded. Ehud Yatom, head of the GSS operations branch, volunteered to provide them with a first-aid kit. This gave him an opportunity to collect visual intelligence on what was going on inside the bus, including

the exact location of each of the hijackers. Information collected by GSS personnel who observed the bus through binoculars corroborated Yatom's depiction.[2]

In the meantime, a Sayeret Matkal team also arrived on the scene. A senior
GSS officer who was at headquarters attested to the fact that Chief of Staff
Moshe Levy, backed by Infantry Corps Commander Yitzhak Mordechai, had decided arbitrarily that Sayeret Matkal would carry out the takeover. At 4:00 a.m.,
several fighters from this unit breached the windows and doors of the bus and
attacked the terrorists with handguns. The operation took about a minute, during
which two of the terrorists and one of the hostages were killed and another seven
passengers were wounded. The frustration of the Yamam fighters after once again
seeing Sayeret Matkal carry out a rescue operation with an unfortunate ending
was so severe that some resigned from the unit.[3]

The drama on Bus 300 would not have become so deeply engraved in the
Israeli collective memory had it not been for the events of the aftermath. The Israeli news media, which closely followed the tumultuous events, reported the
next morning that *four* terrorists had been killed in the takeover operation. The
discrepancy between what had happened the night before and the media report
stemmed from the fact that two of the terrorists who were captured alive had
been executed that night on a direct order from the GSS chief, Avraham Shalom.
Three days later, Israeli newspapers began publishing initial reports on the more
accurate version of the affair. At first, in order to bypass the restrictions of the
military censor, the Israeli media quoted reports from the foreign press. *Hadashot*,
an Israeli newspaper, put an end to the rumors when it printed a full front-page
photo of the two handcuffed hijackers being taken away for interrogation by GSS
operatives. The publication of that photo opened a Pandora's box whose first
casualty was the newspaper itself, which was closed for two days by an admin-
istrative order from the military censor. After that, a commission of inquiry was
established yet its conclusions were distorted due to false testimonies provided by
GSS operatives. In the end, the findings of a second commission of inquiry led
to the GSS chief's resignation. The ramifications of the incident, which came to
be known as the "Bus 300 Affair," were far-reaching. One of the most important
outcomes was the examination of the GSS methods of operation at that time and
the imposition of a series of legal restrictions on the organization's activities.[4]

One fact related to the affair, however, was not given sufficient coverage: Avraham Shalom did not act alone. He interpreted to the best of his understanding
a message relayed to him by Prime Minister Yitzhak Shamir, which stated, "Do
not take any terrorists captive."[5] The GSS, like other intelligence and thwarting

organizations, operates in a twilight zone. It endeavors to translate its sometimes deliberately vague orders from policymakers, and the result can be confusing at the operational level. Covert agencies are required to do everything in their power to achieve results. If they fail, they may discover that there is no one there to back them up.

THE "MOTHERS BUS"

It was only four years later, as a result of a chance mix-up, that the Yamam got its first opportunity to prove itself. During the night of March 6 and 7, 1988, a cell of three PLO activists infiltrated Israel from Egypt, west of Mitzpe Ramon.[6] The three were armed with Kalashnikov rifles, a Karl Gustav machine gun, and hand grenades. At 6:30 a.m., they took over a military vehicle, chased off its passengers, and began traveling north in the direction of Sde Boker. Reports on the incident spread through army and police communication channels, and roadblocks were set up on the vehicle's anticipated route. At approximately 7:15 a.m., the vehicle crashed through a roadblock at the Dimona-Yeruham Junction. Police manning the roadblock took off in pursuit, while the terrorists opened indiscriminate fire. A half-hour later the car stopped at the Aroer Junction where a bus transporting workers to the nuclear facility in Dimona was passing by. The driver and most of the passengers escaped as they saw the armed young men storming the bus, but one man and ten women remained trapped inside. Meanwhile, military and police forces arrived and surrounded the vehicle. The commander of the Negev police region, Haim Benayoun, began negotiations with the hijackers, who demanded that a Red Cross representative be brought in immediately. Not far from the site, Minister of Defense Yitzhak Rabin, Chief of Staff Dan Shomron, and head of the IDF Southern Command Yitzhak Mordecai were assembled. Once again, both police and army takeover units had been called in, but erroneous information regarding the location of the incident had been communicated to Sayeret Matkal's operations room. Their helicopters did not arrive in time, and the commanders in the field had no choice but to give the Yamam the go-ahead.[7]

A Yamam intelligence officer interrogated the women who escaped from the bus and gathered tactical intelligence regarding the precise number of abductors involved and their location in the vehicle. Unit sharpshooters deployed around the bus monitored the terrorists' activities with their binoculars. The information collected by the officer and the sniper surveillance provided the unit commander, Alik Ron, with enough information to prepare an assault plan and present it to the district police commander. Meanwhile, negotiations were proceeding very slowly, with the terrorists making unrealistic demands, including the release of all the Palestinian prisoners held by Israel. When the terrorists realized the negotiators were trying to kill time, they announced that they would begin executing the hostages at half-hour intervals. To prove the seriousness of their intentions, they shot the male hostage, Victor Ram, and Miriam Ben-Yair, one of the female hostages. The order came from military headquarters to carry out the takeover at once. Yamam snipers opened fire on the terrorists while the fighters breached the windows and doors of the bus. The raid took about thirty seconds. Before they were eliminated, the terrorists had time to shoot and kill one more hostage.[8]

In retrospect, this was one of the most complicated rescue missions in Israel's history. The abductors were better armed and more determined than their predecessors. This proof of Yamam's capabilities, however, did not put an end to the decision makers' practice of also calling in Sayeret Matkal during hostage-taking incidents. The initial logic of activating multiple units is clear. A hostage-taking incident can quickly deteriorate, and it is good policy to have adequate forces in place so that, if necessary, they can respond to the worsening situation. What is less logical was the absence of an official policy establishing that whenever both units arrive at a hostage situation, Yamam would carry out the takeover and Sayeret Matkal would act as backup.

ABU JIHAD

One day later, on March 8, 1988, the security cabinet convened to decide on an appropriate response to the hijacking. The intelligence organizations were asked to provide possible targets. Five weeks later, the Israeli government unanimously approved a recommendation to assassinate Khalil al-Wazir, better known as Abu Jihad, the head of the PLO's military arm and Arafat's deputy. Similar to the Spring of Youth operation, this was a complex, high-risk mission involving special forces from the air, land, and sea, as well as Mossad operatives. The painstaking planning of the mission included obtaining information on the layout of Abu Jihad's home in Tunis, the access roads to it, and the target's daily routine. Based on this information, a model of Abu Jihad's house was built in Israel, and special forces teams used it for dry runs through the assassination.[9]

The contingent that ultimately embarked from Haifa Port on April 13, 1988, consisted of two Saar 4.5 class missile boats, which served as a security force; two Saar 4 class boats, which carried the Sayeret Matkal and Shayetet 13 commandos; and a submarine. The boats had Zodiac dinghies onboard that would ferry the commandos to shore and Bell 206 helicopters in case an urgent departure was required. A Boeing 707 airliner accompanied the ships, serving as both transmission station and electronic signal scrambler. Deputy Chief of Staff Ehud Barak commanded the mission from the control room of one of the boats. Sayeret Matkal Commander Moshe (Bogi) Yaalon led the assassination force.[10]

On April 15, the elite force, which by this time was already positioned opposite the Tunisian shore, received the final approval to proceed. Twenty Sayeret Matkal soldiers came ashore. As in the Beirut operation fifteen years earlier, Mossad operatives awaited the commandos on the beach. The forces quickly boarded three cars—two Volkswagen Transporters and one Peugeot 305—that Mossad had rented a few days earlier. That night, Abu Jihad's family returned to their home in the Sidi Bou-Said neighborhood at 11:30 p.m. Abu Jihad's wife and children retired to their beds shortly thereafter, while he went to his study and worked until 1:00 a.m. before heading off to sleep. An hour later, the forces, which had split into four teams, received the order to move into action. Teams A and B approached the building while teams C and D stood guard. Two fighters from team A, one of them dressed as a woman, approached the car in which Ali Abed al-Awal, Abu Jihad's bodyguard, was dozing, and shot him in the head. The commandos also shot a Tunisian maintenance man in the garden. Then they broke into the house and rushed, single file, upstairs to the rooms. Team A went straight to the first-floor bedroom of Abu Jihad, who had been aroused by the noise. He got as far as the doorway, where a hail of bullets met him. One of the commandos later described the "unnatural" sight of Abu Jihad's bullet-riddled body standing upright for several seconds before it finally collapsed. Only then did the officer call for his men to stop firing.

Abu Jihad's wife, Umm Jihad, related afterward that other soldiers who passed her husband's body continued to fire at him, until she yelled at them in Arabic, "*Bas!*"—Enough! Immediately following the shooting, a senior officer entered the room and asked the soldiers to show him the body. The officer bent down and saw Abu Jihad, who was lying face down. He turned the body over with his foot and shot him once more in the head. During this time, the other commandos raided Abu Jihad's study and collected documents. They also confiscated his safe and telephone answering machine. Five minutes later, the teams met the cars that had been waiting for them near the house and sped back to the beach, where the naval commandos awaited them. The Sayeret fighters and Mossad agents then abandoned the cars and boarded the Zodiac dinghies for the journey back to the boats.[11]

The Israeli government continually denied any involvement in the operation.

Two days after the assassination, when Prime Minister Yitzhak Shamir was asked if he knew something about the attack on Abu Jihad's house, he replied, "I heard about it on the radio, just like you."[12] Even so, the flood of rumors that reached the world press left no doubts as to the identity of the assailants.

The main questions were why had Israel chosen to go back to targeting senior Palestinians and why was Abu Jihad singled out? Although he had been a central figure behind the establishment of Fatah's paramilitary frameworks in Jordan and Lebanon, he had lost most of his power after the destruction of the Lebanon-based PLO infrastructure during the First Lebanon War with Israel. Local cells of young people in the Gaza Strip and West Bank had initiated the riots and violent activities, including the hijacking of the bus that triggered the assassination. The exiled PLO leadership was left playing a secondary role.[13]

The answer to these questions is that most of the leaders in Israel were aware of the futility of the assassinations policy, even from the time of Operation Wrath of God in the mid-1970s. As mentioned earlier, the overwhelming majority of the assassinations did not strike significantly at the organizations' ability to operate against Israel, and they certainly did not reduce their motivation to do so. This supports the hypothesis that the assassinations were dictated by the aspirations of politicians to raise public morale, appease Israeli public opinion, and recruit support for the government. No less important was the element of vengeance. Despite the tendency by many to view political decisions as a product of the calculated thought and measured considerations of the costs versus the anticipated results of each operation, one cannot rule out the significance of a basic human instinct that also affects policymakers—the passion for revenge. One of the questions that remain unresolved is whether these assassinations justified exposing hundreds of Israel's most elite fighters to harm as well as mobilizing so many forces from the various branches of the armed forces.[14]

While Israel was risking its most elite units in questionable operations, it also reintroduced the old concept of *histaarevut*. As political unrest in the occupied territories mounted, the Duvdevan, Shimshon, and Yamas special forces were created. The first was designated to operate in the West Bank. The second, which was later dismantled, was assigned to the Gaza Strip, while Yamas was to operate wherever deemed necessary. In light of experience, together with training in the fields of microwarfare and *histaarvut*, the fighters also learned Arabic, including the local dialects. This made it much easier for them to circulate in Palestinian areas. During their training, novice soldiers were required to associate with Palestinian youths and sometimes even take part in protests against the IDF. The operations of the special-forces soldiers sometimes led to amusing situations. During the first intifada (1987–1993), demonstrations mounted by the *shabibeh*, the young people, gained widespread media coverage. One day, the popular Israeli daily newspaper *Yedioth Ahronoth* published a photograph of young Palestinians throwing rocks at an Israeli military vehicle in one of the Gaza Strip refugee camps. The newspaper photographer was not aware of the fact that the local youths were in fact soldiers from the Shimshon Unit. Those units stood in the forefront of the counterterrorism effort during the years of the first intifada.[15]

THE INTIFADA AND EMERGENCE OF HAMAS

While Hezbollah was establishing itself in Lebanon, political changes were taking place in the West Bank and the Gaza Strip as well. Young activists who had been born and raised under the Israeli occupation were filling the upper ranks of the leadership of the Palestinian national struggle. At the same time, the Islamic religious organizations that were groomed in the 1970s by the military administration and the GSS as a counterweight to the Palestinian national movement assumed a political character—the largest of which was Hamas. Throughout the 1970s, Israel was hoping that the Muslim Brothers would serve as a counterforce to the increasing political influence of the PLO in the occupied territories. The broad consensus within the GSS that the Muslim Brothers denounce any kind of violent activity opened the door to allowing local Muslim associations and charities to act freely and acquire substantial political influence, especially at the local level.

The first intifada, which broke out on December 9, 1987, kept GSS handlers and departments busy around the clock. The agency had to cope with violent riots in various towns and villages headed by young people who initially refused to accept the authority of the PLO leadership in Tunis. Thus, instead of the familiar, organized Palestinian enemy, the security establishment was now faced again with local gangs, amorphous social networks whose surveillance and penetration required intensive HUMINT sources.[16]

Hamas, which adhered to the Muslim Brotherhood's worldview, initiated a process similar to the one that had taken place in Lebanon a few years earlier. It took advantage of the smokescreen created by the events of the intifada to tighten its hold on Palestinian society, mainly by providing welfare services, for which there was an ever-growing demand. At the same time, Hamas's political ambitions were kept far from prying eyes and ears. The GSS, whose main efforts were concentrated on dealing with the popular uprising, had to make do with a remote surveillance of the Islamic charity organization. The turning point only came more than a year after the outbreak of the intifada, when two Israeli soldiers were kidnapped and murdered. Avi Sasportas disappeared on February 16, 1989, near the Gaza Strip, and Ilan Saadon was abducted two and a half months later. The kidnappers, who identified themselves as Hamas activists, prompted the GSS to invest greater efforts in gathering intelligence on the movement, which had become one of the main forces to fan the flames of the intifada.[17]

Due to Israel's tight control over the territories and prior acquaintance with the heads of the Islamic charity associations, most of whom had once been welcome visitors to the military administration's offices, the Hamas leadership was identified and charted relatively swiftly. Concurrently, the HUMINT gathering process on the people in charge of the Hamas movement and its operating methods was also intensified.[18]

The kidnapping and murder of the border policeman Nissim Toledano near Jerusalem on December 13, 1992, provided an opportunity for the Israeli government to deport 415 Hamas members, whose identities had been determined in advance by the GSS.[19] The activists were taken across the border to Lebanon in the hope that this would break the organization's backbone and root out the revolutionary Islamic threat from the Palestinian political arena. These hopes were soon dashed.

The Lebanese government refused to accept the deportees into its territory and left them in a tent encampment near the village of Marj al-Zuhur. The deportees' struggle against the harsh Lebanese winter focused world attention on their plight. While world coverage granted the Hamas activists moral support, various organizations, primarily Hezbollah, provided for their material needs. Despite the ideological gaps between Hamas and Hezbollah, the former being Sunni and the latter Shiite, strong ties developed between the deportees and members of the supportive organizations. In addition to the military know-how they conveyed to the Hamas exiles, Hezbollah shared the vast experience it had accumulated in establishing a multifaceted political organization. One year after the expulsion, heavy American pressure on Israel resulted in the gradual repatriation of Hamas deportees to the occupied territories. The political reality to which they returned had changed. The Oslo Accords signed between the Israeli government and the PLO in September 1993 had turned yesterday's enemies—PLO members—into Israel's allies, while the former recipients of favors, supporters of Islamic organizations who strenuously opposed conciliation with Israel, became the main enemy.[20]

IN 1985, THE ISRAELI Defense Forces (IDF), engaged in a war of attrition in Lebanon, withdrew from the Lebanese heartland and redeployed to the "security zone" in southern Lebanon. One of the goals of redeployment was to create a buffer zone between Hezbollah forces, which operated from villages in southern Lebanon, and the settlements in northern Israel. This reflected an initial understanding among policymakers in Israel that the struggle with Hezbollah required the adoption of a defensive model. Nevertheless, the war model was still much more prominent.

ABDUCTIONS

The crews of the two Israeli Air Force Phantom jets that took off on the afternoon of Thursday, October 15, 1986, from Ramat David air base in northern Israel did not anticipate any irregularities. As they approached the first target of their mission near the village of Maghdoushe in Lebanon, they heard a loud explosion, and the plane leading the formation suddenly began to lose altitude. It later turned out that one of the 360-kilogram Marck-55 bombs attached to the fighter jet had prematurely detonated. The pilot, Ishay Aviram, and his navigator, Ron Arad, quickly realized that the fate of their plane had been sealed. Both men activated their ejection seats. The pilot landed in a ravine far from the mission's target and hid there until an Israeli combat helicopter rescued him. Arad, however, was not as fortunate. The moment he touched the ground, Amal militiamen seized him and whisked him off to Beirut.

In early 1988, more than a year after Arad's capture, the Amal organization split up. Mustafa Dirani, who had been in charge of the organization's internal security, left with a small group of supporters and founded a militia called the Resistance of the Believers. Dirani's men kidnapped Arad and held him in a hideaway apartment in the village of Nabi Chit. Dirani had hoped to hand over Arad to Hezbollah in exchange for the organization's sponsorship of his new group. Whatever happened to Arad after that is shrouded in mystery. He was last seen alive on the night of May 5, 1988. On that night, there were skirmishes between IDF forces and Hezbollah militants near Nabi Chit. According to one of the versions of the events that reached Israel, Arad attempted to escape during the chaos and was shot by his guards. Other sources stated that he managed to escape but fell into a nearby ravine and died.[1]

Immediately after Arad's capture, Israel worked frenetically for his release. Uri Lubrani, coordinator of Israel government activities in Lebanon, represented Israel in negotiations with businessman Jamal Said, who mediated for and had close ties with the Amal organization. Despite Israel's high expectations, the negotiations never developed into an agreement. Defense Minister Yitzhak Rabin was still smarting from the harsh public criticism against the government over the 1985 Jibril Exchange. In this swap, which was Israel's most distinctive deviation from its official policy not to negotiate with terrorist groups, it released 1,150 Palestinian and Lebanese prisoners in exchange for three captured Israeli soldiers. Rabin was apprehensive about surrendering to Amal's excessive demands, which included the release of Palestinian prisoners from Israeli jails. The kidnapping of Arad by Dirani's men put an end to the negotiations. In early 1989, Israel renewed diplomatic efforts to obtain information on the missing navigator. A window of opportunity opened when UN Secretary General Perez de Cuellar appointed a special envoy to handle the release of Westerners being held by Hezbollah. The envoy, Giandomenico Pico, formulated a deal that included Israel's release of Lebanese prisoners held by the South Lebanon Army (SLA) in exchange for two Western hostages being held by Hezbollah. That deal, too, did not lead to the disclosure of any significant information about Arad.[2]

Heavy pressure from Arad's family and friends kept Arad's fate on the public agenda in Israel, and the government continued its quest for ways to bring home the captured navigator. The next move, planned shortly before the collapse of the Soviet Union, involved Israel, Hezbollah, the United States, West Germany, and the decaying Soviet empire. Under the terms of the swap, Israel agreed to release hundreds of Palestinian prisoners, as well as two Israeli citizens—Marcus Klingberg and Shabtai Kalmanovich—who were serving long prison sentences for spying for the Soviet Union. In exchange, Israel was supposed to receive information on Arad. The changing of the regime in Moscow, however, led to the dismissal of the deal. Subsequent attempts to get hold of information from Tehran via German sources also proved fruitless.[3]

In light of the futility of diplomatic efforts and continued public pressure, Israel also resorted to other modes of operation. Elite commando units were sent deep into Lebanon to kidnap senior Hezbollah members. The Israeli intelligence community, especially Aman, devised this method, and the Israeli security cabinet supported it for several reasons. First, it was believed that the Hezbollah abductees would provide Israel critical information about Arad's fate and his situation. Second, Israel thought that the kidnappings were one of the only ways to put real pressure on the Hezbollah leadership and the Iranian regime in order to obtain information on Arad's fate or negotiate his release. Later, it would be revealed that none of these assumptions had any solid basis.

On December 15, 1988, a Sayeret Matkal force set up an ambush near the Lebanese town of Tibnin. The unit's mission was to capture Jawad Kasfi, Dirani's operations officer. Kasfi was seized from his car and, along with three of his men, taken to the security zone in southern Lebanon. After a preliminary interrogation, two of the captured men were released, while the other two, including Kasfi, were transferred to Israel. The next kidnapping occurred seven months later. This time the target was more important—Sheikh Abdel Karim Obeid, a highly respected Shiite leader and senior Hezbollah activist. Israel had hoped that his abduction would exert direct pressure on the organization. On July 28, 1989, at 1:00 a.m., a force of thirty Sayeret Matkal commandos landed near Obeid's home village of Jibchit, some five miles north of the security zone. Deputy Commander Amos Ben Avraham led the force, which approached the village at a quick march, identified Obeid's house, and broke into it. The astonished cleric, who was caught in his bed, was ordered to dress and was led away at gunpoint to a helicopter that took him to Israel.[4]

When we take into account the overall outcomes of the abductions policy, the picture is not very flattering to Israeli policymakers. These complicated military operations, which were largely the result of the Arad family's and other Israeli private citizens' pressure on policymakers and the security establishment to bolster the efforts to bring Arad home, endangered the lives of large number of soldiers from the Israeli elite forces, but they had a very little, if any, strategic value. The abductions of Kasfi and Obeid did not result in the revelation of any new information on Arad and did not advance negotiations for his release one iota.[5] Moreover, instead of putting pressure on Hezbollah and the Iranian regime, the abductions actually prompted them to escalate their operations against Israel.

HEZBOLLAH STRIKES BACK

On February 14, 1992, three Israeli soldiers were killed in an attack by the Palestinian Islamic Jihad on an IDF basic training base in Gilad in an operation dubbed Night of the Pitchforks. Two days later Israel responded, but not necessarily aiming for the right target. Israeli Air Force Apache helicopters fired seven missiles at the car of Hezbollah leader, Abbas Musawi. He was killed, along with his wife, Siham, and their five-year-old son, Hussein, who were with him in the car. Hezbollah's response to the elimination of its leader was severe. The target of the first attack was the Israeli Embassy in Buenos Aires, Argentina. The incident took place on March 17, 1992, a little before 3:00 p.m. A suicide bomber drove a Ford F-100 truck laden with about 120 pounds of explosives straight into 910/916 Arroyo Street. Twenty-nine people were killed in the blast. A short while later, the Islamic Jihad organization in Beirut took responsibility for the carnage, stating that it was in response to the Musawi assassination. In those days, before the emergence of global Salafi jihad terrorism, the success of a local organization such as Hezbollah in being able to build an operational infrastructure in a country on the other side of the globe was tantamount to an intelligence bolt from the blue.[6]

After long years of intensive inquiry by Mossad, the following picture of the bombing in Argentina emerged. The masterminds behind the attack were Imad Mughniyah and Mohsen Rabbani. The latter was the cultural attaché at the Iranian Embassy in Buenos Aires but in effect also functioned as representative of the Iranian Intelligence Ministry there. In the earlier groundwork for the operation, a courier was sent on behalf of Mughniyah from Lebanon to Argentina equipped with false documents provided by the Iranian Embassy in Beirut. His mission was to set up a local cell and select the target of the attack. Individuals in the Argentine security system divulged information on the security arrangements of the Israel Embassy to the courier in exchange for bribes. A man who carried a Brazilian identity card showing the name of Elias Griveiro Da Luz purchased the truck the suicide bomber drove. (To this day, the identity of the bomber is unknown.) When they received the signal that the arrangements were complete, three members of Hezbollah who had undergone training in Iran set out for Argentina. The cell, including the suicide bomber, entered Argentina by way of the border with Paraguay, where Mughniyah's courier awaited them. He then took them to Buenos Aires and supervised the execution of the operation.[7]

The escalation between Israel and Hezbollah also became evident in southern Lebanon. The mounting tension between the two sides was discernible mainly in the gradual rise in the number of clashes in the security zone between Israeli and Hezbollah ground forces in the summer of 1993. After Hezbollah fighters succeeded in killing five IDF soldiers on July 8 and 9, and also in the wake of Hezbollah missile attacks on settlements in northern Israel twelve days later, Israel responded forcefully. On July 25, Israeli aircraft and the IDF Artillery Corps began heavily bombarding villages in southern Lebanon where Hezbollah operatives were based. The rationale of the operation, which was termed Din Veheshbon (Accountability), was that the Israeli bombardments would drive masses of Lebanese refugees to flee north toward Beirut. This, in turn, would put pressure on the Lebanese government to force Hezbollah to stop its violent campaign against Israel. The Israeli response indicated an escalation in the use of the war model, given that it was the first time Israel used heavy artillery in its struggle against a subnational armed group except for the PLO. However, this did not prevent Hezbollah from continuing to rain Katyusha missiles on northern Israel, and the rigorous Israeli response had no profound influence on its operational capabilities. After seven days, on July 31, the operation came to an end after Israel and Hezbollah, by means of American mediation, came to a set of understandings. At its core was the agreement that the two sides consented not to take action against civilian populations.[8]

HEZBOLLAH STRIKES AGAIN

Even though the abductions of Kasfi and Obeid did not lead to information on Ron Arad, and despite the escalation of the conflict between Israel and Hezbollah, policymakers in Jerusalem did not abandon the kidnapping policy. The next target was Mustafa Dirani himself. While it seems that Israeli policymakers, Aman, and Mossad operatives already understood that the chances of success in using the abductees as bargaining chips were low, they believed that this time they would succeed in gaining new information on Arad's fate because of Dirani's direct involvement in his kidnapping and confinement.

The method described previously to capture Obeid was repeated, with a few improvements, about five years later. On Friday, May 20, 1994, at 11:00 p.m., two CH-53 Sikorsky helicopters landed near Dirani's home village of Kasser Naba. Two Mercedes cars carrying Sayeret Matkal fighters rolled down the ramps and drove straight to their destination. The soldiers broke into Dirani's house and seized him. This time, however, there were some complications. The force was discovered while they were still in the village, and in the ensuing exchange of gunfire, the commander of one of the units was lightly wounded. Nevertheless, even Dirani's abduction did not budge Hezbollah from its policy of silence concerning

Ron Arad. "We do not understand this language," declared a senior Hezbollah spokesman the morning after Dirani's kidnapping, "and the Israelis will not achieve anything."[9]

Two months later, on July 18, 1994, at 9:53 in the morning, a Renault Traffic commercial vehicle blew up in proximity to a four-story building on 663 Pasteur Street in the heart of a Jewish neighborhood in Buenos Aires. The massive explosion led to the collapse of the Argentine Israelite Mutual Association (AMIA) building on top of its inhabitants. This time the death toll was much worse, at eighty-six fatalities. Once again, the tracks led back to Tehran. Investigation reports issued by Western intelligence agencies indicated that the decision in principal to execute the action was already made in August 1993 in a session of the Iranian Supreme National Security Council. Present were the Iranian spiritual leader, Ali Khamenei; the incumbent president at the time, Hashemi Rafsanjani; the Minister of Intelligence, Ali Fallahian; the officer in charge of intelligence and security in the Office of the Iranian Leader, Mohammed Hijazi; and the Foreign Minister, Ali Akbar Velayati. The green light was given following the IDF attack on the Hezbollah training camp in Baalbek and the abduction of Dirani. This time, as well, the responsibility for carrying out the mission was assigned to Mughniyah's unit. He recruited suicide bomber Ibrahim Hussein Berro, who entered Argentina near the borders of Brazil and Paraguay accompanied by a Hezbollah collaborator by the name of Samuel Salman El Reda, a Colombian of Lebanese origin who was married to an Argentinean citizen.[10]

Nearly ten days before the explosion, the Iranian ambassadors in Argentina, Uruguay, and Chile were summoned to urgent meetings in Tehran and were thus absent from their embassies on the day of the attack. At the same time, the head of the Iranian intelligence station in Buenos Aires, Mohsen Rabbani, also left Buenos Aires. The Iranian intelligence was responsible for the operational aspect of the bombing and relied on a network of local Shiite Muslims. The most prominent figure among these local collaborators was a car dealer by the name of Carlos Alberto Talaldin, an Argentinean of Lebanese Shiite descent, who supplied the booby-trapped car. The Iranian Foreign Ministry furnished Mughniyah's associates with diplomatic papers that allowed them to access Argentina and circulate within its borders freely. This time, as well, Argentinean security people provided information on the security arrangements of the building in exchange for bribes. When Berro arrived at Buenos Aires, the explosives-rigged vehicle was already waiting for him in the public parking lot not far from the Jewish community building. Several hours before the attack, the suicide bomber called up his family in Lebanon. A transcription of the intercepted conversation confirms that he conveyed a message to them according to which he would soon join his brother, who had blown himself up in a car-bomb attack on Israeli soldiers in Lebanon in August 1989. At the end of the conversation, Berro left for the parking lot, started up the car, and blew it up next to the building some five minutes later.[11]

In the first days following the explosion, there was a strong feeling in Israel that the Argentinean police and intelligence service investigation was being conducted in an amateurish manner. According to Yigal Carmon, then counter-terrorism advisor to the prime minister, the Argentinean investigators purposely refrained from interrogating certain suspects, including Carlos Talaldin, who held critical information that may have helped get to the bottom of the affair. Important documents that were presented to the investigating judge and indicated an Iranian connection mysteriously vanished. The frustration in Israel was immense. According to Mossad and the CIA, although Argentine President Carlos Menem made a dramatic denunciation immediately after the explosion, saying, "The animals that committed this attack don't deserve to be among the living," his extensive connections with Iran and Syria led him to sabotage the investigation. This included the rejection of offers by Israel to take part in the investigation as well as a refusal to receive relevant information from it.[12]

Menem, from an Arab family of Syrian descent, grew up in the province of La Rioja, where he also took his first political steps as head of the Syrian-Lebanese Association. In the year 1983, he was elected to the position of the province's governor and six years later became president of the republic. During the course of his presidency, Menem cultivated his connections with the Arab world and improved Argentina's relations with Iran. Mossad claims that he was concerned that the disclosure of the involvement of Iran in a terrorist incident in his country might harm these relations. Menem's motives were also not free of personal interests. A member of the Iranian security services who defected to the West related that the Iranian authorities deposited the impressive sum of $10 million into Menem's personal account in the Bank of Luxembourg in Switzerland. This was to ensure that the investigation would not point an accusing finger at Tehran.[13]

Menem's unwillingness to allow the Israeli intelligence services to take part in the investigations would not have captured the headlines if not for the severe accusations directed at Argentina. These alleged that the Menem administration in fact could have prevented the attack on the Jewish community building but chose not to do anything. On May 31, 1994, forty-eight days before the attack on the AMIA building, representatives of the Argentinean intelligence services

(SIDE) were summoned to the Foreign Ministry and presented with a special message sent from the Argentinean embassy in Lebanon. The message was a specific warning in regard to a terrorist attack against an Israeli or Jewish target in the near future. The information was passed on to neither the Israeli embassy nor the Jewish community. The actions of Menem and his people left a bad taste in the relations between the intelligence agencies of the two countries. Signs of change came only after the events of September 11, 2001, when Argentina joined the Global Coalition against Terrorism, a program established by U.S. President George W. Bush. In March 2003, the head of SIDE, Miguel Angel Toma, visited Israel. After a postponement of many years, he finally delivered the report of the investigation of the attacks to members of the Israeli security establishment.[14]

MOSSAD RETURNS TO LEBANON

Meanwhile, in 1994, frustration in the Israel security establishment grew worse. In Mossad's painstaking investigation that followed the attack on the AMIA building, Mughniyah's name kept cropping up. It was already familiar to intelligence services in the West owing to his involvement in the planning of suicide attacks against the U.S. embassy in Beirut and the Multinational Force bases in Lebanon in the year 1983. One year later, his name was associated with the abduction and murder of William Buckley, chief of the CIA station in Beirut. However, while the bulk of intelligence efforts focused on Mughniyah's activities in Lebanon, he was actually engaged in the cultivation of "sleeper" Hezbollah terrorist cells in other places in the world. These latter efforts had been carried out with the utmost secrecy; even when they came to the attention of the local intelligence agencies, they were treated as a Middle Eastern problem. In this way, instead of detecting the development and expansion of an international terrorist network, each agency concentrated on the activities in its own country and did not share this information with other intelligence services.[15]

Shortly after the second attack in Argentina, Israel initiated a reprisal. Mossad operatives made contact with Ahmed Hallaq, formerly a member of the pro-Syrian Al-Saiqa organization. When they first attempted to entice him into their employment, the agents identified themselves as American government officers and only several months later revealed their real identity. In June 1994, Hallaq was asked to recruit Fuad Mughniyah, a mid-ranking Hezbollah official, to be an informer. Fuad himself was not a particularly interesting objective for Israeli intelligence. His importance was rooted in his family relations: He was Imad Mughniyah's brother. Nearly six months after initial efforts to solicit his services,

Mossad decided to change course. On December 23, 1994, Ahmed Hallaq rigged up a bomb under a Volkswagen car parked right next to a store Fuad owned. When Hallaq received the signal that Fuad was inside the store, the bomb was detonated. As a result of the powerful explosion, Fuad Mughniyah and two passersby were killed. While some sources claimed that Israel's actual intention was to kill Imad while he attended his brother's funeral, others insisted that this was a revenge operation, aiming to hurt Imad by killing his brother, who was a far more accessible target. At any rate, on that very same day, Hallaq and his family fled to southern Lebanon, where a man called "Dani" awaited them and helped them cross the border into Israeli territory. Hallaq was offered the chance to settle down in Costa Rica under a fictitious identity, but he preferred the Philippines. However, five months of dwelling in the "diaspora" were more than enough for him. He demanded that his operators in Israel allow him to return to his homeland. They acceded, providing him with a new identity card with the name of Michel Hir Amin, and put him up in the Christian town of Qlaya, which was then under the control of the IDF and the SLA.[16]

A short time after his repatriation, the Lebanese intelligence services found out Michel Hir Amin's true identity. They did not waste time. They contacted Mofid Nohra, a Hezbollah man whose brother Ramzi was known as a key figure in the drug trade in southern Lebanon and as an Israeli collaborator. Concerned that the Israelis were losing their hold of southern Lebanon and that dark clouds were gathering above, Ramzi searched for a way to atone for the sins of his betrayal and come by a clean bill of health from the Lebanese authorities and Hezbollah. In order to reach this goal, however, he was required to sacrifice Hallaq.

Ramzi Nohra mustered his network of informers in the Qlaya area, and they provided him with details on the identity of the SLA man who was in charge of Hallaq's security. Nohra did not require any special efforts in order to buy the trust of Hallaq's handler and persuade him to impart accurate information on Hallaq's daily routine. The next step was to make direct contact with him. The Lebanese drug dealer learned of Hallaq's weakness for fine whiskey and beautiful women and took advantage of these habits to the full. The two men became friends and began to spend time at Nohra's house in the company of young and attractive girls.[17]

On February 20, 1996, after recruiting his brother Mofid, his friend Maher Touma, and a cab driver named Fadi to the operation, Ramzi Nohra invited Hallaq to another party at his house. However, this time the surprise awaiting Hallaq was far less pleasant. After attempts to put him to sleep by lacing his drink with a drug were unsuccessful, Mofid pulled out a gun. Stunned by this change of events, Hallaq was handcuffed and heaved into the trunk of the taxi. The vehicle picked up speed and set out north in the direction of Beirut. At the IDF roadblock at Jezzine, Nohra flashed documents confirming that he was working in the service of the Israeli intelligence. These papers, together with his fluent Hebrew, persuaded the soldiers that the "agent" was in the midst of a clandestine security assignment in the service of Israel. The taxi passed through the checkpoint with no trouble and a short while later reached the outskirts of Beirut. Hallaq was handed over to the Lebanese security services and Hezbollah. They extracted from him a detailed confession on his contacts with Mossad and Mughniyah's assassination. A military court in Beirut sentenced him to death, and early on the morning of Saturday, September 21, 1996, he was executed by firing squad at the Roumieh prison in Beirut.[18]

GRAPES OF WRATH

The ongoing struggle between Israel and Hezbollah was not restricted to the clandestine sphere of intelligence organizations. It erupted again in April 1996 in what became a full-scale military clash. At the end of 1995, Hezbollah intensified its rocket attacks on northern Israel, violating the Din Veheshbon understandings reached between the two sides three years earlier. These attacks continued despite efforts of the international community, and especially French and American mediators, to lower the flames. On April 9, 1996, a massive shower of Katyusha missiles landed on settlements in northern Israel. Prime Minister Shimon Peres, a great believer in diplomatic solutions to such situations, faced a great dilemma. At the time, Israel was also suffering a string of suicide attacks in its urban centers. Binyamin Netanyahu, Peres's main rival in the elections that were due to be held in May of that year, attacked Peres on his dovish attitude with respect to security issues. Netanyahu claimed that this stance led to the exacerbation of Israel security problems, both inside the country with regard to Palestinian terrorism and at the northern border in the struggle against Hezbollah. Peres realized that if Israel remained aloof to Hezbollah attacks, it would bolster his dovish image and the Israeli public would think he was unsuited to deal with Israel security problems. Therefore, he decided that Israel would respond forcefully this time and ordered the IDF to launch Operation Grapes of Wrath.[19]

On April 11, the Israel Air Force and IDF Artillery Corps began to engage in a heavy shelling of Hezbollah compounds in southern Lebanon, while Israeli ships imposed a blockade on the ports of Tyre and Sidon. As had occurred three years earlier, tens of thousands of Lebanese refugees rushed from southern Lebanon toward the Beirut area while Hezbollah continued to strike northern Israel with Katyusha missiles. It was once more obvious that the Israeli military operation had little effect on Hezbollah operational capabilities. Thus, the second campaign in which Israel used heavy artillery as its main weapon in its struggle against a terrorist group was unsuccessful. The international community also excoriated Israel after an Israeli shell landed in the middle of a UN temporary refugee compound near the village of Qana on April 18, killing 102 citizens and injuring more than 100 others. As a result, both sides and especially Israel were strongly pressured by the international community to bring the clash to its end. On April 27, Israel, Syria, and Lebanon signed what have been called the Grapes of Wrath understandings. Peres, who believed that the operation would increase his chances to win the national election a month later, ironically found that the opposite had occurred. More than 90 percent of Israeli Palestinians decided to boycott the elections because of the tragic Qana events, ultimately resulting in Peres's defeat.[20]

Israeli policy against Hezbollah during this period seems especially puzzling. Despite the futility of previous offensive measures, Israel expanded its war model. Elite IDF forces were repeatedly activated in high-risk operations in Lebanon. Although the abductions yielded no results, policymakers did not hesitate to endanger highly valuable elite forces for the purpose of obtaining information on Ron Arad. Furthermore, as we will see in the following chapters, the Israeli abductions tactic not only failed to coerce Hezbollah into making concessions, but Hezbollah also actually adopted this method and used it against Israel effectively.

The extensive use of air force and artillery corps should also raise questions. Although it had some success in causing harm to Hezbollah leaders and strongholds, in a cost-benefit analysis, Israel seems to be on the losing end. Backed by Iran and other allies around the world, Hezbollah had maximized its advantages as a flexible organization and retaliated in surprising ways and places, thus leading to increased frustration. Moreover, the collateral damage that was caused by Israeli attacks in Lebanon led to worldwide condemnation. Finally, the Lebanese arena serves as ultimate proof of Israel's inability to live up to its own policy of not negotiating with terrorists. The Jibril Exchange served as a milestone for Hezbollah and other enemies in their future strategies against Israel.

THE FIRST INTIFADA WAS engraved in the Israeli collective memory as a popular uprising that was manifested in large demonstrations and riots in the streets of the occupied territories. Yet, toward its final stages in early 1992, terrorism had gained more prominence. In retrospect, this short wave of terrorist attacks, in most cases stabbings of Israeli citizens, seems pale compared to the events that followed, but at the time, the Israeli public was outraged.[1] Despite his hawkish rhetoric, Prime Minister Yitzhak Shamir was perceived as weak and incapable of responding effectively to this wave of attacks. The public was hoping that Yitzhak Rabin, who had reemerged as the leader of the Labor Party and who enjoyed the reputation of a hardliner in security matters, would bring security back to the streets of Israel. On June 23, 1992, Rabin and the Labor Party won the national elections. A year later, it became clear that the leader who had been elected to crack down on terrorism had decided, for the first time in the history of the Israeli-Palestinian conflict, to take the reconciliatory model and was striving to bring peace to the region. However, shortly afterward, the peace road led back to the war model.

INTELLIGENCE ORGANIZATIONS AND THE PEACE PROCESS

In the late 1980s, Adnan Yassin was an aide to the internal security chief of the Palestine Liberation Organization (PLO), Hakam Balawi. Yassin's job included protecting organization members traveling abroad. Those were stormy days for the ruling echelons of the PLO, in exile in Tunis, who were subject to major political turmoil. For the first time, they began to recognize the right of Israel to exist. This decision, along with pressures from the international community, led by the United States, opened a window of opportunity for direct negotiations between the two rival parties, which materialized in the Madrid summit of 1991. Simultaneously, Yassin's private life also underwent several changes. His wife was stricken with cancer and rushed to Paris for treatment, and her devoted husband spent many hours at her hospital bedside. It was not easy for him to be so far from the reassuring confines of the PLO headquarters in Tunis, and he gladly responded to a tall, dark-haired man who approached him in Paris. The man, who spoke fluent Arabic, introduced himself as Hilmi. The two fell into a pleasant conversation in the lobby of the Meridien Montparnasse Hotel, where Yassin spent his time away from the hospital. In a very short time, their conversation shifted to business affairs. The seemingly random encounter wound up in an atmosphere of camaraderie, and the two arranged to meet again as soon as possible. At their next meetings, Hilmi shared his business ideas with Yassin, who responded enthusiastically. They considered several forms of cooperation that might pay off for the both of them. When they were ready to move on to practical matters, Hilmi introduced Yassin to his good friend George, who spoke Arabic with a Lebanese accent. The three of them began to devise business plans, among them importing furniture to Tunis. Yassin swallowed the bait and unwittingly became a central actor in a network masterminded by Mossad in Tunis.

More than four years later, at the height of the Oslo talks between the government of Israel and the PLO leadership, the Palestinian side felt that something was not quite right. It seemed that during the stages of negotiations, Israel was always one step ahead. It was as if the Israelis had a representative of their own among the top ranks of the Palestinian delegation who beforehand would pass on information regarding the PLO positions later presented in the negotiations. The reality was not that far from this impression, and the furniture-importing business of Hilmi and Yassin played a central role. One of the clients in these dealings was the PLO. Mahmoud Abbas, also known as Abu Mazen, one of the heads of the PLO and eventually to become the Palestinian president, was glad to see that an orthopedic chair and a designer table lamp had been placed in his office. What he could not see was that this same stylish office furniture contained equipment that was transmitting sound waves and even fax messages to Mossad headquarters each time Abbas sat on the comfortable chair or turned on the lamp. These were the most sophisticated wiretapping and monitoring devices at Mossad's disposal.[2]

Yassin unknowingly helped Mossad's monitoring network, as well as the operations division. In his capacity as the person responsible for the security of PLO high-ranking officials on their frequent trips abroad, he was among the very few who received precise information on the travel plans of Ataf Basiso, who had been one of the prominent figures in the Black September arm of the PLO during the 1970s. Only a few people were aware of Basiso's planned trip to France in June 1992, and Yassin was one of them. On the Mossad voicemails in Paris and

Rome, messages in the voice of the PLO security man had been left describing Basiso's planned flight itinerary. On June 8, 1992, assassins shot Basiso in Paris, where he died of his wounds. The decision to do away with Basiso was made despite the fact that twenty years had passed since the Munich attack. Moreover, the dispatchers of the assassins knew he had been in close contact with a foreign intelligence service—the French Directorate of Territorial Security (DST). The assassination raised the French giant from its sleep, and it began a close watch of all people who were aware of Basiso's flight plan. Within a short time, a red light flashed above Yassin's name. The information was passed on to Tunisian intelligence, which began to conduct a close surveillance of Yassin and his son Hani. In October 1993, after it was discovered that a Mercedes car they had imported from France to Tunis was packed with explosives and advanced wiretapping devices, the two were arrested. In the interrogation, Yassin broke down and confessed to the accusations made against him. He was later put in an Algerian prison and was released only in 2003 by the Algerian government. The revelation that he worked for Mossad and that he provided the information that led to Basiso's elimination raised the anxiety threshold among the PLO higher ranks. Nor did Israel get away cost-free from the affair. Consequent verification that Mossad was responsible for Basiso's killing on French soil led to a rift between the intelligence communities of both countries.[3]

THE FIRST MAGNA CARTA

The Oslo Accords were devised and discussed initially by representatives of the two sides without the involvement of the Israeli intelligence community. The creation of a Palestinian autonomous entity containing Fatah forces, at the beginning in Jericho and Gaza, and afterward all over the West Bank caught the various organizations unprepared. Thus, as had occurred after the Lebanese invasion eleven years earlier, the signing of the Oslo Accords in September 1993 caused confusion about the division of regions of responsibility among the various intelligence agencies.[4]

Until Arafat and his colleagues settled in Gaza, Mossad and Aman had focused on following the activities of PLO leaders outside the occupied territories, while the GSS had focused on local Palestinian operatives.[5] The arrival of the exiled Palestinian leaders in the territory that had been under the sole and undisputed authority of the GSS produced a new wave of conflicts. Mossad and Aman suddenly lost some of their key targets and were afraid of being demoted and losing resources. This time the conflict had permeated to the research departments of the organizations. The central issue of disagreement was whether Arafat was indeed interested in peace, or if this was just another phase of his original stage plan. After the outbreak of the first intifada, the GSS assessment was that the key to solving the Palestinian problem was political. Arafat and his colleagues were perceived as being the genuine representatives of the Palestinian people and therefore possessing the authority to negotiate in their name. Aman, however, rejected this view out of hand. The agency's assessment was that Arafat had not renounced the option of an armed struggle. Furthermore, the fact that the Oslo Accords had made the PLO preeminent, in Aman's opinion, would strengthen the Palestinian opposition. Ultimately, political pressure would return Arafat to the path of violence. The tension between the intelligence agencies reached such a level that they were unwilling to share information with one another, and that conflict did not remain hidden from the politicians. The prime minister came to doubt the intelligence community that served him, and the government found it difficult to formulate a coherent policy when presented with conflicting assessments. Prime Minister Rabin demanded an end to the crisis. He exerted pressure on the agencies to sign a document—dubbed the Magna Carta—outlining the division of authority between them. According to the agreement, gathering intelligence within the territory of the Palestinian Authority remained the responsibility of the GSS, while Aman was in charge of political intelligence only. Yet the turf wars were not limited to the intelligence organizations. As if twenty years had not passed since the tragedy in Ma'alot and the recommendations of the Horev Committee, Sayeret Matkal and the Yamam were still battling over who should be responsible for hostage-rescue missions.

NACHSHON WACHSMAN

At 11:00 p.m. on Friday, October 14, 1994, the weekend broadcasts of the two Israeli television channels were interrupted for breaking news. The news line appearing at the bottom of the screen said that an announcement from the office of prime minister and the minister of defense, Yitzhak Rabin, was imminent. The subject of the announcement was no surprise to many of the viewers, but they had no idea of the tragic details. Five days earlier, on Sunday, October 9, at around 6:00 p.m., Corporal Nachshon Wachsman had been waiting at the hitch-hiking station near a busy intersection not far from the Ben-Gurion Airport. He wanted to surprise his friend Miriam Aziza, a teacher-soldier stationed near the neighboring city of Ramla, and was trying to stop a passing car. The passengers of the white Volkswagen Transporter that stopped to pick him up did not raise his suspicions; they were all wearing skullcaps and looked like Orthodox Jews. When Wachsman asked if they could give him a ride to Ramla, they responded in fluent Hebrew.[6]

A short while later, three of the passengers attacked the soldier. They hit him, handcuffed him, and moved him to the rear of the large van, which immediately changed direction. Minutes later, they easily passed through the IDF checkpoint near Macabbim-Re'ut and entered the West Bank. From there the trip to the village of Bir Nabala, located between Jerusalem and Ramallah, was brief. Under the cover of darkness the vehicle stopped next to a pleasant two-story house on the outskirts of the village. The terrified soldier was quickly moved into the house and to the living area on the upper floor where he was placed in a small windowless bedroom.

The next morning, after not hearing from their son for a full day, Wachsman's parents became concerned. His father, Yehuda, asked the police for help. At the same time, other family members began an independent search, recruiting a large number of high-school and yeshiva students. They first focused on the Atarot intersection and from there widened the search. Only a small number of police officers joined the search, and the army chose not to take any meaningful steps, reflecting the prevailing view in the security community that this was not a terrorist or criminal incident and that Wachsman would soon be found.

Twenty-four hours later, their assessment changed from one extreme to the other. The Reuters news agency in Gaza City received a videocassette featuring a masked man who identified himself as a Hamas operative. He displayed Wachsman's identity card and an M16 rifle of the type Wachsman had been carrying at the time he entered the van. The man directed his words to the Israeli government and, in exchange for Wachsman, demanded the release of two hundred Hamas prisoners held by Israel, including their leader, Sheikh Ahmed Yassin, who was serving a life sentence in prison for his involvement in the murder of Israeli soldiers and Palestinian citizens accused of collaboration with Israel. The Hamas operative also issued an ultimatum: If the prisoners were not released by October 14, Wachsman would be executed. At 5:00 that afternoon, the heads of all Israeli security organizations met in the prime minister's office in Jerusalem. Since the cassette had surfaced in Gaza and the security forces assumed that it was easier to hide a kidnapped Israeli in Palestinian Authority–administered territory, attention was focused on that southern Palestinian city.

Rabin did not hesitate. He sealed all borders with the Gaza Strip, immediately suspended the peace talks with Arafat, and had Egyptian President Hosni

Mubarak and the U.S. ambassador to the Israeli-Palestinian negotiations, Dennis Ross, apply pressure on him. Rabin demanded a quick end to the crisis, and the pressure paid off. Arafat instructed the heads of the Palestinian security forces to hunt for the soldier vigorously, and that night ninety Hamas operatives were detained. The next day, Wednesday, a second cassette arrived at the Reuters Gaza office; this time Wachsman himself appeared next to one of his kidnappers. The kidnapped soldier, apparently in good health, addressed his government with these words: "They want their prisoners released. If not—they will kill me. That is all." The appearance of this videocassette only strengthened the assessment that Wachsman was being held in Gaza. Consequently, the Israeli security apparatus disregarded messages from Arafat's secretary, Nabil Abu Rodaina, and from Shams Oudeh, the Reuters photographer who had received the cassette, indicating Wachsman was being held in the West Bank. The pressure on Arafat increased and detentions in the Gaza Strip continued.

Despite the assessment that Wachsman was being held in Gaza, GSS agents in the Jerusalem region continued to look for leads. The breakthrough came on Thursday. Following their assumption that the kidnappers had used a rented vehicle, a thorough survey of all vehicles rented in the days preceding the kidnapping led them to an agency in East Jerusalem. One name immediately caught the eye of investigators: Jihad Yaghmour, a well-known Hamas operative from Beit Hanina in northern Jerusalem. Although there was nothing to link Yaghmour to the kidnapping, Carmi Gillon, acting GSS head, asked Attorney General Dorit Beinisch to have him arrested and interrogated using "special means."[7] In the early hours of October 14, Yaghmour broke down and revealed all the details of the kidnapping, including the exact location where Wachsman was being held.

When these facts were received, a meeting was called in the prime minister's office, during which the GSS convinced Rabin that, in light of the intelligence information and familiarity with the cell members, a rescue operation should be immediately planned. The task fell to Major General Shaul Mofaz, commander of the IDF West Bank Division, responsible for the Bir Nabala village. By early morning, the first phase of the operation had already begun with the gathering of visual intelligence on the house and its environs by a surveillance team from the operations branch of the GSS. At the same time, Sayeret Matkal and Yamam fighters were called to the IDF West Bank Division headquarters. Investigators from the GSS briefed the officers of the two units about what Yaghmour had divulged during his interrogation, providing precise details about the layout of the house, Wachsman's exact location, the daily routine of the guards, and how they were armed. The commanders of the units were given the go-ahead to prepare plans for the attack and were asked to present them to the division commander at 2:00 p.m. First, Yamam Deputy Commander David Ben-Shimol made his presentation, leaving a poor impression on his audience. Ben-Shimol sounded hesitant, offered no practical solution for penetrating the village area, and could not offer a backup plan in case something went wrong and the operation took longer than expected. To the surprise of those present, Ben Shimol also demanded improvements and additions to the strike force. From their point of view, this was an unreasonable demand in light of the tight time frame. The presentation made by Sayeret Matkal commander Shachar Argaman was much more promising. Mofaz, a former deputy commander of the Sayeret, and other officers, including former Sayeret commander and incumbent chief of staff Ehud Barak and former Sayeret deputy commander Danny Yatom, weighed both plans and decided to adopt that of the Sayeret.

After the decision was made preparations went into high gear. At the same time that the Sayeret soldiers were being given their final briefing at the West Bank Division headquarters, army and rescue forces were being deployed in Gaza to give the impression that a rescue operation was about to take place there. At 6:00 p.m., the Sayeret soldiers were given orders to begin moving slowly in the direction of the house. Thirty minutes later, when they were already very close, they noticed a Mercedes parked in front of the building. The force was ordered to retreat and apprehend the driver. At 7:15 p.m., the car began to move. It was stopped a safe distance from the house in order to prevent Wachsman's captors from seeing what was going on. Soldiers interrogated the driver, Zacharia Najib, a Hamas activist who had brought dinner to the house, and he confirmed the details they already had.

The special force was divided into two teams, one led by Captain Lior Lotan and the other by Captain Nir Poraz. They received permission to advance toward the house. When they were only a few yards away from it, they hid behind the fence surrounding the building and carried out their final preparations. According to the plan, the raid was to have begun by simultaneously blasting two doors on the ground floor and another one leading to the kitchen on the upper floor. At 7:45 p.m., the three devices went off, but only one breached the building. Nir Poraz was the first to enter. A kidnapper in the living room opened automatic fire on him from a distance of three yards, and Poraz fell. As a result of the ensuing exchange of fire, six more soldiers from Poraz's team were injured, among them the unit commander who had joined the attack forces. At this juncture, the team ceased to function. In the meantime, after a one-minute delay caused by the failure of the initial explosion, Lotan and his soldiers reached the upper floor and gathered in front of the door of the room where Wachsman was being held. One of the two kidnappers guarding Wachsman yelled from inside that if the soldiers did not leave immediately, he would kill the captive. Lotan continued according to plan. He fired at the metal lock, but the door remained secure. An explosive device placed next to the door also failed to blow off the lock. Four minutes later they managed to break down the metal-reinforced wooden door and shoot and kill the two kidnappers. To their deep regret, they found Wachsman dead, shot in the neck and chest a number of times.

There were two IDF losses in the operation—Wachsman and Poraz—and ten officers and enlisted men had been wounded. During the press conference held by the prime minister that same evening, the nation of Israel was told the bitter news. In the days following the failed rescue attempt, besides their sincere regret, sharp criticism of the decision to assign the operation to Sayeret Matkal was heard from within the ranks of the Yamam and even from the IDF.[8]

SUICIDE ATTACKS

In 1993, shortly before the signing of the Oslo Accords, suicide bombing replaced traditional Palestinian terrorist tactics, among which hostage-taking was prominent. The new method originated in Iran during its war with Iraq, and it quickly made its way from Lebanon to the West Bank and the Gaza Strip. While suicide bombers employed in Lebanon by Hezbollah and other organizations in their battle against military forces drove truck or car bombs to compound the damage, Hamas and the Palestinian Islamic Jihad (PIJ) developed a different method. Most of the suicide bombers sent to Israeli cities were young individuals—75 percent were under the age of twenty-four—wearing explosive belts around their waists. The Israeli government placed the responsibility for eliminating this phenomenon on the Palestinian Authority. Indeed, cooperation between the Israeli intelligence services and former rivals from Fatah who had become the intelligence officers of the Palestinian Authority seemed to carry some promise. However, the threat of Hamas and the Islamic Jihad to the stability of Arafat's government in effect prevented his forces from confronting them head-on. At the time suicide terrorism had grown to be the most complicated challenge the Israeli security forces had ever faced.[9]

The transfer of control in Palestinian urban concentrations and villages from Israel to the Palestinian Authority as part of the implementation of the Oslo

Accords dealt a harsh blow to the GSS, which was urgently looking for a solution to the suicide-bomber threat in these areas. Many GSS informants severed ties with their operators, and the intelligence portrayal of political and terrorist activity in Palestinian territory became increasingly blurred. No less problematic was the fact that unlike the PLO, which during its years of operation from Lebanon had maintained a paramilitary structure that included brigades and battalions, the terrorist activities of Hamas and Islamic Jihad came from the heart of the refugee camps. Even though the organizations set up military wings, the similarity between them and a paramilitary group was minimal. The technological arms of Israeli intelligence, which had easily followed the activities of PLO battalions in Lebanon, had difficulty contending with these amorphous structures, a fact that once more highlighted the importance of human intelligence.[10]

Prime Minister Yitzhak Rabin saw the growing frustration of the Israeli public after the optimism of the promise of peace. He wanted to halt the wave of suicide terrorism at any price. Rabin understood that Israel's best remaining tool was interrogations of Hamas and PIJ activists whom the GSS was able to arrest. Rabin rejected the restrictions the attorney general imposed on the GSS with regard to the interrogation techniques used against the prisoners "What kind of attorney general are you?" Rabin shouted at Michael Ben-Yair. "I need to fight terrorism, and you are constantly telling me what not to do. Damnation, tell me what I can do, not what I can't."

It was only a matter of time until the increasing pressures of policymakers on the interrogators of the GSS claimed the life of a detainee. On April 26, 1995, security prisoner Abdel Samed Harizat died at the "Russian Compound," the GSS interrogation facility in Jerusalem. Harizat, who belonged to Taher Kafisha's terrorist cell, one of the most active Hamas networks in the Hebron region, was arrested by the GSS and refused to talk throughout his interrogation. The interrogators introduced "special means." They did not take into consideration that Harizat had a disability and was slight of build. On the afternoon of April 22, the second day of Passover, GSS Chief Carmi Gillon approved orders to continue interrogating Harizat throughout the holiday, as the head of the interrogations branch had requested. Over the course of the eleven consecutive hours of Harizat's interrogation, he was violently shaken twelve times. The interrogation was halted only after a sudden deterioration in his health. He was taken to Hadassah Mount Scopus Hospital, where he died four days later of a subdural hemorrhage. The interrogator who was found responsible for Harizat's death was summoned for a disciplinary hearing and convicted of overstepping his authority, but he was returned to his position in the GSS.[11]

The media's criticism of the GSS led to the hobbling of the organization's interrogations branch. The harsh dispute between Gillon and Ben-Yair filtered down to GSS interrogators. They were unable to achieve a balance between the operational demands required of them and the need to protect themselves legally. Ultimately, this resulted in deteriorating quality in the intelligence they gathered. Ami Ayalon, who replaced Carmi Gillon as head of the GSS, clearly expressed the feelings among the interrogators: "We tell the interrogator: 'Do what you feel is right to save lives and afterward, we will consider whether or not to indict you.' GSS interrogators can no longer rely on such judgments, and I agree with them."[12]

BACK TO THE ASSASSINATIONS

Nasser Issa Shakher is a prime example of this difficulty. Issa served as a liaison between the Hamas network in Ramallah and Yehiya Ayash, "The Engineer." His name surfaced during the investigation of the suicide attack in Ramat Gan on July 24, 1995. He was arrested in Nablus on August 19 and brought in for questioning. Even though he immediately confessed his connection to the attack in Ramat Gan, and despite the high probability that he had information on additional operations planned by the network, his interrogators were not allowed to use "special means" on him. At that point, his cooperation with the GSS interrogators ended. Two days later, on August 21, Sufian Jabarin blew himself up on a Number 26 bus in Jerusalem's Ramat Eshkol neighborhood. Immediately after that incident, the interrogators received permission to use rougher treatment with Issa. Unfortunately, Issa revealed in this interrogation that he had finished planning the Ramat Eshkol suicide bombing just a few hours before his arrest. He also disclosed information about a bomb laboratory in Nablus, where both of the bombs used in the suicide attacks were built. This information led to the arrest of thirty-seven Hamas network members.[13]

The Palestinian groups' ability to continue to initiate suicide attacks in the Israeli metropolitan heartland during 1995 and early 1996 greatly intensified the frustration of the Israeli political and security establishments. Thus, Rabin, meeting with the heads of the intelligence community in September 1995, defined the PIJ and Hamas terrorist activities as a strategic danger to Israel and to the peace process. He ordered the intelligence organizations to coordinate all their efforts to harm these organizations' operational capabilities. Little more than a month after Rabin issued his directive, it was clear that its operational meaning was a return to a modus operandi that Israeli intelligence organizations had already experienced in the past. On October 26, 1995, Ibrahim a-Shawish checked into the Diplomat Hotel in the tourist town of Sliema, located in northern Malta. Very few knew that his real name was Fathi Shikaki and that for more than a decade he had been serving as the head of the PIJ. A few hours later, when Shikaki left the hotel and traveled down the town's main street, someone called out his name. He turned around and was immediately knocked backward by five bullets fired from a pistol, most of them hitting him in the head. A few seconds later, a motorcycle stopped beside the shooter, who jumped aboard, and the two men drove away. Later, it would be revealed that the two were Mossad operatives. In addition, it would soon become clear that this was just the beginning of Israel's endeavor to strike at the heart and soul of Hamas and the PIJ by eliminating their leaders.[14]

YEHIYA AYASH

Yehiya Ayash, "The Engineer," was considered the father of suicide terrorism in the West Bank in the early 1990s. Widely admired, Ayash specialized in preparing explosives and training Palestinian youths to build explosive belts, and he even recruited potential suicide bombers to the ranks of Hamas. Most of the suicide attacks against Israeli targets in the period following the signing of the Oslo Accords were attributed to Ayash, and he became the Israeli security forces' most wanted man. In June 1995, after almost a year of repeatedly evading Israeli forces, who spared no effort in their attempts to track him down, Ayash felt he had found a safe haven. He moved into the home of a former classmate at Birzeit University, Osama Hamad, who lived with his mother in Beit Lahiya in the Gaza Strip.

Ayash seldom left the small room they gave him. Constantly being on the run from his pursuers had taken its toll on him, and he preferred to spend most of his time reading and praying. Yet even the keen senses of "The Engineer," who was known for his meticulous precautions, were subject to the test of time. He did not pay attention to the fact that his friend's uncle, Kamal Hamad, a successful building contractor, was a collaborator with the Israelis and a close friend of Mussa Arafat, commander of Palestinian military intelligence in the Gaza Strip. This was apparently also the reason why Ayash ignored the hiring of his friend Osama as a clerk at Kamal's construction company and as a private tutor for his children. In fact, there was nothing coincidental in Osama's employment—it was ordered by the GSS. Kamal reported to GSS officials that

Ayash had sought refuge at his cousin's home and provided precise information about his daily routine.

Osama, who was unaware of the tightening contacts between his uncle and the Israeli forces, was pleased with the new job offered him. He was even more delighted by the cell phone, a rare possession in those days. Kamal had given it to him, telling him it was for "keeping in touch" at all times. Ayash also benefited from the use of the cell phone, particularly after the landline in the house stopped working, and he lost communication with his family in Rafat, a village on the West Bank. Osama's suspicions were not aroused after his mother's telephone line was inexplicably disconnected, nor by his uncle's request to bring him the cell phone from time to time for adjustments or other reasons. Kamal, who gave the cell phone to his GSS operators, was convinced that the purpose of the "adjustments" was to check on the listening device installed in it.

Just before dawn on Friday, January 5, 1996, Ayash returned quietly to his room after a meeting with Hamas members in Gaza. He prayed and then lay down to sleep. At 8:00 that morning, Osama entered the room, the cell phone in his hand. Ayash's father had called to speak to his son. Osama left the room and stepped away from the door to allow Ayash to speak to his father in privacy. Neither Osama nor Ayash heard the unmanned aerial vehicle that was hovering above the house or the signal it sent to the device Ayash clasped to his ear. Ayash managed to exchange a few sentences with his father before a loud noise split the air. Osama rushed to the room and found his friend lying on the bed, just as he had left him—but now there was a hole in his skull. This wound and the blood spattered on the wall left no doubt that nothing could be done to save "The Engineer."

In retrospect, the decision to eliminate Ayash resulted from several factors. From an operational perspective, it was evident that he was the driving force behind the Hamas suicide-bombing campaign. Prime Minister Rabin had made it clear to GSS leadership in late September 1995 that catching Ayash or eliminating him was one of the organization's first priorities. After Peres replaced Rabin as prime minister in November 1995, GSS constantly kept looking for the operational window of opportunity to complete this task. This opportunity evidently appeared in the last few weeks of 1995.

Other factors included the growing public pressure to avenge those responsible for the suicide attacks as well as the GSS desire to initiate a high-profile operation that would shift the attention of the public and policymakers alike from one of its biggest fiascos, Rabin's assassination by a Jewish Israeli citizen two months before Ayash's death. The elimination of Ayash would not be the end of Israeli attempts to strike at Hamas leaders.[15]

KHALED MASHAL

In the morning hours of September 25, 1997, residents of Amman, the capital of Jordan, could not imagine that their city would soon be transformed into the center of a world-gripping drama in which the Israeli Mossad, the Palestinian Hamas, the government of Jordan, Canadian authorities, and the president of the United States would all be involved. At 10:15 a.m., Khaled Mashal, head of the Hamas Political Bureau, arrived with two bodyguards at his office in the Hila el-Ali neighborhood. At the same time, in Tel Aviv, the head of Mossad, Dani Yatom, and other members of the organization's operations division awaited news from Amman. This was a moment that concluded a two-month effort. On July 30, a Hamas suicide bomber had attacked the Machane Yehuda Market in Jerusalem. The number of casualties was high: 16 dead and 169 wounded. Prime Minister Binyamin Netanyahu summoned Yatom to his office and demanded an immediate response in the form of an assassination. Yatom's problem was that most of the Hamas leaders operated from the West Bank, which was under the responsibility of the GSS. This fact did not discourage him. Backed by the head of the Caesarea operational wing, who was eager to act, Yatom instructed his officers to come up with a list of targets. Given that Mossad was focusing on Europe, all they came up with were a few marginal figures in the organization. Yatom asked for a revised list. This time he asked to expand the search and include Jordan. Among the names that popped up, two seemed especially interesting: Mussa Abu Marzuk, the former head of the Hamas Political Bureau, and Khaled Mashal, his successor. Another suicide attack in Jerusalem on September 4 expedited the preparations. Netanyahu wanted an immediate and proper retaliation. Mossad narrowed the list down to Mashal, the most accessible target.

The two Western-looking men who stood at the entrance to the building appeared to one of Mashal's bodyguards as slightly out of context. During the brief seconds in which the bodyguard hesitated, debating how to react to the presence of the foreigners, they left their place and hastened toward Mashal. One of them opened a soda can and the other sprayed liquid on Mashal's neck. The whole operation took two seconds. Mashal felt as though an insect had bitten on him. One of his bodyguards hit one of the attackers with a newspaper that he held, and both started to pursue the two attackers, who were already making their escape. The two Westerners were just able to reach and climb into a Hyundai car waiting nearby. However, Mashal's guards did not give up. They wrote down the number of the license plate and they chased the car. To their surprise, the car circled around and ended up at the same spot from which it had departed, probably as a result of an error in navigating through the streets of Amman. The bodyguards pounced on the attackers and began struggling with them until a Jordanian police officer who had witnessed the affair called for reinforcements. Together with the police, the bodyguards were able to overpower the two foreigners. The car, which held three more Westerners who viewed the incident from afar, darted off and was quickly swallowed up in the heavy traffic.

At this stage, Mashal was barely able to remain conscious. His stomach began to heave, and he lost his balance. The doctors who admitted him to the emergency room of the medical compound named for King Hussein were not immediately able to establish the source of these symptoms. Several days later, the Jordanian daily *Al-Ra'i* reported that an extensive medical analysis had confirmed that the lethal poison ricin had been injected into Mashal's body.

The first impression of the investigators who received the detainees at the police station was that the two—who were carrying Canadian passports identifying them as Barry Biton and Sean Kendall—had become involved in a chance brawl with Mashal and his people. The police offered them the services of a local lawyer to help them contend with the Jordanian legal system, but, to their surprise, the detainees declined this offer. The police quickly summoned Steve Bennett, the general attaché to the Canadian embassy in Jordan, to the police station in order to discuss the matter with the detainees and make it clear to them that the situation was serious. At the same time, in Tel Aviv, it was already evident to the Mossad chief that the attempt on Mashal's life had indeed failed and that the Jordanian authorities would soon realize that the "Canadian" citizens in Amman were Mossad agents. He contacted Prime Minister Binyamin Netanyahu and reported the developments to him.

In the heated consultations that took place in Jerusalem during the following hours, the prime minister and his advisors decided that their immediate objective was to bring about the release of the detainees and to minimize as much as possible the potential political ramifications of the whole episode. In an urgent phone conversation, Netanyahu spoke with Hussein, the king of Jordan, and asked him to receive the Mossad chief at his palace without delay. Hussein demanded more information from Netanyahu. When he became aware of the development of events, he reacted with great rage and refused to engage in any type of direct dialogue with Netanyahu or his emissaries. In a phone conversation with the president of the United States, Bill Clinton, Hussein raised his concerns regarding the incident. He explained how the Israeli assassination attempt on a Palestinian in the kingdom—where the majority of residents are indeed Palestinians—might lead to a wave of riots that could undermine the stability of the rule of the Hashemite Kingdom. The following hours were nerve-wracking for the highest authorities in both Amman and Jerusalem. Meanwhile, Mashal's condition continued to deteriorate. The troubled king relaxed his attitude somewhat. He agreed to renew contact with the Israelis, but only on condition that Israel provide Mashal with immediate medical attention in order to save his life. Prime Minister Netanyahu was left with no alternative. An Israeli doctor was rushed to the hospital in Amman and injected Mashal with an antidote. Mashal's condition improved to some extent, but the state of crisis between the two countries did not.

King Hussein, who had lost faith in Netanyahu, feared that after the serum had worn off, Mashal's condition would again deteriorate. He demanded that Israel send him the exact formula of the poison injected into Mashal's body. The only Israeli who succeeded in penetrating the wall of hostility surrounding the Jordanian king was his close friend, the former deputy chief of Mossad, Ephraim Halevy, who was at that time Israeli ambassador to the European Union. Two days after the assassination attempt, at a very late hour, Halevy arrived at the royal palace in Amman. He brought with him the formula for the poison and said that Israel was prepared to engage in further confidence-building steps. During this conversation, Hussein agreed to allow the Mossad agents who had fled in their car to the Israeli embassy to leave Jordan. However, Halevy was not able to placate him enough to raise the matter of the release of the two detained agents. At this stage, in Jerusalem it was clear that in the absence of a dramatic Israeli gesture, the chances of their release were very small.

On that very night, Prime Minister Binyamin Netanyahu, Defense Minister Yitzhak Mordechai, and their aides arrived in Amman. They engaged in intensive negotiations with Crown Prince Hassan and with the head of the Jordanian security services General Battikhi. After ten days of global negotiations, and principally due to Clinton's intense intermediary efforts, an agreement was reached by both parties stipulating that Israel would free Hamas leader Sheikh Ahmad Yassin in exchange for the release of the detained Mossad agents in Amman. While for Israel the release of Yassin was a most difficult step because of his senior status, for King Hussein, this was indeed a first-class payoff that helped relieve the existing tensions between the Jordanian monarchy and Islamic movements in his country.

In the upcoming months, a special committee was set up in Israel to investigate the reasons for the operation's failure. The committee's conclusions found the higher ranks of Mossad responsible, leading, eventually, to Yatom's resignation. At the same time, officials from the prime minister's office and from the Foreign Ministry worked hard to restore relations with Jordan and rebuild trust with the Canadian Foreign Ministry, which had recalled the Canadian ambassador in Israel to Ottawa for consultations.[16]

THE SECOND MAGNA CARTA

The gradual collapse of the Oslo process in the late 1990s and the emergence of an unfamiliar type of terrorism reignited the turf wars among the intelligence organizations. At first the struggle was latent, and the first Magna Carta agreement was honored. However, in January 1999, the tension seemed to have compromised the operations of the organizations, and thus the second Magna Carta was signed. This time the document focused on the separation of powers in the counterterrorism realm. If the first agreement gave the GSS a broader territorial deployment than its competitors, this time Aman received priority; it was established that military intelligence assessments would be given preference over those of other agencies. The GSS was forced to make do with relatively reduced responsibilities for gathering thwarting intelligence in the Palestinian arena. Both bodies promised to cooperate fully. The second Magna Carta, however, also failed to bring an end to the dissension. When Ehud Barak was elected prime minister in May 1999, the first signs of conflict were reappearing, this time between the GSS and Mossad. The issue was now who had responsibility for thwarting terrorist attacks that took place inside Israel but were carried out by operatives from outside the country. The disagreement was solved only after a special team appointed by Ehud Barak ruled that such thwarting actions would be the sole responsibility of the GSS.

In addition to the territorial struggles, Prime Minister Barak was forced to deal with a very critical report issued by the state comptroller, which analyzed intelligence community interrelations over the years. The comptroller came to the conclusion that despite the existence of agreements that were to have clearly set out the geographic and functional limits of the various intelligence agencies, no meaningful changes actually occurred. The report warned of several main problems, including the absence of an agreement between the various agencies regarding the training of potential intelligence agents, the unwillingness to share raw intelligence, and duplication in assessment units leading political leaders to receive contradictory assessments. Barak was not in a rush to implement the recommendations of the report. As a former chief of staff, Aman head, and commander of Sayeret Matkal, he had a resolute worldview of intelligence. He attached primary importance to Aman and the GSS while almost completely ruling out the other bodies, particularly the Center for Political Research of the Ministry of Foreign Affairs.[17]

The short-lived hope for peace following the Oslo Accords was shattered with the appearance of suicide-bomber attacks carried out by the Palestinian Islamic opposition movement. The frustration of the policymakers in Israel was deep. Not only had the hope for peace vanished, but the struggle against the terrorists had also become more complicated than ever. The desire to reassure the public led to increasing pressures on the intelligence organizations and the military to offer novel solutions. Yet the security establishment was still adapting to the new political reality, and its various arms were still fighting over their territory. The outcome was the reintroduction of the assassinations policy that later became the trademark of the Israeli counterterrorism effort. However, even as early as the mid-1990s, no proof could be given that the assassinations had any effect on the desire and capabilities of the terrorists to attain their goals.

![black bar]

DESPITE THE SIGNING OF the second Magna Carta during the preparations for Ehud Barak's participation in the Camp David Summit in the summer of 2000, competition between Aman and the GSS once again broke out. Called upon to submit assessments to the prime minister about Arafat's intentions, the agency heads sent contradictory signals and passionately defended their respective positions. In the end, Barak left for the summit not knowing which agency had supplied the most reliable assessment.[1]

THE AL-AQSA INTIFADA

Not even the collapse of the talks and the outbreak of the Al-Aqsa intifada in early October 2000 could bring an end to the conflict between the two agencies, and they continued to advocate opposing views. General Amos Gilad, representative of Aman and former head of its research division, as well as coordinator of government operations in the occupied territories, believed that Arafat and the Palestinian Authority had planned the intifada. In contrast, the GSS claimed that the reality on the streets had dragged the Palestinian Authority into the violence. Naturally, this dispute compromised the ability of the Israeli leadership to formulate policies toward the Palestinian Authority during this most sensitive period of relations between the two entities. When Ariel Sharon became prime minister, he clearly tipped the scales in favor of the GSS. Sharon developed close ties with the head of the agency, Avi Dichter, who a few years later joined him when he established a new political party, Kadima. Aman representatives were concerned that they would be asked for their assessments only as a matter of protocol.

Aman field officers also felt that the GSS had the upper hand. Because of the way in which officers are promoted in the military, intelligence officers serving in the regional commands are usually young and do not have the chance to spend much time in any one position. Consequently, they are far less familiar with local conditions than GSS handlers, who know them down to the last detail. In addition, intelligence-officer training is naturally predisposed to military intelligence, sometimes at the expense of other types of intelligence. Most of these officers are unfamiliar with the handling of human-intelligence operations, and their knowledge of Arabic is limited. In comparison with GSS personnel, they have less experience in formulating full intelligence assessments on the basis of intelligence items and indications that come their way. These conditions, together with the fact that GSS handlers and IDF division commanders share common backgrounds and belong to the same age group, contributed to the preference of the commanders in charge of foiling terrorist operations for GSS information and assessments. During the course of the intifada, GSS handlers joined military units and became those unit intelligence officers during special operations in Palestinian territories. The role of the regional intelligence officer became almost marginal.[2]

The close collaboration between the GSS and the special forces can be explained by other factors as well. Military special units have different areas of responsibility from those of the GSS, eliminating grounds for competition. The most conspicuous collaboration in recent years was between the GSS and the Israeli Air Force (IAF). During the intifada, IAF attack helicopters and unmanned aerial vehicles (UAVs) in effect became the operational arm of the GSS in thwarting operations. Among other assignments, these squadrons carried out strikes on rocket launchers, bombed machine shops and explosives laboratories, and effected targeted assassinations from the air. Police elite units, especially Yamam, also became close allies of the GSS. The window of opportunity for cooperation between these two opened in the first days of the intifada.

During this period, the army avoided intensive operations in the territories controlled by the Palestinian Authority for fear of escalating the situation. When the GSS required a skilled unit to carry out special operations, it came to Yamam. In contrast to the IDF, the police-force chain of command is short, and unit commanders enjoy a relatively free hand in deciding what operational steps to take. The Yamam chief commander during this period was Hagai Peleg, who had previously commanded Egoz, an elite IDF unit. He realized that the GSS could finally provide Yamam with operational opportunities, after many years of standing in the shadow of IDF elite units. The intensifying pace of the incidents, however, required the participation of additional forces. At a meeting that took place in March 2001 in the office of the prime minister, Sharon demanded that the chief of staff and his deputy put counterterrorism high on the IDF list of priorities. To this end, he ordered each IDF elite unit to appoint an outstanding officer as a contact person with the GSS. In the wake of this meeting, the GSS

and the operational units that collaborated with it received all the financial resources and weapons they requested.[3]

SPECIAL FORCES AND COUNTERTERRORISM MISSIONS

Even bureaucratic obstacles, which in the past had precluded direct ties between
the regional desks of the GSS and the IDF special unit headquarters, were sur-
mounted. These units consisted of Sayeret Matkal, Shayetet 13, Sayeret Shaldag,
Egoz, Sayeret Maglan, Duvedevan, and Sayarot (reconnaissance units) of the
four main infantry brigades, Golani, Givati, Paratroopers, and Nahal. Counterterrorism became the most important issue in the eyes of policymakers, and the
government was willing to allocate whatever means necessary to units that were
successful in such missions; and this created fierce competition among the units
as their commanders practically demanded to receive more and more opportunities to prove the superiority of their particular unit. This sometimes led to
extreme scenarios such as the events of April 15, 2002, when Duvedevan and
Sayeret Matkal soldiers were called upon to carry out a high-profile operation
that included the capture of Marwan Barghouti, head of the Tanzim forces in the
West Bank. In order to ensure that they would be the unit chosen for the operation, Duvedevan soldiers hid the truck that was supposed to transfer the Sayeret
Matkal soldiers to the scene.[4]

The decision to assign operations demanding less specialization, such as the
detection and capture of certain objectives or eliminating terrorist cells, to elite
military units requires attention. It is true that the skills developed by special-forces
soldiers who excel in microwarfare are quite suitable to such operations. At issue,
however, is the logic of sending a fighter who has undergone extensive training
in areas such as technological intelligence, targeting laser markers, or dangerous assaults on enemy ports to arrest terrorist suspects in the West Bank. One
argument is that there is simply no alternative. The volume of terrorist incidents
necessitates the participation of all units trained in thwarting operations. Another
argument, also with a degree of logic, insists that participation in such operations helps keep the soldiers in top combat form. Both arguments deserve review.
The training of small units designated for specific missions costs Israel extensive
financial resources. Having soldiers from these groups participate in operations
that members of more conventional military units could perform with equal or
more success is a decision to be made only after careful consideration.

The answer to the first argument can be found in the fact that the IDF has
been quite flexible in responding to the special situations that have continually

arisen. For example, during the first intifada, Duvdevan, Shimshon, and Yamas were already active in their original forms; that is to say, these *mistaarvim* units were carrying out complicated arrests within Palestinian cities and refugee camps. Regular Border Police companies also joined them, and an armored infantry unit was formed with the principal mission of carrying out routine security activities in the occupied territories. With the escalation of the conflict, however, the trend was reversed. Instead of training additional personnel for these tasks, large infantry and armored forces were allocated from both the regular and reserve armies for policing activities in the occupied territories. The fact that during this period the IDF was also occupying the security zone in southern Lebanon created a situation in which most fighting forces were confined to regular security tasks and had less time to train for warfare and specialized activities.[5]

The second intifada, which was much more violent than the first, made the issue even more critical. This time detainees were not young people flying Palestinian flags or spraying slogans in the streets. Now the IDF was being called upon to allocate forces for street battles in the middle of highly populated urban centers. The units that had operated during the previous decade, especially Shimshon, had been disbanded after the signing of the Oslo Accords, and the void they left had to be filled. Egoz, which was left without a purpose after the IDF withdrawal from southern Lebanon, was added on to Duvdevan and Yamas, which had maintained their operational skills throughout this period. The Egoz Unit's soldiers had to transfer their specialized skills in antiguerilla warfare to a new front: the open areas and traffic arteries of the West Bank. Although they were quite successful in their combat relocation to the West Bank, it came at the price of having to sacrifice some of their specific counterguerrilla skills, and it also hindered their preparedness to operate on the Lebanese front when it became necessary.[6]

No less problematic was the situation of Shayetet 13. During the second intifada, the Shayetet soldiers were assigned two main types of missions. The first had to do with raids from or at sea. The operation that received the most attention in the media was Noah's Ark, the January 3, 2002, capture of *Karine A*, a ship carrying weapons from Iran to the Palestinians. In the early morning hours of that day, while the ship was sailing in the southern part of the Red Sea between Saudi Arabia and Sudan, a few IAF helicopters escorted by F-15 aircraft drew near the ship. Before any of the ship's crewmembers understood what the situation was, Shayetet 13 fighters suddenly appeared from the helicopters and were swung down by ropes to the ship's upper deck. In less than eight minutes they overpowered the crew, which did not resist. Following the exposure of a huge arsenal of weapons concealed in the ship, they sailed it to Eilat, arriving at the Israeli port on the following day.[7]

The second type of operations to which Shayetet 13 soldiers were assigned involved the detention of wanted suspects during complex land operations. While Shayetet 13 soldiers are considered the most professional of the IDF elite units for missions of the first type, their skills in carrying out land operations in the West Bank are not necessarily better than those of other units. The decision to supplement the special forces operating in the West Bank with Shayetet 13 was made by the commander of the Israeli Navy, Yedidya Yaari. When he first took up this position, Yaari introduced an approach according to which "enemy ports had become less relevant and the commandos needed to be retrained to work in the alleys of the Casbah." According to Yaari, the intensive microwarfare exercises the naval commandos undergo in their training made them ideal for the new front. This approach was supported by the Shayetet commander, Erez Zuckerman, who had helped to form the Egoz Unit and had functioned as its first commander. In order to integrate Shayetet 13 soldiers into operations in the occupied territories while limiting the impairment of their seaborne capabilities, the unit was divided into task forces. While soldiers who were trained in commando warfare were sent on land missions, their comrades who were more experienced in naval missions were left to train at the unit's base at Atlit. Indeed, the Shayetet enjoyed many operational successes. Furthermore, the fruitful collaboration of naval commandos with the army opened new opportunities for promotion for many of the Shayetet officers within the ranks of the army. However, veteran naval commandos were not happy with the decision. They warned that the "alleys of the Casbah" were not the natural arena for naval commando operations, and their participation in such missions impaired the readiness of the unit to carry out tasks for which it was established.[8]

The effect of switching units from training for war to training for counterterrorism was even more dramatic. Soldiers in the Maglan reconnaissance unit specialize in antitank weaponry. The unit was formed in the mid-1980s and in its early days consisted of soldiers from other elite forces. After a period of structuring, applicants begin to go through its long training regime. Like Sayeret Matkal trainees, Maglan soldiers become highly skilled at land navigation and surveillance. Because their area of expertise is primarily required during wartime, a decision was made to engage these soldiers during low-intensity periods of warfare as "terrorist hunters." The unit developed capabilities that allowed its soldiers to translate GSS-relayed intelligence information into operational programs in a very brief time, sometimes no more than two hours.

Maglan fighters are highly skilled at detaining suspects and carrying out eliminations under difficult conditions. They may be transported to their destinations by helicopter and generally accomplish their missions in a very short time. During the first days of the Second Lebanon War, the consequences of Maglan as well as other special forces spending so much of their time in the territories of the Palestinian Authority were painfully felt. The units, trained for the Palestinian front, found themselves unprepared for the environs and challenges of southern Lebanon. The Hezbollah operated from well-fortified buildings that bore little resemblance to the hiding places of the Palestinian fighters. The Hezbollah's weaponry, especially antitank rockets, came as a surprise to the soldiers.[9]

Even the infantry reconnaissance units, whose main tasks were gathering tactical intelligence and leading their brigades into battle, underwent dramatic changes. During the 1970s, these reconnaissance units, especially Sayeret Golani, would be used as local backup forces in case of terrorist attacks, securing the area until Sayeret Matkal could arrive. From the 1990s, they were given a similar role, usually backing up special operations, especially complex detention operations carried out by elite units, by securing the area and preventing cells of Palestinian fighters from coming in to help their comrades. Reconnaissance units were also allocated to carry out detention operations that did not demand special assault or microwarfare capabilities. In other instances, they were required to carry out decoy operations; that is, they would patrol areas used as bases for Palestinian fighters to try to draw them into attacking the force and revealing themselves. The deployment of the special forces in counterterrorism operations in the West Bank led to new rivalries and reignited old ones.[10]

THE KIDNAPPING OF ELIYAHU GUREL

Even the most ancient battle among the elite takeover units came back to life during that period. Over the years, the number of hostage-taking incidents had diminished, and it seemed that the question of the adoption of the Horev Commission recommendations was no longer relevant. The abduction of taxi driver Eliyahu Gurel on Friday, July 11, 2003, was thus surprising. At 5:00 p.m. on that day, Gurel picked up four passengers—two young men, a young woman, and a girl—who requested that he take them to Jerusalem from the Ben-Gurion Airport. Near Pisgat Zeev, one of the men took out a knife and held it to Gurel's throat. Gurel did not resist and followed instructions to turn the car in the direction of the Beit Hanina village. At this point the woman and girl left the group, and the three men began walking in the direction of Ramallah, where the kidnappers led Gurel to an abandoned factory in Beitunia. After a worried call from Gurel's wife, the police had already begun to search for him. After his taxi was found in the Ramallah area, the Palestinian Authority security forces were also informed. Around noon on Saturday, Gurel called home from his cell phone and said that he had been taken hostage. Representatives of the General Staff negotiating team who were waiting at his house began a dialogue with the kidnappers. The latter's first demand was the immediate release of two thousand prisoners.

On that same day, Shirin Halil, the woman from the taxi, was apprehended in Lod. She gave information about the kidnappers and a general description of the area where Gurel was being held, although she did not know the exact location since he was taken from one hiding place to another every few hours. On Tuesday, the GSS discovered that two of the cell members, Ramez Rimawi and Ahmed Hajaj, had left their hideout and had arrived at the Kalandia Checkpoint near Jerusalem. After a short consultation with Minister of Defense Shaul Mofaz, Deputy Chief of Staff Gabi Ashkenazi, and senior GSS officers, it was decided to detain them immediately. The mission was given to Yamam, backed up by the Duvdevan Unit. During the operation, Rimawi was slightly injured in his leg. Immediately after being detained, the two were interrogated and revealed detailed information about Gurel's location and the identity of his guards. In the evening hours, Sayeret Matkal troops stormed the abandoned building in Beitunia. They overpowered Samir Rimawi and another kidnapper, who were armed only with knives, and found Gurel safe and sound. Even though the collaborative efforts of the two units had been successful, Yamam fighters were once again incensed. They had been deployed to make the arrest, a mission not within their primary expertise, but were not assigned to carry out the rescue. Again, a less suitable force had been awarded their job.[11]

THE ESCALATION OF THE ASSASSINATIONS

Despite the massive military effort in the West Bank, the IDF could not smother the flames of the intifada. Ariel Sharon, this time as prime minister, allowed the GSS to reintroduce Israel's trademark policy in the realm of counterterrorism: assassinations. This time the tactic was ratcheted up a notch and at the same time given a new, more sterile name—"focused preventions," which is closer to the Hebrew original than the more common English term "targeted killings" or, simply, "assassinations." In addition to the new name, the targets, techniques, and frequency of attacks changed. The willingness of the Ariel Sharon administration to increase the use of this method led GSS and Aman think-tank teams to attempt to define criteria that would justify targeting a certain individual. Among others, one drafted document states that assassination is a tool of self-defense designed to stop a terrorist attack that has entered the execution stage when there is no other way to stop it. In contradiction to the Israeli government's approach in the 1970s and the X Commission, the team stressed that assassinations must not become a tool for avenging a target's past deeds. Words, however, are one thing and actions another. As time passed, the aims of the targeted killings assumed a character very similar to that of the assassinations perpetrated by Israel in the past.

The desire of policymakers to take action in response to suicide attacks led them to instruct the security establishment to seek out available targets (see table 8.1). The potential involvement of assassination targets in a future attack on Israel or in the planning of terrorist activities was not a decisive factor in declaring a verdict against them. The escalation of this type of incident was quite dramatic, even in comparison to the days of the X Commission. Now it was no longer necessary to hold quasi-judicial proceedings in order to "convict" a candidate for assassination. The prime minister and the head of the GSS made the decision.[12]

The target of one of the first assassinations in the second intifada was Raed Karmi, a senior Tanzim activist and officer in the Palestinian General Intelligence. Right from the outbreak of the events, the defense establishment gathered intelligence information on Karmi's extensive involvement in attacks against Israeli soldiers and civilians. Among others, he had planned the murder of two Tel Aviv restaurateurs, Etgar Zeituni and Moti Dayan, in Tulkarm on January 23, 2001. He was also behind the assassination attempt on IAF Colonel Natan Barak. The aura of the combat warrior attached to Karmi in the Palestinian street sent the Israeli military into a spin. Senior IDF officers felt they had a score to settle with the man and vowed not to rest until he was dealt with. On January 14, 2002, Karmi was walking from his house to visit his mistress on a route that passed close to a concrete wall. A UAV circling in the skies of Tulkarm transmitted an electronic signal that detonated a powerful bomb planted behind the wall. Karmi was killed instantly. The assassination led to the collapse of the fragile ceasefire between Israel and the Palestinian Authority. After the fact, Defense Minister Benjamin Ben-Eliezer said that Karmi's elimination was "the biggest mistake we made."[13]

Carefully planned assassinations were not the only feature of the increasing aggressiveness of the Israeli response at that point. Reprisal actions were also not

TABLE 8.1 **PROMINENT TARGETED KILLINGS DURING THE AL-AQSA INTIFADA**

DATE	TARGET	ORGANIZATION	POSITION
November 9, 2000	Hussein Muhammad Salim A'bayat	Fatah	Head of the Fatah-Tanzim in Bethlehem
November 30, 2000	Thabit Ahmad Thabit	Fatah	Head of the Fatah-Tanzim in Tul-Karem
April 5, 2001	Iyad Mahmud Naif Hardan	Palestine Islamic Jihad (PIJ)	Head of PIJ forces in Jenin
July 17, 2001	Umar Sa'adah	Hamas	Head of Hamas forces in Bethlehem
July 31, 2001	Jamal Salim Damuni	Hamas	Senior operative of the Hamas military wing in the West Bank
August 27, 2001	Abu-Ali Mustafa a-Zibri	Popular Front for the Liberation of Palestine (PFLP)	Political leader and cofounder of the PFLP
November 23, 2001	Mahmud a-Shuli (Abu Hanoud)	Hamas	Head of the Hamas military wing in the West Bank
January 14, 2002	Raed Muhammad Raif Karmi	Fatah	Head of the Al-Aqsa Martyrs Brigades in the West Bank
July 22, 2002	Salah Mustafa Shehadah	Hamas	Head of the Hamas military wing in the Gaza Strip
March 8, 2003	Ibrahim Makadmeh	Hamas	Spiritual leader and senior operative in the Hamas military wing
June 21, 2003	Abdullah Abd al-Kader Husni al-Qawasmeh	Hamas	Head of the Hamas military forces in Hebron
August 21, 2003	Isma'il Hassan Abu Shanab	Hamas	Political leader and Hamas cofounder
March 22, 2004	Sheikh Ahmad Isma'il Yasin	Hamas	Spiritual and political leader
April 17, 2004	Abd al-'Aziz 'Ali 'Abd al-Hafiz a-Rantisi	Hamas	Senior political leader

TABLE 8.1 **(CONTINUED)**

DATE	TARGET	ORGANIZATION	POSITION
May 30, 2004	Wael Talib Muhammad Nassar	Hamas	Senior operative in the Hamas military wing
October 5, 2004	Bashir Khalil Dabash	PIJ	Head of PIJ forces in the Gaza Strip
October 21, 2004	Adnan Mahmud Jaber al-Ghul	Hamas	Senior operative in the Hamas military wing in the Gaza Strip
September 23, 2005	Muhammad Khalil (Sheikh Khalil)	PIJ	Senior operative in the PIJ military wing
March 31, 2006	Khalil (Abu Yusuf) al-Quba	Popular Resistance Committee (PRC)	Head of the PRC military wing
June 6, 2006	Jamal Abu Samhadana (Abu 'Atiya')	PIJ/PRC	Head of the PRC in the Gaza Strip

Source: NSSC Dataset on Targeted Killings, www.nscc.haifa.ac.il.

a thing of the past. In the evening hours of February 19, 2002, two Palestinian National Security Forces activists, Shadi Saida and Dawoud Haj, arrived at the IDF checkpoint at Ein Ariq, west of Ramallah. They got out of the taxi that had transported them, and under cover of darkness they approached the soldiers manning the checkpoint. They opened fire. Three soldiers were killed and a fourth was wounded, but the attackers had not finished. They broke into a trailer where three off-duty soldiers were resting and killed them, too. Israel responded that very night. A Sayeret Yael force, on its way to arrest some Palestinians wanted for interrogation by the GSS, was notified that their mission had been cancelled and that they were to return to their base immediately. Two hours later they received their new orders. One of the commandos later recalled the events of that night:

> When we arrived at base, our unit commander ran off to the headquarters and when he returned he called us for a briefing. He said: "Six of our soldiers from the Engineering Corps have been killed at the checkpoint and we are going out on a retaliation operation. We are going to kill Palestinian police-men at a checkpoint to avenge the blood of our six soldiers that they killed." An eye for an eye. That was the feeling. They told us that this was a revenge operation and that we were going to take a life for a life at another three or

four checkpoints. And no more. Everyone was excited about the idea of going out to kill people. We were pleased. Since the Intifada began we hadn't had the opportunity to do something with "honor." None of us had notches on our weapons.[14]

The soldiers reached the checkpoint of the Palestinian Police outside Deir es-Sudan, not far from the Israeli settlement of Halamish. The Sayeret soldiers spread out and lay in wait for the policemen, who were in one of the village houses. Three Palestinians who came out were killed in the first burst of gunfire. At the very same time, three teams of the paratrooper elite reconnaissance unit also attacked Palestinian police checkpoints near Nablus. The fact that the police manning those checkpoints had maintained a good working relationship with their Israeli colleagues did not help them. When the sun rose the following morning, eighteen Palestinian policemen lay dead alongside various checkpoints in the West Bank. Recalled one IDF officer five years later,

> That period was rife with terrorism and violent attacks against the armed forces. The army did not have clear targets for responses. The targeted killings [method] had not reached its current level. The IDF's special forces units were inactive. The IDF felt that its hands were tied. A decision was made to switch to the offensive, mainly due to the frustration of the army in face of the Palestinian attacks. Since we regarded the PNA as being involved in terrorism, it became a legitimate target. After an incident like Ein Ariq, we had to respond. A targeted killing can take hours [to plan]. The checkpoints were opportune targets. They were objectives that we could attack within two or three hours. It was a case of the ideal versus reality."[15]

The next milestone was Operation Defensive Shield, which was conducted between March 29, 2002, and April 21, 2002. During this operation, IDF forces occupied all major Palestinian cities and villages in the West Bank, arresting more than 4,200 Palestinians. The operation began as a response to the Passover Massacre at the Park Hotel in Netanya on March 27, 2002. During this operation, the IDF reoccupied cities and refugee camps in the West Bank, which facilitated the partial rehabilitation of the HUMINT infrastructure, but at the heavy price of ruling with an iron fist. The operation also exemplified the difficulties an established regular army unit must confront when fighting clandestine small violent groups that are fortified inside dense urban areas. In Jenin, for example, the Palestinian fighters booby-trapped the entire refugee camp while ambushing the IDF soldiers inside the camp's narrow alleys. Thus, the IDF advance was slow and was accompanied by a relatively large number of casualties. On April 9, thirteen soldiers died in an ambush resulting from several demolition charges that were set off simultaneously. Subsequently, the IDF decided to destroy any building in Jenin that was suspected of providing a hiding place for Palestinian forces. Although the IDF succeeded in renewing their military presence in the Palestinian population centers, the operation actually heightened the motivation of terrorist cells to act, and it also created fertile ground for the expansion of the ranks of these groups.[16]

TOWARD A DEFENSIVE MODEL

Between 2000 and 2004 there were 157 suicide attacks in which 507 Israelis were killed (see figure 8.1). The combination of the intensity of these attacks, the difficulty in obtaining ample information on the cells that had initiated them, the futility of the assassination policy, and the serious physical and moral damage to the Israeli home front led the GSS to advocate the introduction of a defensive model. The most ambitious effort was the construction of the Separation Fence.

FIGURE 8.1 **SUICIDE ATTACKS AND TARGETED KILLINGS DURING THE AL-AQSA INTIFADA**

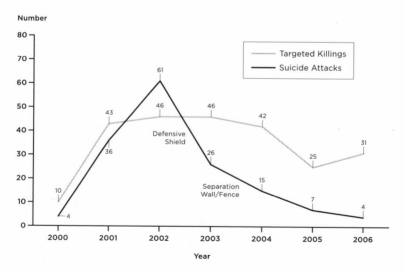

Source: NSSC Dataset on Palestinian Terrorism, www.nssc.haifa.ac.il

The primary goal of the fence was to create a physical buffer between the West Bank and Israeli territory and thereby prevent the infiltration of suicide bombers into urban centers. The erection of the fence began in May 2002 despite the opposition of the military intelligence, which claimed that the fence would not be effective enough and argued that Israel continue to employ mostly offensive measures. In June 2003, Israel completed the northern part of the fence and in the ensuing months was also able to build a concrete wall surrounding Jerusalem.[17]

Indeed, the construction of the fence has proved its effectiveness in halting suicide terrorism. From June 2003 to April 2007, there were thirty-seven suicide attacks in Israel. Only on three occasions did a suicide bomber penetrate the fence. All other attacks occurred inside the West Bank or were perpetrated in the central and southern parts of the country. Previously, between 1993 and mid-2003, 34.6 percent (35 out of 101) of the suicide attacks occurred in northern Israel, areas that from mid-2003 were protected by the Separation Fence. In addition, Jerusalem, which until 2003 was the most attractive target for suicide attacks, became a relatively safe area after the erection of the wall on the city's eastern border. While between 1993 and 2003 the city suffered thirty suicide attacks, the number was reduced to three in 2004 and to zero in the ensuing years.

It was evident that the erection of the fence, combined with IDF repeated blockades on areas and cities in the West Bank, proved to be an effective strategy against the Palestinian suicide-attack campaigns. The problem is that political considerations took over the process of building the Separation Fence—specifically the Israeli government's desire to include a large number of Israeli settlements in the area west of the fence. The inevitable result was an extensive Israeli annexation of Palestinian territories and the consequent inability of many villagers to reach their own fields or nearby villages. An obstacle that succeeded in protecting Israeli residents in the short term became another significant factor in increasing Palestinian enmity toward Israel.[18]

The disappearance of the suicide attacks from the Israeli streets should be credited also to complementary defensive mechanisms that were implemented alongside the erection of the fence. Several municipalities adopted laws obligating restaurants, bars, coffee shops, and businesses that involve public gatherings to post a security guard at the entrance to their establishments. These guards were added to thousands of other guards who have been protecting public buildings such as government offices, hospitals, and shopping centers since 1998, following the passage of legislation in the Knesset. In some cases this proved to be very effective, as on April 29, 2003, when a security guard in a coffee shop in Tel Aviv prevented a suicide bomber from bursting into the shop, eventually leading to an explosion at the entrance. Although three people died in the event, the head of Israeli police in the Tel Aviv District admitted that the guard had saved the lives of dozens, who would have died if the perpetrator had been able to set off the explosion inside the coffee shop. This was not the only case; between 1993 and 2007, on fourteen different occasions, guards prevented attacks or were able to force the suicide attacker to detonate before arriving at his destination.[19]

In addition, public transportation security was intensified. In 1994, when suicide attacks on buses began to spread to the cities of Israel, the Ministry of Transport established the Unit for the Protection of Public Transport. Approximately four hundred graduates of IDF combat units were enlisted into this unit. The training of the unit's recruits was based to a great degree on terrorist-identification procedures developed by the GSS in the 1960s and 1970s in response to the wave of plane hijackings by Palestinian organizations. Three years after its formation, there was a temporary decrease in suicide attacks, and the Unit for the Protection of Public Transport was dismantled, its functions transferred to the Yoav, Horev, and Nitzan police units. However, toward the end of 2001, following an increase in suicide attacks, the unit was reconstructed. While the unit guards covered only a small number of the bus lines (less than 5 percent), their presence on main bus lines helped somewhat to reduce the public fears and gave it the feeling that some security measures were being implemented in order to defend Israel's most popular form of public transportation.[20]

COUNTERING THE FINANCING OF TERRORISM

Another method that falls under the defensive category is the attempt to block the flow of money intended for terrorist purposes. During the course of Operation Defensive Shield, the GSS and Aman were able to seize documents that revealed a small aspect of the fundraising complex of Hamas and the Islamic Jihad in the countries of Western Europe. To the satisfaction of the Israeli intelligence services, in several cases it was possible to draw a direct line between a "charitable society" that operated in Europe and local terrorist cells. For example, a Hamas foundation that was active in Great Britain, Interpal, transferred funds to the families of suicide bombers. The same society was also employed as a Hamas conduit for transferring donated money from Palestinian charitable societies in Switzerland, South Africa, and Belgium. On another occasion, evidence led to a Palestine solidarity fund (Compagnie Beneficent de Solidarité avec Palestine) in France that supplied millions of dollars to Hamas each year. This intelligence information served as a basis for a series of appeals that Israel submitted to the relevant countries in the attempt to prevent the continued operation of the foundations in their jurisdiction. In some of the cases, the appeals were heeded. In August 2002, the German Interior Ministry ordered the closing of the German branch of the Hamas-run Al-Aqsa Charitable Foundation, one of the organization's money raising centers in Europe. Ten months later, the government of the Netherlands also announced that it would not allow the foundation to continue to raise funds on its territory. Denmark and Belgium were the last countries to restrict fundraising activities in their territories after the European Union declared Hamas a terrorist group in September 2003.[21]

Across the Atlantic, actions taken against financiers of terrorism were even more adamant as reflected in the story of Sami Al-Arian, professor of computer science at the University of South Florida. Al-Arian was for many years the object of the keen interest of both American and Israeli intelligence agencies. He was born in Kuwait to a Palestinian family in 1958 and at the age of seventeen immigrated to the United States after being accepted for engineering studies at Southern Illinois University. His impressive academic achievements paved the way to a doctoral program at the University of North Carolina. After completing his studies, he obtained a teaching position at the University of South Florida and was soon promoted to full professor. Along with the cultivation of an impressive academic career, Al-Arian also became a prominent spokesman for the Palestinian cause in the United States, and in 1991 he founded the World and Islam Studies Enterprise (WISE). During the course of the 1990s, there were growing fears both in the United States and Israel that the institute was providing patronage to the activities of the Palestinian Islamic Jihad organization in the United States. Furthermore, they suspected that Al-Arian stood at the head of a group of Palestinians who were raising funds earmarked for suicide operations in the cities of Israel and aid to families of suicide bombers. On February 20, 2003, FBI agents arrested Al-Arian. His trial, which a prosecutor called an "Israeli-American coproduction," lasted more than two years. A substantial part of the case was based on evidence that American authorities received from Israeli intelligence agencies, which, over a significant length of time, had intercepted correspondence and phone calls Al-Arian had conducted with his colleagues in Damascus and Ramallah. Although in the court of first instance Al-Arian was acquitted, in the retrial, completed in April 2006, the scales were tipped against him. Al-Arian was sentenced to fifty-seven months in prison for offenses related to the financing of terrorist activities. He is slated for deportation from the United States at the end of his prison term.[22] The case of Al-Arian seems to demonstrate that a major portion of the cooperation between intelligence and law-enforcement agencies concludes in the filing of an indictment pertaining to offenses associated with the financing of terrorism.

Other actions taken by Israel have included raids of banks in the West Bank and the seizing of funds from accounts suspected of financing sources for terrorist networks. The most famous action against Palestinian banks was conducted on February 5, 2004, against a branch of the Arab Bank in Ramallah. This bank held the accounts of more than one hundred families of suicide bombers. According to Israeli sources, the Palestinians and their supporters in Arab and Western countries have found circuitous means of keeping the embers of the struggle burning by transferring large sums of money to charitable funds and straw companies. In a local political reality based on primordial ties, it is very difficult to prevent the head of a charitable organization from transferring money to a brother or cousin active in a terrorist cell. In many cases the same charitable funds were actually involved in humanitarian activities.[23]

On January 25, 2006, the Palestinian Authority conducted a general election in which Hamas won 76 out 132 seats and subsequently assembled a new government with Ismail Haniya, head of Hamas, as its prime minister. The economic embargo imposed on the Hamas government stimulated Palestinians to find creative ways to transfer funds. In a few cases, cash was smuggled on the bodies of leaders returning from visits to other countries. For example, Sammy Abu Zahary, a Hamas spokesman, tried to smuggle in hundreds of thousands of euros hidden in a money belt while returning to the Gaza Strip from a trip to Qatar in June 2006. That December, Mahmoud A-Zahar was not allowed to enter Gaza Strip after he tried to smuggle $20 million in his luggage. In other cases, the relatively uncontrolled border between Egypt and the Gaza Strip and the tunnels dug between the Egyptian and Palestinian sections of Rafah provided a route for smuggling activities. GSS efforts to avert the transfer of these funds can be compared to Sisyphus eternally rolling his boulder up the hill.[24]

If the construction of the fence ostensibly showed that the Israeli understood that the Palestinian groups had adopted a nonhierarchical structure and that local cells had become the driving force behind most of the suicide attacks, the targeted assassinations and, to some degree, the attempt to stop the flow of resources into the hand of the terrorists, should have raised eyebrows. The elimination of leaders, which back in the 1970s and 1980s had proved severely limited in its deterrent effect, became a truly double-edged sword during the years of the Al-Aqsa intifada. Attacks on prominent figures in the Palestinian leadership heightened the desire for revenge against the Israelis and were a shot in the arm for the localization of terrorism. The national leaders lowered their profiles and slackened what little control they still had over the local cells. Thus, the GSS found itself operating against groups such as the Popular Resistance Committees, a militia based on the Samhadana clan from Rafah, and the Army of Islam, from the Darmush clan in Gaza City, which, among other things, was responsible for the kidnapping of the Israeli soldier Gilad Shalit in July 2006.[25]

ON FRIDAY, MAY 26, 2006, the Al-Jazeera television network reported that a Mercedes coupe had burst into flames in Sidon, a coastal city in southern Lebanon. The two passengers in the car were Mahmoud al-Majzoub, also known as Abu Hamza, a member of the Palestinian Islamic Jihad (PIJ) and its liaison in the southern Lebanon area, and his brother Nidal al-Majzoub. Both were severely injured in the explosion and a short while later died of their wounds. Conflicting news reports were broadcast throughout the course of the day on the various communication networks. The PIJ claimed that Israeli intelligence agents had laid a large explosive device along the route usually taken by Abu Hamza and detonated it with a remote control mechanism as his car passed by. In contrast, Lebanese security sources said that the bomb was rigged up in the car itself and activated when he started the car.

The ambiguity in regard to the details of the assassination was not due to journalistic carelessness. The full story was made public only weeks later. An announcement issued by Lebanese Minister of Defense Elias Murr revealed that the assassins had used particularly sophisticated means. As the Lebanese security forces suspected from the very beginning, a highly powerful explosive device had indeed been planted in the car, specifically, in the car door. However, it did not go off as the car's ignition was turned on. Abu Hamza had been filmed on the ground as he walked toward his car, and then the same film reverted to a real-time image of an Israeli Air Force (IAF) plane hovering above. When it was clear that Abu Hamza had taken his place next to the steering wheel, the plane transmitted an electronic signal that activated the bomb and blew up the car and its occupants.[1]

Murr's announcement was made only after an intense investigation that led to the discovery of a group of twenty Lebanese civilians who were Mossad collaborators. Members of the network received the booby-trapped car door from Israel. Two Israeli specialists with forged identities arrived in Sidon and installed the door in Majzoub's car with the help of network members. The architect of the network was Mahmoud Kassem Rafa, a fifty-nine-year-old Druze from the town of Hasbaya. Before the IDF withdrawal from Lebanon in May 2000, he served in the South Lebanon Army (SLA) at the rank of colonel. Rafa's past as an SLA officer placed him high on the list of targets of Lebanese military intelligence, but his wanted status did not prompt him to take the requisite precautions. His ostentatious and lavish lifestyle stood in direct contrast to the meager means one would expect from a former SLA officer. This standard of living only fueled the suspicions against him, and after a long period of surveillance and wiretapping his phone calls, security officers raided Rafa's villa and arrested him. A search of his house uncovered sophisticated visual-intelligence equipment and forged documents that he used to help Mossad people infiltrate Lebanon. During his interrogation, Rafa divulged that Israeli forces had recruited him as far back as 1994. The mission he had been assigned was the mobilization of Lebanese civilians to Mossad operations all over the country.[2]

The killing of Abu Hamza had been the swansong of the network's activities. This was preceded by a series of other assassinations, which included high-ranking Hezbollah officials Ali Hassan Dib, a senior Hezbollah operative responsible for Hezbollah administration over the southern Lebanon area, and Ali Hussein Saleh, a senior Hezbollah operative who was responsible for the connection with terrorist groups in the West Bank. A third target was Jihad Jibril, the son of Ahmad Jibril, the founder and commander of the Popular Front for the Liberation of Palestine–General Command. Jihad Jibril was in charge of PFLP-GC operations in the West Bank at the beginning of the second intifada.[3]

THE ROAD TO THE SECOND LEBANON WAR

Three years earlier, there was renewed hope that nearly a decade after Dirani's kidnapping, the pressure on the Hezbollah leadership was beginning to have some effect. A three-stage deal between Israel and Hezbollah was drafted. In the first stage, Israel agreed to release nineteen Lebanese detainees who were held as bargaining chips, with Dirani heading the list. These detainees were kept away from the public eye in a one-story structure in the heart of a military base near Kibbutz Metzer. Aman Unit 504 was in charge of running the detention facility, called Barak 1391. These nineteen were to be joined by more than four hundred security prisoners held in Israeli jails. In exchange, Hezbollah promised to release the bodies of three Israeli soldiers who had been abducted by the organization in October 2000, as well as a kidnapped Israeli civilian, Elhanan Tannenbaum. The three soldiers had been snatched while on a routine patrol along the security fence at the Lebanese border on the morning of October 7, 2000. After a number of roadside charges were detonated as their vehicle drove past, Hezbollah militants seized the mortally wounded soldiers. Hezbollah refused to disclose any information regarding the condition of the Israeli soldiers throughout the duration of their captivity. Tannenbaum was an IDF reserve colonel whom Iranian intelligence personnel had kidnapped in early October 2000 while he was visiting Abu Dhabi. The Iranians then turned him over to Hezbollah. His abduction was part of a complex plan Hezbollah had concocted to kidnap a senior Israeli army officer. After Hezbollah learned that Tannenbaum was involved in drug dealing, an Israeli Arab contacted him, and the two became partners. Tannenbaum did not know that this partner, Kais Obeid, also had close contacts with Hezbollah. In October 2000, after the two had met in Brussels, Obeid convinced him to go to Abu Dhabi to close a highly profitable drug deal.[4]

The first stage of the prisoner exchange was carried out successfully in January 2004. In the second stage of the deal, Israel was supposed to release the remainder of the Lebanese prisoners, including Samir Kuntar, who was seventeen years old in April 1979 when he infiltrated the shore of Nahariya, leading a cell of PLF activists. After a long night of murder, during which Kuntar and his cohorts slaughtered twenty-eight-year-old Danny Haran and his four-year-old daughter Einat, as well as two Israeli policemen, Kuntar was caught and later sentenced to four life sentences. Over the years, Kuntar had become an important symbol in Lebanon, and Hezbollah had been hankering after his release in order to lionize him and add glory to the organization. In exchange for Kuntar, Hezbollah representatives promised to provide Israel with authoritative information on Ron Arad's fate. During the second-stage negotiations, Israel demanded credible information on Ron Arad, before releasing the Lebanese prisoners. Hezbollah refused, and contacts between the two sides were suspended. Two years later, Hassan Nasrallah claimed that Ron Arad was "dead and lost," and that if the organization had had any information on Arad it would have used it to close the deal with Israel and bring about the release of Lebanese prisoners jailed in Israel.[5]

THE ISRAELI INVASION

Hezbollah's successes in its negotiations with Israel were not lost on the Palestinians. On June 25, 2006, eight men from Hamas, the Army of Islam, and the Popular Resistance Committees penetrated an IDF outpost near Kerem Shalom, close to the border with the Gaza Strip. The men, armed with antitank missiles, hand grenades, and light firearms, split into three groups. One force attacked an armored personnel carrier, while the second stormed an IDF position and attacked the three soldiers manning it. The third group assailed a Merkava III tank from the 188th Armored Brigade with missiles and grenades. Two of the four-member crew, Commander Hanan Barak and driver Pavel Slotzker, were killed instantly, and the other two were wounded. The attackers took Gilad Shalit, one of the soldiers, hostage and quickly led him to the border fence. They blasted a hole in the fence using explosives they had brought with them and then disappeared. Israel responded with a massive assault against infrastructure targets in the Gaza Strip and an extensive wave of arrests of senior Hamas activists. Even so, neither the bombardment nor the arrests precipitated the release of the abducted soldier.[6]

On July 12, an army patrol consisting of two armored Humvees carrying seven reserve soldiers set off on a routine patrol along Israel's border fence with Lebanon near the rural community of Zar'it. At about 9:00 a.m., Hezbollah began shelling IDF positions along the border. Using the commotion caused by the heavy mortar fire as cover, Hezbollah set up an ambush for the patrol vehicles. As the latter approached, the guerillas launched rocket-propelled grenades at the Humvees. Three soldiers were killed in the attack and four others were wounded. The attackers took two of the wounded, Ehud Goldwasser and Eldad Regev, to the Lebanese side of the border. Similar to the abduction in October 2000, long moments passed before news of the kidnapping reached the IDF regional division headquarters. In a desperate attempt to stop the kidnappers, a tank was sent in pursuit of the Hezbollah men. The tank was soon damaged by an antitank mine, and all four of its crewmembers were killed. Infantry soldiers dispatched to assist in the pursuit remained behind with the burning tank to protect it, thus frustrating any chances of stopping the kidnappers, who disappeared on the roads leading into southern Lebanon.[7]

This kidnapping operation prompted the Israeli government to make a swift decision and immediately embark on a military campaign in Lebanon that became known as the Second Lebanon War. While regular forces were involved in widespread aerial and ground strikes, Israeli special forces sought to obtain information on the kidnapped soldiers as well as the location of missile launchers. They encountered great difficulties, primarily because of the disparity between the relatively low operational capabilities of the Palestinian forces they confronted during the Al-Aqsa intifada and the much more sophisticated operational capabilities of the Hezbollah forces in southern Lebanon. Thus, Israeli elite forces failed to make the required adjustments, as demonstrated by the following events, which unfolded on July 19.

Toward nighttime on that day, a force from Sayeret Maglan took position near the village of Marun A-Ras in order to prepare for its mission: to locate and disable Hezbollah launchers in the area. The Israeli soldiers first came across a system of Hezbollah underground fortifications that seemed to be deserted. While trying to breach the steel doors of the bunkers with the inadequate tools they had in their possession, they were attacked in a surprise ambush by Hezbollah fighters, who killed two of their men almost immediately. As the morning hours arrived, the fierce battle continued, and the Maglan men were not able to retreat to Israeli territory. Forces from the Egoz Unit, which were deployed nearby on the Israeli side of the border, rushed in to assist them. Anticipating the ploy, Hezbollah fighters armed with guns and antitank rockets attacked the Egoz troopers just a few minutes after they crossed the border. Five Egoz men were killed, and many others were injured. The battle continued and the gunfire was so heavy that only the next day were the bodies of the IDF fatalities recovered from the battleground.[8]

In addition, Israel decided during this war once again to undertake abductions of its own for bargaining power. This time the IDF's attempts to kidnap Hezbollah activists were even less successful than in the past. During Operation Sharp and Smooth, Sayeret Matkal and Shaldag commandos infiltrated the city of Baalbek. While the Sayeret men took over the local hospital, which also served as Hezbollah headquarters, the Shaldag unit made their way to the town's Sheikh Habib quarter, where senior Hezbollah members lived. Once there, they took five men hostage, one of whom bore the same name as the organization's leader, Hassan Nasrallah. Shortly thereafter, though, he was released along with the others when it turned out they were not affiliated with the organization. On August 4, Israel again tried to kidnap Hezbollah high-ranking officers without too much success. A Shayetet 13 force infiltrated the Lebanese coastal city of Tyre from the sea and took control of a five-story building where the Hezbollah men were supposed to reside. The latter however refused to surrender and, during the fight, seven Hezbollah operatives were killed and eight Shayetet men were injured. The Hezbollah officers escaped.[9]

The overall picture of activation of special forces reveals that those operations, which were highly publicized in the Israeli media, succeeded somewhat in lightening the spirits of the Israeli public, as at least some Israel leaders had intended; yet Israel actually continued to endanger its elite units in operations that seldom suited their qualifications and whose strategic benefits were questionable. This was in particular displayed in an operation that was executed four days after the war had ended and UN Security Council decision 1701 was affirmed. On the night of August 18–19, IAF CH-53 Sikorsky helicopters set down two Jeeps and about a dozen Sayeret Matkal soldiers wearing Lebanese army uniforms near the village of Boday, not far from the city of Baalbek. Their mission was to infiltrate the Hezbollah headquarters in the village for intelligence-gathering purposes and if possible kidnap organization operatives. But, after discovering that the headquarters had already been evacuated, they decided to double back to their meeting point. They did not take a different route as a precaution in the event that a villager might notify Hezbollah of their presence. This is apparently what happened, and the consequences were fatal. Hezbollah forces set up several road-blocks in the vicinity. When the Sayeret Matkal team reached one of these posts, they pretended that they belonged to the Lebanese Army, but their disguise was discovered almost immediately. During the fight that broke out, the unit lost a veteran, heavily decorated officer, Lieutenant Colonel Emanuel Moreno; another officer was seriously injured.[10]

Israel's and Hezbollah's kidnappings and retaliations illustrate one of the major pitfalls encountered by Israeli civilian and military leaders. Israel has repeatedly declared that it will not negotiate with terrorists; yet, like other countries, it has found it impossible to stick to that statement. In addition to their commitment to Israeli soldiers and civilians, as well as the desire to see captives safe in the arms of their loved ones, Israeli prime ministers have invested great efforts on the hostages' behalf. They are usually under tremendous pressure from the families of the hostages and public opinion, and politicians are extremely sensitive to such pressures. The problem is that the public is fickle. Along with the intense pressures it applies in order to obtain the hostages' release, the public equally objects to paying an excessive ransom for them—particularly when it concerns the release of security prisoners.[11]

Policymakers have chosen the military course as an elegant way around this predicament. If this course does not lead to any new information, at least Israel's leaders broadcast a decisive message to the public concerning their commitment "to bring the boys home," even if by means of very risky commando operations that are purposely leaked to the media. The problem is that, thus far, such military actions and kidnappings have not achieved the desired results—quite the opposite. They have caused Israel to be viewed as a paper tiger, increased the motivation among anti-Israel militant groups to abduct more soldiers and civilians, and heightened the risk to soldiers in elite units who are sent to the enemy's home front on hostage-taking operations.

Furthermore, for the first time in its history, in this war, the Israeli heartland sustained a devastating rocket offensive for over a month. More than 3,970 missiles landed in cities, small settlements, and army bases in the north of Israel. Despite the intensive efforts of the IAF and ground forces to reduce its operational and launching capabilities, Hezbollah continued its artillery strikes until the final hours of the war, firing off an average of two hundred missiles per day. The consequences were unprecedented. Forty-four Israeli citizens died, and more than two thousand were injured. In addition, more than 300,000 residents left their homes in the bombarded areas and sought alternative dwellings in their relatives' homes or at hotels.

The financial consequences were no less severe. For more than a month, industry in northern Israel was almost totally inoperative, and tourism halted. The total costs for the Israel economy were estimated at around $4 billion. In the face of such consequences, it comes as no surprise to find the following statement in the Winograd Commission's report: "No level of public support during the time of a military crisis can justify unctuous behavior when the political leaders need to decide whether to embark on a war or other military actions."[12]

███████████

SINCE THE DAY OF its Declaration of Independence in 1948, Israel has been plagued by terrorism. Though it never declared war on terror or even developed a coherent doctrine for coping with the challenge, both policymakers and the heads of the security establishment have perceived terrorism as an act of war and have thus continuously applied the war model as the major route of response. Despite a few periods of decline, over the years the threat of terrorism has not diminished. It has actually become increasingly more acute and lethal (figure 10.1). Moreover, Israel's main successes in reducing the threat of terrorism cannot be attributed to the war model but to the few times in which the defensive model was applied. Terrorism should thus not be considered an act of war but a psychological tactic used by paramilitary groups. Furthermore, terrorism can rarely be considered a threat to the state's national security. In most cases, its main effect is a sense of insecurity within the civilian population.

It has been argued that sovereign states suffer from an inherent difficulty in their attempt to cope with this amorphous threat.[1] Yet terrorists suffer from their own limitations. Most prominently, unlike threats that are posed by other states, the physical damage that terrorists can cause is limited. The only times when terrorism can turn into a national threat, if we exclude the use of weapons of mass destruction (WMD), which have not so far been proven as effective tools in the hands of terrorists, is when an intelligence organization and the armed forces put the struggle against terrorism at the top of their agendas and act accordingly. This is tantamount to undermining the state's national-security interest in favor of the struggle against a secondary threat. The war model for countering terrorism is flawed not only because it undermines civil liberties, as many have argued in the past,[2] but also because it is simply unsuitable for the challenge of terrorism and causes the security establishment to deviate from dealing with other, more imminent threats.

So why has Israel stuck to this model and actually pressured its security establishment to offer new ways of defeating terrorism time and time again? The

FIGURE 10.1 **PALESTINIAN TERRORIST ATTACKS ON ISRAELI TARGETS, 1948–2006**

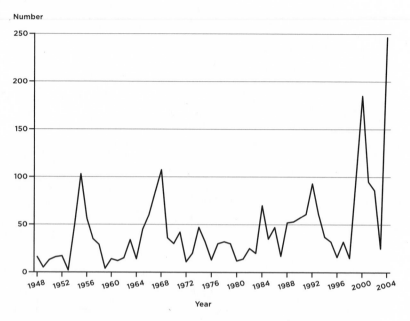

Source: NSSC Dataset on Palestinian Terrorism, www.nssc.haifa.ac.il

public and the politicians are more sensitive to terrorism than to other threats because of its impact on civilians and the sense of insecurity it instills.[3] Frustration in the face of terrorist attacks and the panic they create leads policymakers to dismiss the fact that military power suffers from inherent limitations in the struggle against nonstate actors, including groups that use terrorism. Policymakers are eager to satisfy the public with an immediate and decisive response. Hence, they are more open to offensive responses that are offered to them by the intelligence community and the armed forces than they are to long-term defensive measures. There are close ties between policymakers and the armed forces in Israel, and the fact that many of the decision makers were formerly high-ranking officers, often in elite units, most notably Sayeret Matkal, increases their inclination to use offensive responses. In this reality, the police are almost entirely excluded from the decision-making circle, and hence the criminal-justice model has little chance of being implemented. The defensive model is applied only following attempts at offensive responses that have proven to be futile.

One of the major obstacles in reforming the counterterrorism policy is that heads of the various branches of the security establishment are aware of the policymakers' distress and their desire to respond promptly. Thus, regardless of their primary duties, they elevate the response to terrorism to the top of their agendas. By doing so, they hope to secure the flow of resources to their agencies and enhance their reputations. In the upper echelons, this may include decisions to form new units or wings within units that already exist, to divert forces to counterterrorism missions, and to acquire new technologies for such missions. Mid-ranking officers within the various forces feel similar pressures. In order to perform well against terrorism, they overload their units, which in most cases have completely different primary roles, and engage in competition with other units regarding seniority in this type of warfare. The outcome, as proven in the Israeli case, is that despite the innovative spirit and the fierce competition among the various forces, most initiatives lead to either short-term successes or outright failures. More important, consumed by the notion that the struggle against terrorism should be on top of their agendas, intelligence organizations tend to sublimate other considerations to this goal and thus either overlook or even indirectly give rise to more severe threats. The preparedness of the armed forces, which constantly innovate and train in microcounterterrorism tactics, to cope with other threats is also undermined. The application of the war model thus leads to an escalating cycle of terrorism as well as to distressing outcomes in other arenas.

CURRENT AND FUTURE CHALLENGES

As with many terrorist events that have not cost lives, most of Israel's citizens have forgotten the explosion at the country's largest fuel and gas facility that took place on May 23, 2002. I did not know much about the circumstances of that incident until one Friday morning in late December of that year. At that time I was teaching a seminar on terrorism, part of the master's-degree program for students at the University of Haifa who were members of the security establishment. The small classroom in which the course was held fostered a degree of intimacy among the students. In the first row, slightly apart from the other students, sat a mild-mannered man who occasionally made comments revealing his deep familiarity with the subject we were discussing. Few Israelis would recognize this man's name—Rafi Taterka—but there is no one in the intelligence community who has not heard of him. Taterka, who began his career in the operations branch of the GSS, rose through the ranks until he was head of the branch and then deputy head of the entire organization. About five years after his retirement from the

GSS, Taterka was appointed CEO of Petroleum and Energy Infrastructures, the government company responsible for Israel's oil and gas reserves.[4]

Part of the seminar coursework involved the presentation of an outline of each student's final paper in front of the class. Rafi had a different idea. Instead of describing the subject of his seminar paper, he presented the class with his company's report on the internal investigation into the terrorist attack perpetrated by the Silwan cell of Hamas against the Pi Glilot oil and gas depot. The cell's members had managed to attach a one-kilogram explosive charge to a tanker truck and to explode the charge by remote control after the truck had entered the protected compound. Taterka promised an experience we would not soon forget, and he was good on his word. The in-depth investigation included a minute-by-minute silent video portrayal of the attack, as captured by security cameras positioned in various locations at Pi Glilot. The picture of the tanker truck exploding and bursting into flames at the diesel storage area is still deeply engraved in my memory. The shocking aspect of the attack has nothing to do with the results. No lives were lost, and there were no injuries. The cold sweat that drenched my back and the shocked expressions frozen on the faces of the other students were the result of the scenario running through our heads, in which the tanker truck had exploded not in front of the diesel storage area, but rather in front of the gas storage area a few dozen meters away. This could have been Israel's 9/11. The Pi Glilot facility is located on the outskirts of Tel Aviv, and a few hundred meters away, on the other side of the highway, is Israel's intelligence city—a series of military bases and civilian facilities that serve Aman and Mossad.[5]

In the years since the attack, Palestinian militant groups have upgraded their abilities in guerrilla warfare and terrorism. "Necessity is the mother of invention," as the popular saying goes. Despite Israel's unceasing efforts to seal the border between the Gaza Strip and Egypt, whose entire length is just over 7.5 miles, local entrepreneurs still managed to find all sorts of ways to smuggle weapons, ammunition, and money from Sinai into Gaza. The drip of weapons turned into a flood in January 2008, when Hamas activists took down the wall between Gaza and Egypt. Smugglers also use the 130-mile-long border between Israel and Sinai, which, following the opening of the Gaza-Egyptian border, became a highly sensitive area due to the success of armed Palestinians in infiltrating the Sinai Desert and using it as a point of departure for attacks in Israel. Not only have the groups engaged in terrorism become a greater challenge, but their tactics have also become more sophisticated over the years, a fact that requires the heightened alertness of the security establishment. Throughout the Al-Aqsa intifada, the

Palestinians increased their use of high-trajectory weapons, due to Israel's success in foiling suicide attacks.[6]

At first the rockets were short-range Qassams fired from the Gaza Strip toward northern Negev communities. As the intifada progressed, Grad missiles with a range of ten miles appeared on the scene. The Palestinian factions, frustrated at the limited effects of the rockets in comparison to suicide attacks, are constantly striving to increase their effectiveness. One of the ways to do this is to smuggle the missiles into the West Bank or manufacture them there. In one such attempt three Palestinians were arrested on October 5, 2005, after trying to smuggle technological information on rocket production to the West Bank from Gaza. Unlike the Gaza Strip, launching rockets from the West Bank threatens installations such as the Ben-Gurion Airport and large urban centers, including the Tel-Aviv metropolitan area. The rockets are not the only threat hanging over Israel's residents. Terrorists do not usually limit themselves to a single tactic, but rather tend to use every method that proves its efficacy (see figure 10.2). Thus, for

FIGURE 10.2 **PALESTINIAN TERRORIST ATTACKS ON ISRAELI TARGETS BY TACTIC, 1993–2007**

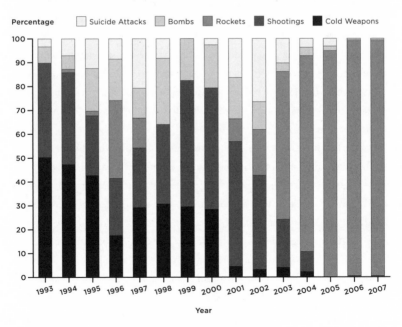

Source: NSSC Dataset on Palestinian Terrorism, www.nssc.haifa.ac.il

example, the Palestinian networks have never stopped their attempts to kidnap Israelis for bargaining purposes. In most cases the kidnap victims are soldiers, but these groups have stressed in the past that they also view civilians as legitimate targets. Israel must also continue to be on guard against suicide bombers. Even though the security establishment has managed to set up mechanisms over the years to make the dispatching of suicide bombers into Israel very difficult, the militants find it hard to abandon this method because of its great effectiveness. There are large numbers of Palestinians ready to strap an explosive belt around their waists and strike at targets in Israel and around the world, and these are certainly still a cause for worry. Another formidable threat is the potential use of force multipliers. Even though conventional terrorism has proven to be the most effective means of causing the maximum number of victims, attacks that make use of such multipliers produce a strong psychological effect.[7]

Palestinian terrorism is not the only front where Israel has found itself with no definitive response. The assassination of Imad Mughniyah on February 12, 2008 in the Kfar Suseh neighborhood of the Syrian capital brought to the headlines the name of the archterrorist, who for over two decades was responsible for some of the most horrific attacks against Israeli and other Western targets while staying out of the spotlight. During the Second Lebanon War, Hezbollah successfully sowed terror on the Israeli home front by launching rockets against civilian population centers. Eight months after the war, Israeli civilians learned that one of those rockets had landed in the heart of Haifa's oil-refinery compound, where there is a large concentration of hazardous substances. Similar to the Pi Glilot incident, here too, luck played a major role. The rocket, one of 124 that landed in the Haifa Bay area during the war, exploded in an open space, and no major disaster occurred.[8]

In the first months of 2008, most estimates are that while Hezbollah still cannot operate and function freely in southern Lebanon, as it was able to before the July–August 2006 war, the military wing of the organization under the leadership of Mughniyah was able, with the aid of Iran and Syria, to restore large parts of its artillery capabilities and arsenal, especially regarding short and mid-distance missiles.[9] Hence, the war did not change the basic strategic balance between the two sides. Even the assassination of Mughniyah, who was an invaluable asset for Hezbollah and Iran, will not have a significant impact. He trained a number of potential successors over the years. Furthermore, the war exemplified again, as in the 1980s during Israel struggle against the PLO and as in the 1990s against Hezbollah, and even in the last few years against the Palestinian groups operating in the Gaza Strip, that Israel, for all its military superiority, has not found an effective offensive response to artillery attacks initiated by terrorist groups.

Additionally, powerful players such as Hezbollah, Iran, and Syria, which are interested in maneuvering proxy players in the Palestinian arena and controlling the intensity of the violence in the West Bank and Gaza Strip, are constantly trying to transfer funding and munitions to the various Palestinian networks and in certain cases to train their people. Mughniyah was a major facilitator of this endeavor. Religious divisions between Sunni and Shiite regimes seem to be less relevant when it comes to the struggle against Israel. Syria, for example, where most of the residents are indeed Sunni, helps Iran in transferring weapons shipments to Hezbollah and is even in direct contact with that organization, supplying it with intelligence concerning Israel. Iran, which is predominantly Shiite, has supported all the Palestinian factions throughout the Al-Aqsa intifada, especially Hamas and Islamic Jihad, which are faithful to a radical Sunni doctrine. The cargo ship *Karine A,* which was attempting to smuggle weapons and ammunition to Gaza but was intercepted by Shayetet 13, is just one example of the efforts invested by Tehran in aiding the Palestinian struggle. A simpler method of providing assistance has always been funding and/or remuneration. The Iranian rulers, as well as the Saudi royal house, which follows a Wahhabi Sunni ideology, have deposited huge sums of money in the personal bank accounts of senior Hamas activists. Saddam Hussein's secular Baathist regime preferred to help families of suicide bombers directly by depositing $15,000 in the personal bank accounts of each Palestinian family with a son who carried out a suicide attack.[10]

Finally, yet important, is the threat posed by the global jihadi movement. After the American invasion of Afghanistan and the destruction of Al-Qaeda's organizational infrastructure, the latter became an amorphous coalition of groups all over the world, called the global Salafi jihad, or "Al-Qaeda 2.0." Though many believe that the main target of the network is the United States, it has also proved that it is interested in and capable of striking at Israeli and Jewish targets in Israel and around the world. Through the years, Al-Qaeda and local groups inspired by the global-jihad ideology have committed a number of terrorist attacks against such targets. These have included a truck-bomb explosion near a synagogue on the island of Djerba, Tunisia, on April 11, 2002; a suicide bombing in the Israeli-owned Paradise Hotel in Mombassa, Kenya, on November 28, 2002; and the firing of a shoulder-launched rocket against an Israeli Arkia Airlines plane at the same location and on the same day. A year later, on November 15, 2003, two suicide bombers attacked a synagogue in Istanbul, Turkey, and five days later a suicide bomber detonated a device near the Israeli consulate in Istanbul. The anti-Israeli operations by Al-Qaeda affiliates continued in April 2004 with a double attack on recreation sites in the Sinai Peninsula filled with Israel tourists; the Hilton Taba Hotel and the Ras A-Satan recreation village were both struck by car bombs. Finally, in the summer of 2005, global Salafi jihad militants succeeded in surprising Israel by launching a Katyusha rocket from Jordanian territory toward the resort town of Eilat.[11]

Among the most challenging threats Israel faces today are attacks by terrorists who are not Palestinians or even Arabs. The risk emerges from countries where terrorists enjoy unlimited freedom of movement—mainly Africa and the Middle East, but not only there. The salient example of such an activity is the case of two British youths of Pakistani origin who volunteered to commit a suicide attack at a bar in Tel Aviv called Mike's Place at the behest of Hamas and the Al-Aqsa Martyrs Brigades. Twenty-two-year-old Asif Mohammed Hanif, a resident of the town of Hounslow near London, and Omar Khan Sharif from Derby, who was five years older than his friend, had become acquainted when they had visited Damascus at the same time in order to pursue their Islamic studies. Both were associated with the Al-Muhajiron ("The Immigrants") group that was active in England and believed in war against the West. A friendship developed between the two, and the rumor soon spread that the two wanted to offer themselves in the name of the struggle against Israel. On April 12, 2003, they reached the Jordanian side of the Allenby Bridge, presented their British passports at the border checkpoint, and asked for permission to enter Israel. The two aroused the suspicion of an airport security guard, and a GSS officer questioned them on the purpose of their visit in Israel, the route they had taken before arriving at Israel, and the people they intended to meet. In the end, the interrogation did not yield any cause for further detention, and they were allowed into the country.

Hanif and Sharif enjoyed complete freedom of movement in Israel. First they traveled to Gaza, and after a short stay there they visited Tel Aviv, Jerusalem, Nablus, and Ramallah. At the end of their tour, they returned to Gaza, where they made contact with members of the Hamas military wing. The British pair introduced themselves to the local people as peace activists and made sure to link up with representatives of international humanitarian organizations and to visit institutions that granted welfare services to the Palestinians. On April 29, more than two weeks after they had gained entrance to Israel, they joined a group of Italian journalists traveling to Tel Aviv. The journalists' vehicle was not checked, according to the policy that was customary then, and from there it was not very far to the youth hostel on 48 Ha'yarkon Street. On the wall of the hostel, the two found an invitation in English to music evenings at the neighboring bar, Mike's Place. The next day, at a late hour, they left the hostel and made their way to the bar. While they were waiting at the entrance to the building, Sharif's explosive device, rigged up in a Koran, had a technical failure. While the detonator exploded the main charge failed to go off. Hanif decided to carry out the operation on his own. At 1:00 a.m. a strong blast was heard from the area of the bar. Ten minutes later, the police received a report about a man who was seen running away from the vicinity of the explosion. The man, Omar Sharif, tried to enter the lobby of the nearby David Intercontinental Hotel, but the security guard at the entrance pushed him back. Sharif rushed outside and stopped a taxi. He had just about got into the car when the security officer who had pursued him arrived in time to pull him out of the cab. Despite the joint efforts of the officer and the driver to restrain him, Sharif was still able to escape and fled toward the beach. After combing the area, the police found only his jacket and explosive device. On May 12, his body washed up on the shore.[12]

Most of the onus of gathering intelligence in such cases fell on the shoulders of Mossad, which now had to monitor social networks operating in the Middle East, Asia, Africa, and Europe. Israeli intelligence's familiarity with some of these regions is very limited. Furthermore, the increase in Islamic immigration to the West has now created a situation in which almost every major city in Europe, America, and Australia has a widespread network of mosques, as well as Islamic education and welfare institutions. The ability of a small organization such as Mossad to obtain intelligence on all the sites that may potentially develop into extremist action–oriented cells is also very limited. This is emphasized by the fact that Mossad knew nothing of the 9/11 plot. Furthermore, the only partial cooperation offered by local intelligence agencies does not effectively help Mossad to thwart terrorism.[13]

POLICY RECOMMENDATIONS

Is it possible to be better prepared for these challenges? Over the years, terrorism aimed at Israel has become more aggressive, and the civilian home front has become the front line. The Israeli war model, which has also been replicated in other countries, has not proven to be a success in meeting its goals. In order to effectively contend with terrorism, it is incumbent to transfer the bulk of counterterrorism activity to alternative models. Citizens of democratic states must realize that terrorism pursues democracies wherever they may be and every so often will rear its head. Policymakers should refrain from making empty promises of being able to entirely eradicate terrorism.[14] During times of terrorism, policymakers must exhaust all available resources in the framework of the conflict so that they may reduce its intensity and lower violence to tolerable levels. This could be achieved by applying elements from the reconciliatory model. Moreover, since terrorism is a type of psychological warfare, politicians should fight the temptation to boost the morale of the public through sophisticated assassinations of terrorist leaders. The assassinations do not meet this goal. The public is aware that assassinations usually lead to retaliations by the terrorists and thus instead of feeling more secure, civilians feel more threatened. Policymakers themselves intensify the fear by warning the public of the unavoidable revenge. Hence, not only do such assassinations not undermine the capabilities of the various terrorist groups to attack, but they also intensify the terrorists' desire to prove their viability by amplifying the psychological fear factor. Clear and honest statements by politicians who tell the public that terrorism, despite its horrific outcomes, rarely poses a major threat to the state's national security would be welcome in that connection. Such statements would reassure the public and undermine the attempts of the terrorists to create a continuous state of fear, chaos, and mistrust of the public in its leaders. Beyond mitigating the psychological impact of terrorism, policymakers should allocate resources and formulate a defensive model that consists of three main stages: prevention, crisis management, and reconstruction.

At the prevention stage, it is extremely important to assess frequently the level of threat posed by terrorists. Preventive intelligence is essential, since it enables the security forces to implement effective selective prevention procedures. Yet even in the absence of accurate information, it is of the essence to try to bring different pieces of information together and to assess the risks on yearly, monthly, weekly, and daily bases. Such risk assessments are essential to planning more effective protection mechanisms for attractive targets in times of danger. These include the physical protection of targets, the allocation of resources for technological solutions, and the employment of a sufficient number of guards at strategic places. It is also important to deploy trained rescue forces if the risk seems immediate.

At the crisis-management stage, it is essential to design and implement routine procedures that will ensure a flow of relevant information to all the emergency forces after an attack. This is important in preventing too many or too few rescue forces from being sent in, as well as in ensuring that the forces can enter and leave the attack site unobstructed, whether by clearing urban traffic arteries or by the use of roadblocks. When an attack occurs, temporary headquarters should be set up at the site to synchronize the entrances and departures of the emergency forces and to coordinate activities inside the area. Moreover, a framework that defines the roles and routines of all actors participating in postattack crisis management is essential. Finally, since the first persons to encounter and provide information about terrorist attacks are usually members of the public, governments should try to educate the public on how to respond to such attacks.

In the reconstruction stage, it is important to treat the direct victims and their families, as well as other individuals who have been affected by an attack. Such treatment should follow a long-term plan that would allow state authorities a degree of flexibility, enabling them to tailor different solutions for the different victims. At the end of the day, the goal should be a speedy and effective recovery for the victims, both physically and psychologically. No less important is putting businesses back on track as quickly as possible. This could be achieved by offering them various incentives such as tax relief. Most important, it is the duty of policy-makers to mitigate the psychological effects of terrorist attacks immediately, using every media outlet, and thus to undermine the very goal of the terrorists.

On a different front, efforts to suppress channels of cash flow to terrorists should be reassessed. Groups such as Hamas are almost impenetrable when attempting to pin down their financing sources. In contrast to its image in the West, the group is first and foremost a social movement that runs a ramified system of charity and relief institutions. A significant part of the monies that are collected in the West is sent to these institutions out of a genuine desire to assist the Palestinian population, which is in dire need of health and welfare services. The relatively amorphous structure of the Hamas leads to situations in which the heads of the charity mechanisms in Gaza at the same time support terrorist cells and may transfer part of the funds to them, either directly or indirectly. The bulk of these pecuniary transfers are conducted on a local level and are not registered or documented, another fact that makes efforts to block the cash flow particularly difficult.[15]

Even more complicated are the attempts to block the support of states. Iran, which over the last few years has become a major source of funding for the various Palestinian groups, has a ramified network of financial, security, and intelligence organizations that can overcome different barriers set by Israel. Hence, it can be assumed that despite a few successes in revealing attempts to channel funds to groups of terrorists, many more such attempts remain hidden from intelligence organizations. Since terrorist attacks, either suicide operations or rocket barrages, are relatively cheap, and given that the various terrorist networks do not seem to have been weakened over the years, it appears that the campaign to crack down on the financiers of these groups has not been very successful.

INTELLIGENCE AND THE ARMED FORCES

Despite the proven success of the defensive model, policymakers and the heads of the security establishment are unlikely to give up the war model easily. Still, I think it important to make some recommendations for intelligence organizations and the armed forces to consider.

Israel's intelligence organizations, headed by the GSS, have indeed developed impressive capabilities. They have helped to intercept acts of terrorism while still in the planning stages and to strike at terrorists and their leaders. Terrorists are skilled at eluding intelligence efforts, however, and they will continue to be so. It is impossible to monitor every terrorist cell and thwart every attack. In order to contend with terrorists effectively, intelligence and thwarting forces have to be as flexible as the terrorists—a virtually impossible task as well. Therefore, instead of implementing organizational reforms that will end up in a new series of struggles between the various agencies, the agent model that is employed in the United States should be adopted, with certain adjustments. The idea is to establish a main headquarters for the struggle against terrorism that will serve as the hub of a network that will send out its arms to each and every one of the various intelligence and thwarting forces. The establishment of such a headquarters will not require any far-reaching organizational reforms or a massive investment of resources. At the same time, it will enable daily coordination among the various bodies and a rapid deployment of the necessary resources when a terrorist threat is detected by one of the intelligence organizations. Representatives of all the forces in charge of coping with terrorism will be stationed full-time at the headquarters. Their job will be real-time coordination among the various organizations. The prime minister's advisor for coping with terrorism or an intelligence advisor will supervise the headquarters, as the Agranat Commission and the Committee of Inquiry Into the Intelligence System in Light of the War in Iraq recommended.[16]

The basic requirements for the position of advisor should be a deep familiarity with all aspects of terrorism and with the capabilities and limitations of the intelligence and thwarting forces. The advisor must have the ability to analyze contradictory intelligence assessments, to present the leadership with as clear picture as possible while distinguishing between assessments based on intelligence and those based on guesswork, and to offer viable alternatives for coping with each challenge. Other important duties of the advisor would include the assessment of various counterterrorism policies that have been implemented in the past as well as by other countries and a careful drawing of conclusions from such experiences. These conclusions will become highly valuable for the creation of a framework for an official counterterrorism policy. This new model should not replace the war model altogether, but rather should incorporate successful elements from alternatives, including the criminal-justice and the reconciliatory models.

The advisor would have to be close to but independent of the prime minister. One of the advisor's main functions would be to prevent the leadership from acting under public or political pressure, to offer alternative models of response, and to help leaders instill a sense of security in the civilian population. Another no less important function would be to serve as an unbiased arbiter in the event of struggles between organizations. The position of advisor would not be at the expense of the triennial evaluation of the regional and functional sectors of the responsibilities of each of the intelligence organizations and the redefining of the borders of each sector in keeping with changing circumstances. A permanent committee whose role would be defined by law would conduct this evaluation. Participants in the discussions would include representatives of the parliamentary system, the prime minister's advisor, and heads of the intelligence organizations. A clear division of fields of activity that would be sensitive to the changing types of threats could mitigate the extent of interorganizational struggles.

In the area of international cooperation, the picture actually looks brighter. Global terrorism has opened an unprecedented window of opportunity for Israel. Most of the countries around the globe are afraid of terrorist attacks against their citizens. This fear has found public expression in the signing of international treaties against terrorism and increasing intelligence cooperation among friendly states. Even though many countries are not interested in formal or even informal friendly ties with Israel, the importance of intelligence cooperation sidelines such issues. Israel still enjoys significant prestige, mainly in the human-intelligence field. The intelligence organizations of many countries are glad to benefit from the knowledge Israel has developed and receive information from this country.[17] Since the Israeli intelligence community does not have unlimited resources, it, too, can benefit from the assistance of intelligence organizations from rich countries that are spearheading the development of high-tech intelligence-gathering instruments and their use in the struggle against terrorism. Before intelligence organizations around the world can express openness to the idea of cooperation with Israel, however, Israel will have to give up its longstanding habit of violating the sovereignty of other states. In an era of multiple and increasingly sophisticated threats, Israel cannot afford to jeopardize strategic cooperation with potential allies in the war against terrorism.

Adjustment is also necessary in the thwarting sphere. In late 2006, Israel's Channel Two television broadcasted a segment in which the Israeli Defense Forces (IDF) revealed for the first time the existence of a counterterrorism military school. The soldiers who were training there appeared in the broadcast while practicing takeover scenarios developed during a period of hostage taking incidents. The segment, which was broadcast four months after the Second Lebanon War, was designed to relay a firm message: Israel is prepared for the struggle against terrorism. More than anything else, however, it showed that the IDF is ready to contend with incidents whose chances of occurring are low.

The major lesson learned from the Second Lebanon War is that military units must become more professional in their fields of specialization. Tracking down and arresting terrorists is not a mission that requires the assignment of elite units. In many countries that adhere to the criminal-justice model, police forces carry out this task. Yet given the volume of terrorism with which Israel has to cope, police forces by themselves will not be able to counter this challenge. That said, much of the burden can be transferred to the Border Police as well as to soldiers who would be trained specifically for such missions. In December 2005, six independent battalions, including the armored infantry, established back in the days of the first intifada, were concentrated under the Kfir (900) Brigade. Each battalion is under the command of a different regional brigade in the West Bank and is designated to operate against Palestinian fighters in an area familiar to its soldiers. The soldiers themselves go through a specialized seven-month training period in microwarfare to prepare themselves for the operations to which they will be assigned. With the support of Yamam, the elite *mistaarvim* units Duvdevan and Yamas, the border police, and the unmanned-aerial-vehicle and helicopter squadrons, the Kfir brigade soldiers should be the operational arms of the GSS in the occupied territories and enable their comrades from the Armored Corps, the Infantry Corps, and the elite units to focus on their own training and to fulfill their original, designated purposes in times of emergency. The successful Sayeret Matkal and Shaldag operation on Syrian soil in September 2007 is a prime example of the great potential of the special units, when they are not occupied with side missions that do not correspond with their qualifications and their original objectives. While Sayeret Matkal soldiers gathered crucial intelligence and evidence that Syria was building a nuclear facility, the Sayeret Shaldag men used their special laser position-pinpointing equipment to make it feasible for the Israeli Air Force to attack and eradicate it. Hence, the Yamam should remain the sole counterterrorism SWAT team, while the elite military units should be removed from the counterterrorism scene and be deployed for such missions only if they serve the purpose of training them to perform better in their designated fields of expertise.

At the time that this book was written, there was no end in sight to Israel's conflict with the Palestinians or with the Arab world in general. The conflict, which used to be territorial in nature, has changed in recent years, becoming an ideological and theological dispute as well. This significantly worsens the situation with regard to the challenges of terrorism. The chances of reducing the levels of violence seem slimmer than ever, as the players are not only Palestinian groups plotting to strike at Israeli and Jewish targets, but also Sunni and Shiite cells all over the world, who are ideologically committed to the destruction of the State of Israel.[18]

This book focuses entirely on Israel's struggle against terrorism, which has so far not been extensively researched, at least not with respect to its operational dimension. Even so, it must be recalled that together with the terrorism threat, the Israeli security establishment is constantly contending with strategic threats from other sources. Worth mentioning, among others, are the Iranian nuclear threat, the risk of war with the states bordering on Israel, and the risk of the rise of other radical regimes in the region. While terrorism tends to occupy the public as well as policymakers, it is imperative to understand and internalize the psychological dimension of terrorism and the limitations of the use of force in a nonsymmetrical struggle. It is time to give other counterterrorism models a chance while diverting the war model to where it belongs: strategic threats posed by state actors.

███████████

INTRODUCTION

1. Ronald D. Crelinsten, "Terrorism and Political Communication: The Relationship Between the Controller and the Controlled," in Paul Wilkinson and Alasdair M. Stewart, eds., *Contemporary Research on Terrorism* (Aberdeen: Aberdeen University Press, 1987), 3–23; Ronald D. Crelinsten, "Terrorism, Counter-Terrorism, and Democracy: The Assessment of National Security Threats," *Terrorism and Political Violence* 1, no. 2 (1989): 242–269; Ronald D. Crelinsten, "Analyzing Terrorism and Counter-terrorism: A Communication Model," *Terrorism and Political Violence* 14, no. 2 (2002): 77–122; Ronald D. Crelinsten and Alex Schmid, "Western Responses to Terrorism: A Twenty-five Year Balance Sheet," *Terrorism and Political Violence* 4, no. 4 (1992): 332–333.

2. Paul Wilkinson, *Terrorism and the Liberal State* (London: Macmillan, 1986), 125.

3. For example: Peter Chalk, "EU Counter-terrorism, the Maastricht Third Pillar, and Liberal Democratic Acceptability," *Terrorism and Political Violence* 6, no. 2 (1994): 103–145; Peter Chalk, "The Liberal Democratic Response to Terrorism," *Terrorism and Political Violence* 7, no. 4 (1995): 10–44; Peter Chalk, *West European Terrorism and Counter-Terrorism: The Evolving Dynamic* (London: Macmillan, 1996); Peter Chalk, "The Response to Terrorism as a Threat to Liberal Democracy," *Australian Journal of Politics and History* 44, no. 3 (1998): 373–388; Ronald D. Crelinsten, "The Discourse and Practice of Counter-terrorism in Liberal Democracies," *Australian Journal of Politics and History* 44, no. 1 (1998): 389–413; Crelinsten, "Terrorism and Political Communication," 3–23; Crelinsten, "Terrorism, Counter-terrorism, and Democracy," 242–269; Crelinsten and Schmid, "Western Responses to Terrorism," 307–340; Charles Dunlap, "The Policeization of the Military," *Journal of Political and Military Sociology* 27, no. 2 (1999): 217–232; Ariel Merari, "Deterring Terrorists," paper presented at the Terrorism Beyond the 21st Century conference, Oklahoma City, April 2000, 16–19; Fernando Reinares, "Democratic Regimes, Internal Security Policy and the Threat of Terrorism," *Australian Journal of Politics and History* 44, no. 3 (1998): 351–371; Ken G. Robertson, "Intelligence Terrorism and Civil Liberties," in Wilkinson and Stewart, *Contemporary Research on Terrorism,* 549–569; David T. Schiller, "The Police Response to Terrorism: A Critical Overview," in ibid., 536–548; Paul Wilkinson, "Pathways Out of Terrorism for Democratic

Societies," in ibid., 453–465; G. Davidson Smith, *Combating Terrorism* (London: Routledge, 1990).

4. Boaz Ganor, *The Counter-Terrorism Puzzle: A Guide for Decision Makers* (New Brunswick, N.J.: Transaction Publishers, 2005), 27–28, 39–40.

5. Crelinsten and Schmid, "Western Responses to Terrorism," 318–322; Mohammed M. Hafez and Joseph M. Hatfield, "Do Targeted Assassinations Work? A Multivariate Analysis of Israel's Controversial Tactic During the Al-Aqsa Uprising," *Studies in Conflict and Terrorism* 29, no. 4 (June 2006): 359–382.

6. "Palestinians Support the Ceasefire, Negotiations, and Reconciliations Between the Two Peoples, But a Majority Opposes Arrests and Believes That Armed Confrontations Have Helped Achieve National Rights," Public Opinion Poll no. 3 (December 2001); "While Indicating Important Shifts in Palestinian Public Attitudes Toward the Intifada and the Peace Process, PSR Poll Shows Significant Support for the Appointment of a Prime Minister and Refusal to Give Confidence in the New Palestinian Government," Public Opinion Poll no. 6 (November 2002); "With Arafat's Popularity Reaching Its Highest Level in Five Years, Three Quarters of the Palestinians Support the Maxim Restaurant Suicide Bombing and Two-Thirds Believe the Roadmap is Dead," Public Opinion Poll no. 9 (October 2003); "After Four Years of Intifada, an Overwhelming Sense of Insecurity Prevails Among Palestinians Leading to High Levels of Support for Bombing Rocket Attack on One Hand and to High Levels of Demand for Mutual Cessation of Violence and Questioning the Effectiveness of Armed Attacks on the Other," Public Opinion Poll no. 13 (September 2004). All published by the Palestinian Center for Policy and Survey Research, www.pcpsr.org (accessed May 27, 2007).

7. Graham H. Turbiville Jr., "Preface: Future Trends in Low Intensity Conflict," *Low Intensity Conflict and Law Enforcement* 11, nos. 2–3 (Winter 2002): 155; Tamir Barkawi, "On the Pedagogy of 'Small Wars,'" *International Affairs* 80, no. 1 (January 2004): 19–37; Mark Kramer, "The Perils of Counterinsurgency: Russia's War in Chechnya," *International Security* 29, no. 3 (Winter 2004–2005): 5–62; Melissa S. M. Bazarian, "Whither the Iraqi Insurgency: Prospects for Counterinsurgent Success," *Low Intensity Conflict and Law Enforcement* 13, no. 1 (Spring 2005): 24–53; Ivan Arreguín-Toft, *How the Weak Win Wars: A Theory of Asymmetric Conflict* (New York: Cambridge University Press, 2005); John A. Nagl, *Learning to Eat Soup with a Knife: Counterinsurgency Lessons from Malaya and Vietnam* (Chicago: University of Chicago Press, 2005); Zeev Maoz, "Evaluating Israel's Strategy of Low-Intensity Warfare, 1949–2006," *Security Studies* 16, no. 3 (July–September 2007): 319–349; David Tucker, "What's New About the New Terrorism and How Dangerous Is It?" *Terrorism and Political Violence* 13, no. 3 (Autumn 2001): 1–14; Eli Carmon, "The Role of Intelligence in Counter-terrorism," *Korean Journal of Defense Analysis* 14, no. 1 (Spring 2002): 119–139; Gordon H. McCormick, "Terrorist Decision Making," *Annual Review of Political Science* 6

(June 2003): 473–507; Shaul Mishal and Maoz Rosenthal, "Al Qaeda as a Dune Organization: Toward a Typology of Islamists Terrorist Organizations," *Studies in Conflict and Terrorism* 28, no. 4 (July–August 2005): 275–293; Robert A. Pape, "The Strategic Logic of Suicide Terrorism," *American Political Science Review* 97, no. 3 (August 2003): 343–361; Stephen Marrin, "Homeland Security Intelligence: Just the Beginning," *Journal of Homeland Security* (November 2003), www .homelandsecurity.org (accessed May 27, 2007); Marco Cepik, "Sistemas nacionais de inteligencia: Origens, logica de expansão e configuração atual" (National Intelligence Systems: Origins, the Logic of Expansion, and Current Configuration), *Dados* 46, no. 1 (2003): 75–127; Walter W. Burke, *Organizational Change: Theory and Practice* (Thousand Oaks, Calif.: Sage Publications, 2002); Charles R. Wise, "Organizing Homeland Security," *Public Administration Review* 62, no. 2 (September 2002): 131–144; Uriel Rosenthal, "September 11: Public Administration and the Study of Crises and Crisis Management," *Administration and Society* 35, no. 2 (May 2003): 129–143; John R. Deni, "The NATO Rapid Deployment Corps: Alliance Doctrine and Force Structure," *Contemporary Security Policy* 25, no. 3 (December 2004): 498.

8. Adam Grissom, "The Future of Military Innovation Studies," *Journal of Strategic Studies* 29, no. 5 (2006): 905–934; Amy B. Zegart, *Spying Blind: The CIA, the FBI, and the Origins of 9/11* (Princeton: Princeton University Press, 2007), 16–17.

9. Grissom, "The Future of Military Innovation Studies," 907; Michael Horowitz, "The Diffusion of Military Power: Causes and Consequences for International Politics" (PhD dissertation, Harvard University, 2006), 38; John W. Soule, "Problems in Applying Counterterrorism to Prevent Terrorism: Two Decades of Violence in Northern Ireland Reconsidered," *Terrorism* 12 (1989): 31–46; Brian Martin, "Instead of Repression," *Social Alternatives* 25, no. 1 (2006): 62; Christopher Davy, "Managing Risk and Uncertainty: An Approach to Counterterrorist Planning," in Alan Thompson, ed., *Terrorism and 2000 Olympics* (Canberra: Australian Defense Center, 1996), 165; Aharon Yariv, "Countering Palestinian Terrorism" in Ariel Merari, ed., *On Terrorism and Combating Terrorism* (Frederick, Md.: University Press of America, 1985), 4; Ariel Merari and Shlomi Elad, *Foreign Terrorism: Palestinian Terrorism Abroad (1968–1986)* (Tel Aviv: Hakibbutz Hameuhad, 1987), 118; Daniel G. Arce and Todd Sandler, "Counterterrorism: A Game-Theoretic Analysis," *Journal of Conflict Resolution* 49, no. 2 (April 2005): 183–200; Nathaniel N. Keohane and Richard G. Zeckhauser, "The Ecology of Terror Defense," *Journal of Risk and Uncertainty* 26, nos. 2–3 (March 2003): 201–229.

10. Barry R. Posen, *The Sources of Military Doctrine: France, Britain, and Germany Between the World Wars* (Ithaca, N.Y.: Cornell University Press, 1984); Ganor, *The Counter-Terrorism Puzzle*, 251–265; John W. Soule, "Problems in Applying Counterterrorism to Prevent Terrorism," 31–46; Brian Martin, "Instead of Repression," 62; Jonathan Stevenson, "Pragmatic Counter-terrorism," *Survival* 43,

no. 4 (2001): 35–48; Jordan J. Paust, "Executive Plans and Authorizations to Violate International Law Concerning Treatment and Interrogation of Detainees," *Columbia Journal of Transnational Law* 43, no. 3 (2005): 811–863; Philip Rumney, "The Effectiveness of Coercive Interrogation: Scholarly and Judicial Responses," *Crime, Law and Social Change* 44, no. 4–5 (December 2005): 465–489; Dov Waxman, "Terrorizing Democracies," *Washington Quarterly* 23, no. 1 (Winter 2000–2001): 15–19; Herb Keinon, "Civil Rights vs. Security," *Jerusalem Post,* September 10, 1999; Elizabeth S. Silker, "Terrorists, Interrogation, and Torture: Where Do We Draw the Line?" *Journal of Legislation* 31, no. 1 (2004): 191–215; Yaakov Peri, *Strike First* (Tel Aviv: Keshet, 1999), 150–152; Ephraim Halevy, "On the Right for Renunciation and Duty for Loyalty," in Hezi Karmel, ed., *Intelligence for Peace* (Tel Aviv: Yedioth Ahronoth and Hemed, 1998), 194–197; Yehoshafat Harkabi, "Tangled Between Intelligence and Captain," in Avi Kober and Zvi Ofer, eds., *Intelligence and National Security* (Tel Aviv: Maarachot, 1987), 439–453; Shlomo Gazit, "Assessment of Intelligence and Captain," in ibid., 459–469; Ephraim Halevy, *Man in the Shadows: Inside the Middle East Crisis with a Man Who Led Mossad* (Tel Aviv: Matar, 2006), 146–151.

11. Richard K. Betts, *Enemies of Intelligence: Knowledge and Power in American National Security* (New York: Columbia University Press, 2007); Terry Terriff, "Innovate or Die: Organizational Culture and the Origins of Maneuver Warfare in the United States Marine Corps," *Journal of Strategic Studies* 29, no. 3 (June 2006): 480; Michael Eisenstadt, "Israel's Approach to Special Operations," *Special Warfare* (January 1994): 22–29; Ariel Levite, "The Gulf War: Tentative Military Lessons for Israel," in Joseph Alpher, ed., *War in the Gulf: Implications for Israel* (Boulder, Colo.: Westview Press, 1992), 148; Reuven Shapira, "Continuous Struggle for Prestige Gone Public," *Haaretz,* December 21, 1997; Moshe Zonder, *The Elite Unit of Israel* (Jerusalem: Keter, 2000), 302–303.

12. Stephen Peter Rosen, *Winning the Next War: Innovation and the Modern Military* (Ithaca, N.Y.: Cornell University Press, 1991).

13. The method of researching intelligence, including the research of intelligence organizations, is based on the study of official documents, news articles, books, and position papers that deal with various aspects of intelligence. Since the intelligence field deals with subjects that are hidden from the public eye, there is an extensive use of profile interviews with people who played key roles in the intelligence community, both in the past and present. They can provide a glimpse into the intelligence world. Among the books in the intelligence field that use this method are Alfred Maurer, Marion D. Tunstall, and James M. Keagle, *Intelligence: Policy and Process* (Boulder, Colo.: Westview Press, 1985); Jeffrey Richelson, *Foreign Intelligence Organizations* (Cambridge, Mass.: Ballinger, 1988); Wesley K. Wark, *Espionage: Past, Present, Future?* (Ilford, UK: Frank Cass, 1994); Michael Herman, *Intelligence Power in Peace and War* (Cambridge: Royal Institute of International Affairs, 1997); and Mark M. Lowenthal, *Intelligence: From Secrets to Policy* (Washington, D.C.: CQ Press, 2000).

CHAPTER ONE **THE EMERGENCE OF ISRAEL'S COUNTERTERRORISM DOCTRINE**

1. Yoav Gelber, *Growing a Fleur-de-Lis: The Intelligence Services of the Jewish Yishuv in Palestine, 1918–1947* (Tel Aviv: Ministry of Defense, 1992), 1:14–27; Asa Lefen, *The Roots of the Israeli Intelligence Community* (Tel Aviv: Ministry of Defense, 1997), 21; Efraim Dekel, *The Story of Shai* (Tel Aviv: Davar, 1953), 144–145.

2. Zvi El-Peleg, "'The Arab Revolt': Causes, Development, and Results," in Mordechai Naor, ed., *Days of Wall and Stone (1936–1939)* (Jerusalem: Yad Yitzhak Ben-Zvi, 1987); Yehuda Lapidot, *The Birth of an Underground: Etzel in the 1930s* (Tel Aviv: Brith Hayalei Etzel, 2001); Ezra Danin, *Zionist in Every Condition* (Jerusalem: Kidum, 1987), 147; Celia E. Rothenberg, "A Review of the Anthropological Literature in English on the Palestinian 'Hamula' and the Status of Women," *Journal of Arabic and Islamic Studies* 2 (1998–99): 24–48; Samith K. Farsoun and Christina F. Zacharia, *Palestine and the Palestinians* (Boulder, Colo.: Westview Press, 1997), 24–26; Sharif Kanaana, "Survival Strategies of Arabs in Israel," *MERIP Reports* 41 (1975): 6–7.

3. Danin, *Zionist in Every Condition*, 33, 124–134; Ian Black and Benny Morris, *Israel's Secret Wars* (London: Warner, 1992), 8–10; Lefen, *Roots of the Israeli Intelligence Community*, 116–118; Mordechai Naor, ed., *Lexicon of Haganah* (Tel Aviv: Ministry of Defense Publishers, 1992), 294, 340; Arie Shalev, *The Intifada: Causes and Effects* (Tel Aviv: Papirus, 1990), 32–33; Yehuda Sluzki, "From Defense to Struggle," in Ben-Zion Dinor, ed., *The Book of Haganah History* (Tel Aviv: Maarachot, 1964), 939–967; Yehoshua Porat, *From Riots to Revolt: The National Palestinian Movement, 1933–1939* (Tel Aviv: Am Oved, 1979), 174–175.

4. Sluzki, "From Defence to Struggle," 774–778; Yigal Eyal, "The British Army's Repression of the Palestinian Arab Revolt, 1936–1939" (PhD thesis, University of Haifa, 1993), 334–398; El-Peleg, "The Arab Revolt"; Jeffrey Herf, "Convergence: The Classic Case of Nazi Germany, Anti-Semitism, and Anti-Zionism During World War II," *Journal of Israeli History* 25, no. 1 (March 2006): 74–75.

5. Danin, *A Zionist in Every Condition*, 220; Black and Morris, *Israel's Secret Wars*, 44–45; Lefen, *Roots of the Israeli Intelligence Community*, 226–253; Gelber, *Growing a Fleur-de-Lis*, 318, 507, 729.

6. Lefen, *Roots of the Israeli Intelligence Community*, 89–92, 95; Gelber, *Growing a Fleur-de-Lis*, 499–500, 516–525.

7. "7 Jews Killed by Arab Fire," *Haaretz*, December 1, 1947, 1; Yaacov Markovetzky, "Battles on Haifa and Nearby Areas in the Independence War," in Mordechai Naor and Yossi Ben-Artzi, eds., *Haifa in Development, 1918–1948* (Jerusalem: Yad Yitzhak Ben-Zvi, 1989); "36 Killed and 45 Wounded in a Deadly Arab Attack on Medical Workers in Sheikh Jarrah Neighborhood," *Haaretz*, April 14, 1948; Yehuda Lapidot, *In Flame of Revolt: Etzel in Jerusalem* (Tel Aviv: Ministry of Defense Publishers, 1996).

8. Danin, *A Zionist in Every Condition*, 205–208; Meir Pail, *Independence* (Tel Aviv: Ministry of Defense Publishers, 1990), 26; Palestinian Academic Society for the Study of International Affairs, "Palestinian Personalities," www.passia.org;

Baruch Kimmerling and Joel Migdal, *Palestinians: The Making of a People* (Jerusalem: Keter, 1999), 132; Yoav Gelber, *Independence Versus Nakba* (Or Yehuda: Kinneret, Zmora-Bitan, and Dvir, 2004), 41, 47–54.

9. Lefen, *Roots of the Israeli Intelligence Community*, 92, 114, 237–242; Gelber, *Independence Versus Nakba*, 61, 80.

10. Yeroham Cohen, *By Light and in Darkness* (Tel Aviv: Amikam, 1969), 47–49; Yeroham Cohen, "'Mista'arvim'—Palmach Arab Unit," *Maarahot* 297 (1985): 44–45; Oded Granot, "Intelligence Corps," in *IDF and Its Corps: Encyclopedia of Army and Security* (Tel Aviv: Revivim, 1981), 8:18; Cohen, *By Light and in Darkness*, 61.

11. Samuel M. Katz, *Soldier Spies: Israel Military Intelligence* (Novato, Calif.: Presidio Press, 1992), 42, 47.

12. Haggai Eshed, *One-Man Mossad: Reuven Shiloah, Father of the Israeli Intelligence* (Tel Aviv: Edanim, 1988), 120; Gelber, *Growing a Fleur-de-Lis*, 516–517.

13. Yoav Gelber, "Reuven Shiloah—Contribution to Development of Israeli Intelligence," in Hezi Carmel, ed., *Intelligence for Peace* (Tel Aviv: Miskal, 1998), 42; Eshed, *One Man Mossad*, 129–130; Reuven Miran, "One Man Mossad," *Haaretz*, October 29, 1997.

14. Eshed, *One-Man Mossad*, 129–130; "History," *HaMossad leModi'in u le Tafkidim Meyuhadim*, Mossad Web site, www.mossad.gov.il (accessed February 6, 2008); Shlomo Nakdimon, "Death of the Spy," *Makor Rishon* 289 (February 28, 2003): 14–17.

15. Hillel Cohen, *Good Arabs: The Israeli Security Service and the Israeli Arabs* (Jerusalem: Ivrit, 2005), 10; Benny Morris, *The Birth of the Palestinian Refugee Problem Revisited* (Cambridge: Cambridge University Press, 2004); Naseer Hasan Aruri, ed., *Palestinian Refugees: The Right of Return* (London: Pluto Press, 2001); Gelber, *Independence Versus Nakba*, 382–384, 387; Kimmerling and Migdal, *Palestinians*, 169; Avi Plascov, *The Palestinian Refugees in Jordan, 1948–1957* (London: Frank Cass, 1981).

16. Yair Bauml, "The Military Government Over Israeli Arabs and Its Cancellation: 1948–1968," *Hamizrach Hahadash* 53 (2002): 133–156; Yair Bauml, "Relations Between the Israeli Establishment and the Arabs in Israel: Policy, Principles, and Actions in the Second Decade, 1958–1968" (PhD thesis, University of Haifa, 2002), 153–156, 159; Cohen, *Good Arabs*, 37–47; Yaacov Peri, *Striking First* (Tel Aviv: Keshet, 1999), 34–40; Raanan Cohen, *The Political Development of the Israeli Arabs in Light of Their Voting in the 1984 Electoral Campaign* (Tel Aviv: University of Tel Aviv), 117–122; Yaacov Caroz, *The Man with Two Hats* (Tel Aviv: Ministry of Defense, 2002), 80–83; Black and Morris, *Israel's Secret Wars*, 141.

17. Dan Soen and Mustafa Mashhour, "The Influence of the Clan in the Political Life of an Arab Village in Israel," *Orient* 25, no. 2 (Spring 1984): 257–269; Zeev Schiff and Raphael Rothstein, *Fedayeen: The Story of Palestinian Guerrillas* (London: Valentine and Mitchell, 1972), 4–5; Benny Morris, *Israel's Border Wars, 1949–1956: Arab Infiltration, Israeli Retaliation and Countdown to the Suez*

War (Tel Aviv: Am Oved, 1996), 18–20; Rafi Sutton and Yitzhak Sasson, *Men of Secrets, Men of Mystery* (Jerusalem: Idanim, 1990); Black and Morris, *Israel's Secret Wars,* 120–121.

18. Shabtai Tevet, "Old Versions, New Versions," *Haaretz,* September 16, 1994; Nir Hefetz and Gadi Bloom, *The Shepherd: Life Story of Ariel Sharon* (Tel Aviv: Miskal, 2005), 88–101; Uzi Benziman, *Sharon: An Israeli Caesar* (New York: Adama Books, 1985), 42–45, 52; "Unit 101," IDF Paratroopers Web site, http://202.org .il/Pages/tagmul/y101/unit101.php (accessed February 9, 2008); Interview with Yoav Gelber, Haifa University, October 10, 2006; Benny Morris, "The Israeli Press and the Qibya Operation, 1953," *Journal of Palestine Studies* 25, no. 4 (Summer 1996): 40–52; Hani Ziv and Yoav Gelber, *The Bow Bearers* (Tel Aviv: Ministry of Defense, 1998), 203.

19. Yosef Argaman, *It Was Top Secret* (Tel Aviv: Ministry of Defense, 1990), 19–20, 24–28; Benny Morris, *Israel's Border Wars, 1949–1956* (Oxford: Oxford University Press, 1997), 359–360; Yohai Sela, "Assassination of Colonel Hafez," Omedia, www.omedia.co.il (accessed February 9, 2008); Michael Bar-Zohar and Eitan Haber, *The Quest for the Red Prince* (Tel Aviv: Zmora, 1984), 144–147; Ehud Yaari, *Egypt and the Fedayeen, 1953–1956* (Givat Haviva, Israel: Center for Arabic and Afro-Asian Studies, 1975), 29–30.

CHAPTER TWO **THE PATH TO THE DEFENSIVE MODEL AND BACK**

1. Oded Granot, "Intelligence Corps," in *IDF and Its Corps: Encyclopedia of Army and Security* (Tel Aviv: Revivim, 1981), 8:74; Eitan Haber, "Syrian Attempts to Sabotage Foiled," *Yedioth Ahronoth,* January 14, 1965; "Thwarted Attempt of Palestinian Terrorists to Damage Water Infrastructure," *Haaretz,* January 15, 1965; "Three Jordanians Members of Fatah Attacked in Ramat Hakovesh," *Haaretz,* May 26, 1965.

2. "Suddenly I Felt I Was Flying in the Air," *Maariv,* October 9, 1966.

3. Interview with Rafi Malka, former GSS executive officer, August 22, 2006; Ian Black and Benny Morris, *Israel's Secret Wars* (London: Warner, 1992), 248–249; Yaakov Peri, *Striking First* (Tel-Aviv: Keshet, 1999), 45–54; Yossi Melman and Dan Raviv, *The Imperfect Spies* (Tel Aviv: Maariv, 1990), 154–156; David Ronen, *The Year of the Shabak* (Tel Aviv: Ministry of Defense, 1989), 26; Tom Segev, *1967: Israel, the War and the Year That Transformed the Middle East* (New York: Metropolitan Books, 2007), 487; Israel Ministry of Foreign Affairs, "Which Came First—Terrorism or 'Occupation'?" (March 2002), www.mfa.gov.il (accessed February 16, 2008); Ehud Yaari, *Fatah* (Tel Aviv: Lewin Epstein, 1970), 87–88; Christopher Dobson, *Black September: Its Short, Violent History* (New York: Macmillan, 1974), 75–78; Andrew Gowers and Tony Walker, *Behind the Myth: Yasser Arafat and the Palestinian Revolution* (New York: Olive Branch Press, 1992), 51.

4. Mark Tessler, *The History of the Israeli-Palestinian Conflict* (Bloomington: Indiana University Press, 1994), 376–377, 660.

5. Samuel M. Katz, *Soldier Spies: Israel Military Intelligence* (Novato, Calif.: Presidio Press, 1992), 212–213; Rafael Eitan, *Raful* (Tel Aviv: Maariv, 1985), 108–109; Yasser Arafat, "A Discussion with Yasser Arafat," *Journal of Palestine Studies*, 11, no. 2 (Winter 1982), 8; David Hirst, "Yasser Arafat," *Guardian*, November 11, 2004.

6. NSSC Dataset on Palestinian Terrorism, http://nssc.haifa.ac.il; Hani Ziv and Yoav Gelber, *Sons of the Bow: One Hundred Years of Struggle, Fifty Years of IDF* (Tel Aviv: Ministry of Defense, 1998), 278.

7. Zeev Schiff and Raphael Rothstein, *Fedayeen: The Story of Palestinian Guerrillas* (London: Valentine and Mitchell, 1972), 229–230; Black and Morris, *Israel's Secret Wars*, 238; Shlomo Shpiro, "Intelligence Services and Political Transformation in the Middle East," *International Journal of Intelligence and Counterintelligence* 17, no. 4 (October–December 2004), 579. For a thorough review of Israeli-Jordan secret relations, see Moshe Zak, *King Hussein Makes Peace: Thirty Years of Secret Talks* (Ramat-Gan: Bar Ilan University Press, 1996).

8. David Raab, *Terror in Black September: The First Eyewitness Account of the Infamous 1970 Hijackings* (New York: Palgrave Macmillan, 2007); Oriya Shavit, "Precedent of Black September," *Haaretz*, April 10, 2002; Dobson, *Black September*, 36–37; Andrew Gowers and Tony Walker, *Behind the Myth: Yasser Arafat and the Palestinian Revolution* (New York: Olive Branch Press, 1992), 81; Zeev Schiff and Ehud Yaari, *Intifada* (Tel Aviv: Shocken, 1990), 229–230; Black and Morris, *Israel's Secret Wars*, 238; Katz, *Soldier Spies*, 267; Bruce Hoffman, "All You Need Is Love: How the Terrorists Stopped Terrorism," *Atlantic Monthly*, December 2001.

9. Ronen, *The Year of the Shabak;* interview with David Maimon, former military governor of the Gaza Strip, February 25, 2007; Uzi Benziman, *Sharon: An Israeli Caesar* (New York: Adama Books, 1985), 115; "Sayeret Rimon," Israeli Special Forces and Special Operations Database, www.isayeret.com/content/units/disbanded/rimon.htm (accessed February 16, 2008); David Ronen, "And in the Terrorists' Role: Mistaarvim," *Maariv*, Saturday Supplement, March 25, 1994; David Maimon, *The Evincible Terror: Terror Oppression in Gaza Strip, 1971–1972* (Tel Aviv: Steimatzky, 1993), 169.

10. "GSS and Aman: Responsibility Division," *Haaretz*, November 16, 2000; Gad Shimron, *The Mossad and Its Myth* (Jerusalem: Keter, 2002), 123; Gabriel Weimann, "The Theater of Terror: Effects of Press Coverage," *Journal of Communication* 33, no. 1 (December 1983): 38–45; Gabriel Weimann, "Media Events: The Case of International Terrorism," *Journal of Broadcasting and Electronic Media* 31, no. 1 (1987): 21–39; Gabriel Weimann and Conrad Winn, *The Theater of Terror* (New York: Longmans, 1994); Brian Michael Jenkins, *International Terrorism* (Los Angeles: Crescent, 1974); Naftali Lavie, "The Israelis Still Held in Algiers," *Haaretz*, July 24, 1968; "The Implementation of 'Gesture' Begins: Five of Sixteen Released," *Haaretz*, September 18, 1968; "Representatives of Red Cross

Met with Sixteen who had Been Released in 'Gesture,'" *Haaretz,* September 5, 1968; Mitchell Bard Geoffrey, *The Complete Idiot's Guide to the Middle East Conflict* (Tel Aviv: Alpha Books, 2002), 377–378; Moshe Zonder, *The Elite Unit of Israel* (Jerusalem: Keter, 2000), 109; interview with Michael Koubi, former GSS interrogator, April 26, 2007; Moshe Betser and Robert Rosenberg, *Secret Soldier: The True Life Story of Israel's Greatest Commando* (New York: Atlantic Monthly Press, 1996), 84; Malka interview.

11. Aaron Klein, *Striking Back: The 1972 Munich Olympics Massacre and Israel's Deadly Response* (Tel Aviv: Miskal, 2006) Simon Reeve, *One Day in September: The Full Story of the 1972 Munich Olympics Massacre and the Israeli Revenge Operation "Wrath of God"* (New York: Arcade, 2000), 36. "1972: Israeli commandos storm hijacked jet," *BBC,* http://news.bbc.co.uk/onthisday/hi/dates/stories/may/9/newsid_4326000/4326707.stm (accessed February 17, 2008).

12. Zonder, *Elite Unit,* 22–23, 25, 30–31; Amos Harel, "The Price of the Choice of the Shayetet's Commander," *Haaretz,* July 7, 2004; Roni Hadar, "The Daring in the Enemy's Home Front," *Haaretz,* March 3, 2006; Shimron, *The Mossad and Its Myth,* 133–134.

13. For an analysis of the alliances among the various terrorist groups during the 1960s, see Eli Carmon, *Coalitions Between Terrorist Organizations: Revolutionaries, Nationalists and Islamists* (Leiden: Martinus Nijhoff, 2005), as well as Carmon's PhD thesis, "Coalitions of Terrorist Organizations," University of Haifa, 1996.

14. Amos Hadar, "Twenty Killed and Fifty Wounded in Terrorist Attack at Lod Airport," *Haaretz,* May 31, 1972; Edgar O'Ballance, *The Language of Violence: The Blood Politics of Terrorism* (San Rafael, Calif.: Presidio Press, 1979), 151–152; Patricia G. Steinhoff, "Portrait of a Terrorist: An Interview with Kozo Okamoto," *Asian Survey* 16, no. 9 (September 1976): 837–838; "The Killers Changed Their Plan," *Haaretz,* June 1, 1972; Amos Hadar, "Caught Terrorist: The Operation Was Meant To End with our Death," *Haaretz,* June 1, 1972.

15. Malka interview; Lisa Beyer, "Is This What We Really Want?" *Time,* September 16, 2001; Paulo Prada and Daniel Michaels, "Israel Airport Is Safe but Hard to Emulate," *Wall Street Journal,* September 17, 2001; Jacoby, "What Israeli Security Could Teach Us," *Boston Globe,* August 23, 2006; Ellis Shuman, "El Al's Legendary Security Measures Set Industry Standards," *Israel Insider,* October 3, 2001.

16. "Biography of Gassan Kanafani," www.palestineremembered.com/Acre/Acre/Story168.html (accessed February 17, 2008); Dalia Karpel, "Writer Under Influence," *Haaretz,* Saturday supplement, April 13, 2005; Eitan Haber, "Revenge Now," *Yedioth Ahronoth,* October 3, 2005, 6–7; "Beirut Blast Kills Guerilla Leader," *New York Times,* July 9, 1972; "Death of Guerilla," *Time,* July 24, 1972; Uri Dan, "Munich—Repeated Screening," *Makor Rishon,* February 12, 2006.

17. Moshe Zonder, "Shooting and Not Crying," *NRG,* July 27, 2001; Dan, "Munich—Repeated Screening"; Ron Maiberg, *Code Name: Bayonet,* Dragoman

Films Distribution, 2006; Reeve, *One Day in September*, 1–19; "The Munich Massacre," *BBC*, http://news.bbc.co.uk/sport2/hi/olympics2000/907614.stm; Alexander Wolff, "When The Terror Began," *Time*, August 25, 2002.

18. Timeline, Jewish Agency for Israel, www.jafi.org.il/education/jafi75/timeline6c .html; Alexander B. Calahan, "Countering Terrorism: The Israeli Response to the 1972 Munich Olympic Massacre and the Development of Independent Cover Action Teams," Federation of American Scientists, www.fas.org/irp/ eprint/calahan.htm (accessed February 17, 2008).

19. Richard Girling, "A thirst for vengeance," *Times Online*, www.timesonline.co.uk (January 15, 2006); Edwin Eitan, "Assuming Syrians Killed Syrian 'Journalist' in Paris as Revenge," *Yedioth Ahronoth*, November 14, 1972.

20. Michael Bar-Zohar and Eitan Haber, *The Chase After the Red Prince* (Tel Aviv: Zmora, 1984), 39; Melman and Raviv, *The Imperfect Spies*, 164; "Israeli Killed in the Center of Madrid," *Haaretz*, January 28, 1972; Steven Stewart, *The Spymasters of Israel* (New York: Ballantine Books, 1982), 280–282; Yosef Aziel, "Arab Killer Followed Israeli, Spoke with Him, and Then Shot Him," *Yedioth Ahronoth*, January 28, 1973.

21. Melman and Raviv, *The Imperfect Spies*, 166; Alan Hart, *Arafat: Terrorist or Peacemaker?* (London: Sidgwick & Jackson, 1984), 248–249, 309–310; Abu Iyad and Eric Rouleau, *My Home, My Land: A Narrative of Palestinian Struggle* (New York: Times Books, 1981), 112–113; NSSC Dataset on Palestinian Terrorism, http://nssc.haifa.ac.il.

22. "And Now, Mail-a-Death," *Time*, October 2, 1972; Yeuda Belu, "The Hunt For Black September," www.e-mago.co.il/Editor/history-833.htm.

23. Ariel Merari and Shlomi Elad, *Foreign Terrorism: Palestinian Terrorism Abroad (1968–1986)* (Tel Aviv: Hakibbutz Hameuhad, 1987), 169; Maiberg, *Code Name: Bayonet;* Yossi Melman, "Golda Didn't Give an Order," *Haaretz*, February 18, 2006); Eitan Haber, "Revenge Now," *Yedioth Ahronoth*, Holiday Supplement, October 3, 2005, 6–7; Klein, *Striking Back*, 136; Bar-Zohar and Haber, *The Chase After the Red Prince*, 160.

24. "PFLP Admits That Kubaysi Who Was Murdered in Paris Was One of Its Leaders," *Haaretz*, April 8, 1973; Bar-Zohar and Haber, *The Chase After the Red Prince*, 161; "Official Confirms: Israel Methodically Killed PLO Leaders," *Associated Press*, November 23, 1993; Zonder, "Shooting and Not Crying."

25. Maiberg, *Code Name: Bayonet;* Zonder, *Elite Unit*, 59–60; Mike Eldar, *Flotilla 13* (Tel Aviv: Maariv, 1993), 469–480.

26. Maimon interview; Doug Mellgren, "Norway Solves Riddle of Mossad Killing," *Guardian*, March 2, 2000.

27. Calahan, "Countering Terrorism"; Klein, *Striking Back*, 152; Ariel Merari and Shlomi Elad, *Foreign Terrorism: Palestinian Terrorism Abroad (1968–1986)* (Tel Aviv: Hakibbutz Hameuhad, 1987), 56; Yossi Melman, "Golda Didn't Give an Order"; Melman and Raviv, *The Imperfect Spies*, 166; Uri Dan, "Munich— Repeated Screening."

28. John W. Soule, "Problems in Applying Counterterrorism to Prevent Terrorism: Two Decades of Violence in Northern Ireland Reconsidered," *Terrorism* 12 (1989): 31–46; Brian Martin, "Instead of Repression," *Social Alternatives* 25, no. 1 (2006): 62.

CHAPTER THREE **RESCUING HOSTAGES**

1. "Terrorists Killed Worker and Wounded Eight in Attack on Car That Drove to Fassouta from Ata," *Haaretz,* May 16, 1974; "Report of the Investigation Commission on Ma'alot Events," *Yedioth Ahronoth,* July 11, 1974; Yehuda Ariel and Atallah Mansour, "'This Is the Police Looking for Terrorists'—With These Words, Terrorists Burst Into Yosef Cohen's Family Apartment in Ma'alot, Killed Them, and Took Schoolchildren Hostage," *Haaretz,* May 16, 1974; Zeev Schiff, "Security Forces Didn't Prepare Special Caution Measures," *Haaretz,* May 16, 1974; Moshe Zonder, *The Elite Unit of Israel* (Jerusalem: Keter, 2000), 108–116; Moshe Dayan, *Milestones: Autobiography* (Jerusalem: Idanim Publishers, 1975), 721; Yitzhak Ben-Horin, "I Told the Pupils to Sing 'Hatikva' and Let's Finish this Thing in a Respectful Way," *Maariv,* May 16, 1974; "Twenty Killed and Seventy Wounded in Ma'alot," *Haaretz,* May 16, 1974; interview with Baruch Fein, former Sayeret Matkal soldier who participated in the Ma'alot operation, March 22, 2007.

2. "Division of Responsibility Between the Police and the IDF in the Struggle Against Terrorism," *Haaretz,* July 11, 1974; interview with Alik Ron, former commander of the Israeli Police Northern Command, March 5, 2007.

3. Ron Shiyovitz, "YAMAM," *Police Mirrors* 201 (September–October 2004): 26; Moshe Givati, *Abir 21* (Jerusalem: Reut, 2003), 60, 65; Shimon Rapaport, "Mother Ship Sailed from Beirut; Collected Terrorist near Tyre," *Maariv,* March 8, 1975; Merav Crystal, "Suddenly I Wanted to Live," *Ynet,* www.ynet .co.il (March 7, 2007); Avi Raz, "I Was Hostage for Six Hours," *Maariv,* March 7, 1975; "This Is How Negotiations with the Terrorists Were Conducted with the Assistance of Hostage Kochava Levi," *Maariv,* March 6, 1975; Zonder, *Elite Unit,* 38.

4. Yaacov Erez, "Six Terrorists Killed in Savoy; Five Israelis Killed and Twenty-Three Wounded," *Maariv,* March 6, 1975; "How Negotiations Were Conducted"; Raz, "I Was Hostage for Six Hours"; Yehoshua Kahana, "Eight Terrorists Were Members of Elite Unit Who Had Been Groomed by Abu Iyad," *Maariv,* March 9, 1975; Zonder, *Elite Unit,* 306.

5. Zonder, *Elite Unit,* 89, 174, 306–307; Assaf Mitzna, "Uzi Had to Be There," *NRG,* March 3, 2000; Dalia Karpel, "Artist from a Leper House," *Haaretz,* July 13, 2005; Yifat Gadot, "Six Israelis Killed in Savoy Hotel," *NFC,* www.nfc.co.il.

6. Zonder, *Elite Unit,* 20, 309; Shlomo Gazit, "Risk, Glory, and the Rescue Operation," *International Security* 6, no. 1 (Summer 1981): 118–127.

7. "Top Secret: The Elite Units," Channel 2, November 4, 2006; Avigdor Shachan, *Operation Thunderball* (Ramat-Gan, Israel: Masada, 1993), 14, 32; Yeshayahu

Ben-Porat et al., *Entebbe: Flight 139* (Tel-Aviv: Zmora-Bitan, 1991), 138, 323–324; Lauren Gelfond Feldinger, "Back to Entebbe," *Jerusalem Post,* June 30, 2006; interview with Entebbe hostage Yitzhak Hirsch, October 5, 2006.

8. Louis Williams, "Entebbe Diary," *Toronto Star,* July 6, 1986; Shachan, *Operation Thunderball,* 15, 48; Ben-Porat, *Entebbe,* 26–30; Hirsch interview; interview with Entebbe hostage Yaacov Cohen, October 27, 2006.

9. Cohen interview; Hirsch interview; Shachan, *Operation Thunderball,* 16; Yitzhak David, *I Have Come Back from Entebbe* (Tel-Aviv: Zohar, 1977), 33; Yeshayahu Ben-Porat et al., *Entebbe Rescue* (New York: Delacorte Press, 1977), 27; Sefi Hendler, "Here Is Your Captain, We Have Been Hijacked," *NRG,* www.nrg .co.il (June 29, 2001); Ben-Porat, *Entebbe,* 45; Mordechai Gur, "Decision-Making Process: Planning the Operation," www.mota.co.il/antebe.htm (accessed February 10, 2008).

10. Williams, "Entebbe Diary"; David, *I Have Come Back from Entebbe,* 51, 53, 131–138; "Israeli Airborne Commandos Rescue 103 Hostages Held in Uganda by Hijackers of French Airliner; 31 Killed in Airport Clash," *Facts on File World News Digest,* July 10, 1976; Shachan, *Operation Thunderball,* 62; Gur, "Decision-Making Process"; Uri Dan, *Operation Uganda* (Jerusalem: Keter, 1976), 50; Zonder, *Elite Unit,* 9; Hirsch interview.

11. David, *I Have Come Back from Entebbe,* 158, 169–170; Shachan, *Operation Thunderball,* 29–30; Zonder, *Elite Unit,* 139–140.

12. Shachan, *Operation Thunderball,* 32, 79; Sharon Rofeh-Ofir, "Exclusive: The Mossad Took Pictures, the Entebbe Operation Began," *Ynet,* www.ynet.co.il (July 1, 2006); Zonder, *Elite Unit,* 139.

13. Shachan, *Operation Thunderball,* 33, 100–101; Gur, "Decision-Making Process"; Dan, *Operation Uganda,* 50; Hagai Huberman, "We Obtained Intelligence in Travel Agencies," *Hatzofeh,* July 9, 2006; Rofeh-Ofir, "Exclusive."

14. Rofeh-Ofir, "Exclusive"; Shachan, *Operation Thunderball,* 36–37, 101–103; Williams, "Entebbe Diary"; Gur, "Decision-Making Process"; Cohen interview; Zonder, *Elite Unit,* 140; Shimon Peres, *Entebbe Diary* (Tel Aviv: Idanim, 1991), 81.

15. Ben-Porat, *Entebbe,* 314; Ben Caspit, "First Publication: Government Diaries of Entebbe Operation," *NRG,* www.nrg.co.il (July 7, 2006); Zonder, *Elite Unit,* 143.

16. Williams, "Entebbe Diary"; Zonder, *Elite Unit,* 146; Tali Lipkin-Shahak, "The Main Player," *Maariv,* Weekend Supplement, June 16, 2006; Shachan, *Operation Thunderball,* 129–130; Ben-Porat et al., *Entebbe Rescue,* 130–131; Cohen interview.

17. Iddo Netanyahu, *Sayeret Matkal at Entebbe: The Testimonies, Documents, Facts* (Tel Aviv: Miskal, 2006), 140, 142; Moshe Betser and Robert Rosenberg, *Secret Soldier* (New York: Atlantic Monthly Press), 259; Cohen interview. The role of Yoni Netanyahu, chief commander of the Sayeret Matkal, in the operation later became a significant bone of contention between the Netanyahu family

and other soldiers in the elite unit. The known facts are that at the time of the hijacking, Netanyahu was engaged in a military exercise in Sinai. He joined the special forces as they drilled for the operation as late as Thursday, July 1. There were many objective difficulties that stood in his way. He was required to learn details of the intricate operation quickly and help find solutions to logistic complications that were liable to crop up in an operation so deep in the heart of Africa. According to the testimonies that piled up over the years, Netanyahu was also going through a personal crisis at the time, which apparently had an effect on his performance as commander.

18. Netanyahu, *Sayeret Matkal at Entebbe,* 212; Zonder, *Elite Unit,* 150.

19. Dan, *Operation Uganda,* 62, 64–65; Eyal Ben, "Why Did They Forget Our Hero?" *Ynet,* www.ynet.co.il (July 2, 2006); David, *I Have Come Back from Entebbe,* 200; Hirsch interview; Cohen interview; Ben-Porat, *Entebbe,* 14; Anat Fitusi-Farhi, "30th Anniversary of Operation Entebbe," *Geffen Hamoshava,* www.gfn.co.il (June 7, 2006); Sharon Rofeh-Ofir, "'Motta Said: Yoni's Death is His Own Fault'; Bibi Stepped Outside, Angered," *Ynet,* www.ynet.co.il (July 2, 2006); Zonder, *Elite Unit,* 149; Hendler, "Here Is Your Captain"; Netanyahu, *Sayeret Matkal at Entebbe,* 212, 250, 309, 312, 328; Shachan, *Operation Thunderball,* 270; Zonder, *Elite Unit,* 151; Williams, "Entebbe Diary."

20. Iddo Netanyahu, *Yoni's Last Battle* (Jerusalem: Geffen, 2002), 220–221; "Entebbe Raid: 'Subject for Songs and Legends,'" *New York Times,* July 5, 1976; Drew Middleton, "Key to Raid Success," *New York Times,* July 5, 1976; Zonder, *Elite Unit,* 154.

21. Farouq Nassar, Associated Press, April 1, 1978; Naftali Lavi, "Israelis Still Held in Algiers," *Haaretz,* July 24, 1968; Edgar O'Ballance, *Language of Violence: The Blood Politics of Terrorism* (San Rafael, Calif.: Presidio Press, 1979), 84–90.

22. Dan, *Operation Uganda,* 19–20; Ben-Porat, *Entebbe,* 74–76; Yossi Melman, "Golda Didn't Give an Order," *Haaretz,* February 18, 2006.

23. Aaron Klein, *Striking Back: The 1972 Munich Olympics Massacre and Israel's Deadly Response* (Tel Aviv: Miskal, 2006), 181; Yossi Melman, "One Hundred Percent Israeli," *Haaretz,* May 12, 2006.

24. Zvi Tal, "Meir Peretz Who Slept in the Children Nursery and Was Held as a Hostage: For Eight Long Hours I Was Suspended Between Life and Death," *Yedioth Ahronoth,* April 8, 1980; Emmanuel Elnecave, Ilan Kfir, and Yair Amikam, "To the Sound of Crying Babies, IDF Soldiers Rushed Inside the Children Nursery and Killed Five Terrorists," *Yedioth Ahronoth,* April 8, 1980; Yehoshua Halamish and Eliezer Rotenshtreich, "Iraq Behind a Terrorist Organization," *Yedioth Ahronoth,* April 8, 1980; Yaacov Erez, "Israel Checking Response to Terrorist Attack on Kibbutz Misgav Am," *Maariv,* April 8, 1980; Zeev Schiff, "Part of the Electronic Fence Didn't Work Because of Mishap," *Haaretz,* April 9, 1980; Emmanuel Elnecave, Ilan Kfir, and Yair Amikam, "Representatives from All the Villages Came to Cheer Up and Help Misgav Am Citizens," *Yedioth Ahronoth,* April 8, 1980.

25. Tal, "Meir Peretz"; Yitzhak Ben-Horin, "Four Hours Esti Shani Hid in the Shower, Knowing That Her Husband Was Already Dead and Worried About Her Son," *Maariv,* April 8, 1980; Yaacov Erez, "Before They Were Killed, Terrorists Cold-bloodedly Killed Kibbutz Secretary and Two-Year-Old Tot," *Maariv,* April 8, 1980; "Armed with Only a Screwdriver, the Kibbutz Secretary Tried to Stop the Terrorists," *Maariv,* April 8, 1980.

26. Erez, "Before They Were Killed"; interview with Roi Feiga, former soldier in the Sayeret Matkal, December 2, 2006; Yaacov Erez, "IDF Officer Who Led the Soldiers Remembers the Operation in Misgav Am: 'Battle Was Conducted from Half a Meter,'" *Maariv,* April 8, 1980; Elnecave, Kfir, and Amikam, "To the Sound of Crying Babies."

27. Elnecave, Kfir, and Amikam, "To the Sound of Crying Babies"; Erez, "Before They Were Killed"; Alex Fischman, "No Second Bullet," *Hadashot,* March 11, 1988.

28. Zonder, *Elite Unit,* 188–189; "Armed with Only a Screwdriver"; Tal, "Meir Peretz"; Amir Oren, "To Germany and Back," *Haaretz,* Saturday Supplement, January 30, 2004.

29. Gazit, "Risk, Glory, and the Rescue Operation," 121, 135–137; Ron interview; Ira Sharkansky and Yair Zalmanovitch, "Improvisation in Public Administration and Policy Making in Israel," *Public Administration Review* 6, no. 4 (July–August 2000): 326; Zonder, *Elite Unit,* 309; interview with Rafi Malka, former senior GSS officer, August 22, 2006.

CHAPTER FOUR **THE LEBANESE PUZZLE**

1. "Civil War Seen Easing Guerrilla Pressure on Israel in Fatahland," *New York Times,* September 24, 1970; Avner Yaniv, *Dilemmas of Security: Politics, Strategy, and the Israeli Experience in Lebanon* (New York: Oxford University Press, 1987), 104; Yezid Sayigh, "Palestinian Military Performance in the 1982 War," *Journal of Palestine Studies* 12, no. 4 (Summer 1983): 17–19; Edgar O'Ballance, *Language of Violence: The Blood Politics of Terrorism* (San Rafael, Calif.: Presidio Press, 1979), 228–238; Zeev Schiff, "Chief of Staff Hofi: Clear Signs That the Terrorists Came from Lebanon," *Haaretz,* April 12, 1974; "Database of Terrorist Incidents, 1970–1979," CDISS, www.cdiss.org.

2. Oded Granot, "Intelligence Corps" in *IDF and Its Corps: Encyclopedia of Army and Security* (Tel Aviv: Revivim, 1981), 8:141–164; interview with Gershon Ekstein, former IDF commander, October 11, 2006; interview with Lior Lotan, former head of the General Staff Negotiating Team, March 12, 2007; Shlomo Gazit, "Risk, Glory, and the Rescue Operation," *International Security* 6, no. 1 (Summer 1981): 111–135.

3. Meron Medzini, ed., *Israel's Foreign Relations: Selected Documents* (Jerusalem: Ministry of Foreign Affairs, 1977–1979), 359–362; Ofer Grosbard, "Personality Study of Menachem Begin" (PhD dissertation, George Mason University, 2004), 358; "Yadin: We Shall Speak with Terror Organizations Only in Language They Understand," *Yedioth Ahronoth,* March 15, 1978.

4. Major George C. Solley "The Israeli Experience in Lebanon, 1982–1985," www
.globalsecurity.org/military/library/report/1987/SGC.htm (accessed February 11, 2008); Mitchell Bard, "The Lebanon War," www.jewishvirtuallibrary
.org/jsource/History/Lebanon_War.html (accessed February 11, 2008); "Database of Terrorist Incidents, 1970–1979"; Zeev Schiff and Ehud Yaari, *Israel's
Lebanon War* (New York: Simon & Schuster, 1984).

5. Yossi Melman, *Abu Nidal: Profile of a Terrorist Organization* (Tel Aviv: Hadar,
1984), 116–117; Jane Metlikovec, "Bullet Ended Career," *Herald Sun* March 5,
2003; "3 Convicted in Shooting of Israeli Ambassador," *New York Times,*
March 6, 1983.

6. Shimon Schiffer, *Snow Ball: The Story Behind the Lebanese War* (Tel Aviv: Idanim
Publishers, 1984), 93; Schiff and Yaari, *Israel's Lebanon War,* 100–103, 181–193;
Eliezer Zafrir, *Imbroglio: Traffic Policemen in Lebanese Entanglement* (Tel Aviv:
Miskal, 2006).

7. "The New Alliance," *Journal of Palestine Studies* 8, no. 1 (Autumn 1978): 160;
Zafrir, *Imbroglio,* 83; Shimon Schiffer, *Lebanon War Secrets* (Tel Aviv: Idanim,
1984), 53; Schiff and Yaari, *Israel's Lebanon War,* 27; interview with Yossi Chen,
former head of the GSS Northern Command, February 12, 2006.

8. Zafrir, *Imbroglio,* 91, 175; Yaari and Schiff, *Israel's Lebanon War,* 104, 287, 308.

9. Anat Kurtz, David Tal, and Maskit Burgin, *Islamic Terrorism and Israel* (Tel
Aviv: Papirus, 1993), 32; Commission of Inquiry Into the Events at the Refugee
Camps in Beirut, *Final Report* (Jerusalem, 1983), 100–104.

10. Zafrir, *Imbroglio,* 87; Schiffer, *Lebanon War Secrets,* 39; interview with Aviezer
Yaari, former head of the Amin Research Division, January 29, 2007; Chen
interview; Dudi Cohen, "Hezbollah Founder: We Have Ability and Courage
to Launch Zilzal 2," *Ynet,* www.ynet.co.il (August 3, 2006); "Fadlallah, Sheikh
Muhammed Hussein," National Memorial Institute for the Prevention of Ter-
rorism, www.tkb.org/KeyLeader.jsp?memID=5784 (accessed February 11, 2008);
Kurtz, Tal, and Burgin, *Islamic Terror and Israel,* 27; Ronen Bergman, *Point of
No Return* (Or Yehuda, Israel: Kinneret, 2007), 146–147; Uri Blau, "If I Was a
Palestinian," *Haaretz,* December 23, 2006; Nissim Levy, *A Year Without Birds*
(Tel Aviv: Am Oved, 2006).

11. Yaari interview; Chen interview; Robert A. Pape, "The Strategic Logic of
Suicide Terrorism," *American Political Science Review* 97, no. 3 (August 2003):
343–361; Augustus R. Norton, "Hizballah and the Israeli Withdrawal from
Southern Lebanon," *Journal of Palestine Studies* 30, no. 1 (Autumn 2000): 22–35;
Raphael Israeli, "A Manual of Islamic Fundamentalist Terrorism," *Terrorism and
Political Violence* 14, no. 4 (Winter 2002): 23–40; Reuven Erlich, "Portrait of
Ghazi Kanaan, Designer and Implementer of the Syrian Order in Lebanon, and
Handler of Palestinian and Lebanese Terrorists Serving the Syrian Régime,"
www.intelligence.org.il/eng/eng_n/kanaan.htm (accessed February 11, 2008);
Shimon Shapira, *Hizballah: Between Iran and Lebanon* (Tel Aviv: Hakibbutz
Hameuchad, 2000), 162–163; Ian Black and Benny Morris, *Israel's Secret Wars*

(London: Warner, 1992), 428; On Levy, "The Task: Killing, as Many as Possible," *Davar*, March 20, 1992; Shaul Mishal and Avraham Sela, *The Hamas Wind: Violence and Coexistence* (Tel Aviv: Miskal, 2006), 56–59; interview with Arie Livne, former head of the GSS Southern Command, January 25, 2007.

12. Black and Morris, *Israel's Secret Wars*, 394; Kurtz, Tal, and Burgin, *Islamic Terror and Israel*, 30–33.

13. Bergman, *Point of No Return*, 182–187; "GSS and Aman: Division of Responsibilities," *Haaretz*, November 16, 2000; Knesset Foreign Affairs and Security Committee, "Report on the Committee of Enquiry Into the Intelligence System in Light of the War in Iraq" (March 2004), A:43–45, 61–62, 66–68.

14. Interview with Hezi Kalo, former head of the GSS Human Resources Division, May 22, 2006; Yaacov Peri, *Striking First* (Tel-Aviv: Keshet, 1999), 110; Chen interview; Black and Morris, *Israel's Secret Wars*, 399; Bergman, *Point of No Return*, 185.

15. Ronen Bergman, "Blinded Ducks," *Haaretz*, May 14, 1999, 35–38; Bergman, *Point of No Return*, 184–189; Amir Oren, "Military Command Opposes Self-Restrained Policy," *Haaretz*, October 8, 2000; Yossi Melman, "Our Brothers, Persians," *Haaretz*, November 22, 2006; Chen interview.

16. Kalo interview; Bergman, *Point of No Return*, 186; Chen interview; interview with Yaacov Amidror, former head of Aman research division, April 12, 2007.

17. Carmi Gillon, *Shin-Beth Between the Schisms* (Tel Aviv: Lemiskal, 2000), 183–186; Chen interview.

18. Ludo Block, "Evaluating the Effectiveness of French Counter-terrorism," *Terrorism Monitor* 3, no. 17 (September 8, 2005): 6–8; Dexter Filkins, "The Plot Against America," *New York Times Book Review*, August 6, 2006.

CHAPTER FIVE **NEW CHALLENGES FROM THE WEST BANK AND GAZA**

1. Ron Schleifer, *Psychological Warfare in the Intifada: Israeli and Palestinian Media Politics and Military Strategies* (New York: Academic Press, 2006), 37–41.

2. Ezra Yanov, "The Houses of the Terrorists Were Demolished," *Maariv*, April 15, 1986. Yosef Walter, "These Guys Came Like Angels—They're Excellent Professionals," *Maariv*, April 15, 1984; Ezra Yanov, "Soldier Lilly Lazar: 'I Was in the Toilet and Saved,'" *Maariv*, April 15, 1986; Yosef Walter, "The Story of Yitzhak Sela, Who Chased After the Bus: I'm at the Ashdod Junction, the Bus Has Been Hijacked," *Maariv*, April 15, 1986; Ronen Bergman, "I'm an Orphan," *Haaretz*, February 12, 1999; Mordechai Alon, "Ehud Yatom from Bus 300 Affair Talking," *Yedioth Ahronoth*, Saturday Supplement, July 26, 1996; Yosef Walter, "IDF Warns: Terrorist Organization Will Try to Intensify Terrorist Activity Against Civilian Targets," *Maariv*, April 15, 1986; Alex Fishman, "No Second Bullet," *Hadashot*, April 13, 1987; interview with Michael Koubi, former GSS interrogator, April 17, 2007.

3. Yair Fidel and Uri Milstein, "Yamam Operated After Years of Frustration," *Hadashot*, March 8, 1988; Walter, "These Guys Came Like Angels"; Baruch Nae,

"Terrorist Hid Behind Irit," *Maariv,* April 15, 1984; Walter, "IDF Warns"; Alon, "Ehud Yatom"; Fishman, "No Second Bullet"; interview with N., former senior officer in GSS, April 1, 2007.

4. Alon, "Ehud Yatom"; Yechiel Gutman, *A Storm in the GSS* (Tel Aviv: Yedioth Ahronot, 1995), 19, 23–25; Yossi Melman and Dan Raviv, *The Imperfect Spies* (Tel Aviv: Maariv, 1990), 235; Carmi Gillon, *Shin-Beth Between the Schisms* (Tel Aviv: Miskal, 2000), 362–371; Ian Black and Benny Morris, *Israel's Secret Wars* (London: Warner, 1992), 403–406; "Report of State Inquiry Commission for the Investigation on Interrogation Methods of Shabak in the Field of Hostile Terrorist Activity" (Jerusalem, 1987).

5. Black and Morris, *Israel's Secret Wars,* 408.

6. Dan Avidan, "Fatah Took Responsibility: We Avenged Limasol," *Davar,* March 8, 1988. Officially, the names of the terrorists were not released; however, the Arab press published many different names for them. The most common were Abdallah Clab, Muhammad Abed El-Kader, Abu El-Zalp, and Muhammad El-Hanapi. All of them were in their twenties, came from the Rafah refugee camp, and had joined Fatah together.

7. Eitan Rabin and Reuven Pedahzur, "Three Killed in the Blood Bus in the South," *Haaretz,* March 8, 1988; Emmanuel Rosen and Uri Binder, "This Is How Everything Happened: The Hijack, Chase and the Takeover," *Maariv,* March 3, 1988; Shmuel Tal, "Commander of Command Learning Base: I Was Offended Personally by the Officers' Response," *Hadashot,* March 9, 1988; "Mothers Bus," *Maariv,* March 3, 1988; Fishman, "No Second Bullet"; Koubi interview.

8. Interview with Alik Ron, former commander of the Israeli Police Northern Command, Yamam and Shaldag, March 5, 2007; Moshe Givati, *Abir 21* (Jerusalem: Reut, 2003), 76; Rosen and Binder, "This Is How Everything Happened"; Ben Caspit, "'Bastards Terrorists Killed Me'—Daisy Wrote in Her Farewell Letter to Her Children," *Maariv,* March 8, 1988; "Snipers Shot Into the Bus and After a Few Seconds the Yamam Soldiers Were Inside," *Maariv,* March 8, 1988.

9. Jill Smolowe, "Middle East Assignment: Murder," *Time,* May 2, 1988; Moshe Zonder, "This Is How the Sayeret Matkal Assassinated Abu Jihad," *Maariv,* July 4, 1997.

10. Robert Fisk, "Microchip Murder Squads Do Israel's Dirty Work," *Independent,* April 13, 2001; Neil C. Livingstone and David Halevy, *Inside the PLO: Covert Units, Secret Funds, and the War Against Israel and the United States* (New York: Morrow, 1990), 47–48; Moshe Zonder, *The Elite Unit of Israel* (Jerusalem: Keter 2000), 240; Baruch Shai and Meir Suissa, "Iron Lady," *NRG,* www.nrg.co.il (May 5, 2003).

11. Livingstone and Halevy, *Inside the PLO,* 53, 56–57; Oriya Shavit and Jalal Bana, "Child of the Revolution," *Haaretz,* Saturday Supplement, April 20, 2001; Zonder, "How the Sayeret Matkal Assassinated Abu Jihad"; Moshe Zonder, "Bogi," *NRG,* www.nrg.co.il (March 29, 2002).

12. John Kifner, "Israel's Silence Reinforces Belief Its Commandos Killed P.L.O. Aide," *New York Times*, April 18, 1998.

13. Livingstone and Halevy, *Inside the PLO*, 38; Zonder, *Elite Unit*, 248.

14. Zeev Schiff, "Thwarting: From Ticking Bomb to Ticking Infrastructure," *Haaretz*, September 10, 2003; Yossi Melman, "Once Assassinations Were Last Resort; Today They Are Done Wholesale," *Haaretz*, March 24, 2004; Diana Bahur-Nir, "Ami Ayalon: Without Political Hope, Yassin Assassination Was a Mistake," *Ynet*, www.ynet.co.il (March 24, 2004); Steven R. David. "Fatal Choices: Israel's Policy of Targeted Killing," Begin-Sadat Center for Strategic Studies, www.biu.ac.il/SOC/besa/david.pdf (accessed February 14, 2008); Daniel Byman, "Do Targeted Killings Work?" *Foreign Affairs*, 85, no. 2 (March–April 2006): 95–112; Yossi Melman, "Assassinations Policy Unnecessary," *Haaretz*, November 12, 2000; Mia M. Bloom, "Palestinian Suicide Bombing: Public Support, Market Share, and Outbidding," *Political Science Quarterly* 119, no. 1 (Spring 2004): 85.

15. Givati, *Abir 21*, 84–85, 93, 98–100; "Border Guard," www.police.gov.il (accessed February 14, 2008); Shlomi Zipori, *Justice in Disguise* (Tel Aviv: Agam, 2004), 59–60.

16. Arie Shalev, *The Intifada: Causes and Effects* (Tel Aviv: Papirus, 1990), 32–33; Zeev Schiff and Ehud Yaari, *Intifada* (Tel Aviv: Shocken, 1990), 168–177, 225, 253; "What Started 'The First Intifada' in 1987?" *Palestine Facts*, www.palestinefacts .org/pf_1967to1991_intifada_1987.php (accessed February 14, 2008); Eitan Y. Alimi, *Israeli Politics and the First Palestinian Intifada* (London: Routledge, 2007), 135–136; Koubi interview; interview with Arie Livne, former head of the GSS Southern Command, January 25, 2007.

17. William Sheppard, *Sayyid Qutb and Islamic Activism: A Translation and Critical Analysis of Social Justice in Islam* (New York: E. J. Brill, 1996); Avraham Sela and Shaul Mishal, *The Hamas Wind: Violence and Compromise* (Tel Aviv: Miskal, 2006), 216–217; Roni Shaked and Aviva Shabi, *Hamas: Palestinian Islamic Movement* (Jerusalem: Keter, 1994), 123; The Nightmare Is Back," *NRG*, www.nrg.co.il (June 25, 2006); Gillon, *Shin-Beth Between the Schisms*, 194–195; Livne interview; Koubi interview.

18. Lior Ben-David, "Terrorist Organizations Fighting Against Israel," www.knesset .gov.il/mmm/data/pdf/m01048.pdf (accessed February 14, 2008); Mishal and Sela, *The Hamas Wind*, 56–59; Shmuel Hadad, "Yassin Interrogator: I Discovered a Man Who Was Highly Eager to Kill Jews," *Ynet*, www.ynet.co.il (March 22, 2004); Livne interview.

19. Ian Black, "Regional Weapon with a Long History," *Guardian*, December 18, 1992; "Remarks by Prime Minister Rabin on Israel Television Following an Attack on a Bus in Tel Aviv, October 19, 1994," Israel Ministry of Foreign Affairs Web site, www.mfa.gov.il (accessed February 14, 2008); Ehud Yaari, "The Metamorphosis of Hamas," *Jerusalem Report* 3, no. 18 (January 14, 1993): 24–26.

20. "Profile of the Hamas Movement," Israel Intelligence Heritage and Com-

memoration Center, www.intelligence.org.il/Eng/eng_n/pdf/hamas_e0206
.pdf (accessed February 14, 2008); "Profile: Hamas' Mahmoud Zahhar," *BBC*,
http://news.bbc.co.uk/2/hi/middle_east/4653706.stm (January 27, 2006); interview with Yossi Chen, former head of the GSS Northern Command, February
4, 2007; Shaked and Shabi, *Hamas*, 270–279, 325–326; Sela and Mishal, *The
Hamas Wind*, 99–100; Nahman Tal and Anat Kurtz, "Hamas: Radical Islam in
a National Struggle," www.tau.ac.il/jcss/memoranda/memo48su.html (accessed
February 14, 2008); Gillon, *Shin-Beth Between the Schisms*, 194–195.

CHAPTER SIX THE GLOBAL CHALLENGE OF IRAN AND HEZBOLLAH

1. "Hanging on a Helicopter Skid, Major Aviram was Rescued and Returned to
   Israel," Israeli Air Force Web site, www.iaf.org.il (accessed February 20, 2008);
   Moshe Tuval, "Ron Arad Parachuted from a Phantom Over Sidon," *Haaretz*,
   May 22, 1994; Yossi Melman, "Is Ron Arad Worth More?" *Walla*, http://news
   .walla.co.il (May 14, 2005); Ran Edelist and Ilan Kfir, *Ron Arad: The Mystery* (Tel
   Aviv: Miskal, 2000), 93.

2. Interview with R., former senior officer in Mossad, January 11, 2007; interview
   with U., former senior officer in Israeli intelligence, January 10, 2007; Edelist and
   Kfir, *Ron Arad*, 137–165.

3. R. interview; U. interview; Melman, "Is Ron Arad Worth More?"

4. Edelist and Kfir, *Ron Arad*, 91; Moshe Zonder, *The Elite Unit of Israel* (Jerusalem: Keter, 2000), 234, 254–255; Tuval, "Ron Arad Parachuted"; Paul Taylor,
   "Lebanese Prisoners Held by Israeli Ally Key to Hostage Fate," *Reuters*, May 7,
   1990; Nadav Ze'evi, "The Architect of the Sayeret Matkal," *Maariv*, Saturday
   Supplement, July 4, 1997.

5. Edelist and Kfir, *Ron Arad*, 197, 200; Eitan Rabin, "Arens Considering Appointment of Investigator Who Will Investigate the Arad Affair," *Haaretz*, May 6,
   1992; Clyde Haberman, "Israelis Abduct Guerrilla Chief from Lebanon," *New
   York Times*, May 22, 1994.

6. Ariela Ringel-Hoffman and Galit Yamini, "Mossad Determined: It's Possible to
   Leave the Security Zone," *Yedioth Ahronot*, Saturday Supplement, July 25, 1997;
   "Hezbollah Activities Geared Toward Israeli Arabs in Effort to Boost Terrorism
   against Israel and Collect Intelligence," Israel Intelligence Heritage and Com-
   memoration Center, www.terrorism-info.org.il/malam_multimedia/html/final/
   sp/6_04/si_8d_04.htm (accessed February 20, 2008); Eitan Rabin and Guy
   Bechor, "IDF Assassinated Hezbollah General Secretary Musawi; Head of the
   Organization: Intensify Jihad Against Israel," *Haaretz*, February 17, 1992; Mar-
   cela Valente, "Argentina: No Suspects Found in Israeli Embassy Bombing," IPS-
   Inter Press Service, March 17, 1998; "Recordatorio de las victimas del atentado,"
   Israeli Embassy to Argentina Web site, http://buenosaires.mfa.gov.il (accessed
   February 16, 2007); Andrew Meisels, "Israel Suspects Iran Link in Blast," *Wash-
   ington Times*, March 20, 1992; Clyde Haberman, "Israel Vows 'Painful Punish-
   ment' for Bombing in Argentina," *New York Times*, March 19, 1992; Robert Fisk,

"Islamic Jihad Claims Argentine Bombing," *The Independent,* March 19, 1992; "Argentina Issued Search Warrant for Hezbollah Men Responsible for Bombing in Israeli Embassy," *Haaretz,* September 5, 1999; Ephraim Kam, *From Terror to Nuclear Bombs: The Significance of the Iranian Threat* (Tel Aviv: Ministry of Defense Publishers, 2004); Yossi Melman, "Imad Mughniyah Still Walks Free," *Haaretz,* December 12, 1997.

7. Kam, *From Terror to Nuclear Bombs,* 274; Ronen Bergman, "Terror with Address," *Haaretz,* Saturday Supplement, December 20, 1996; Blanca Madani, "New Report Links Syria to 1992 Bombing of Israeli Embassy in Argentina," *Middle East Intelligence Bulletin* (March 2000), www.meib.org/articles/0003_s1.htm (accessed February 20, 2008); "Argentina Issued Search Warrant."

8. "Operation Accountability," www.globalsecurity.org/military/world/war/lebanon-accountability.htm (accessed February 20, 2008); Michael Brecher and Jonathan Wilkenfeld, *A Study of Crisis* (Ann Arbor: University of Michigan Press, 1997), 299–300.

9. Eitan Rabin, Aluf Ben, and Guy Bechor, "Israel Will Use Information on Ron Arad That Darani Will Provide in Order to Put Pressure on Iran," *Haaretz,* May 22, 1994; Edelist and Kfir, *Ron Arad,* 261; Eitan Rabin, "The Soldiers Raided Dirani's House in Lebanon, Seized Him from His Bed, and Brought Him in a Helicopter to Israel," *Haaretz,* May 22, 1994.

10. Akiva Eldar, Eitan Rabin, and Aluf Benn, "Mossad Personnel Dispatched to Argentina for Bombing Investigation; 27 Dead and 70 Wounded," *Haaretz,* July 20, 1994; Zeev Schiff, "Iranian Committee Permitted Bombing," *Haaretz,* March 18, 2003; "Ali Akbar Hashemi Rafsanjani," Iran Chamber Society, www.iranchamber.com/history/arafsanjani/akbar_rafsanjani.php (accessed February 20, 2008); Daphna Vardi, "Arab Newspaper Reported on July 14th: Iran Permitted Hezbollah to Avenge Aerial Bombing of Their Training Camp," *Haaretz,* July 20, 1994; Daniel Santoro, "Argentine Judge Assesses Video Seeking Hizballah Link with AMIA Bombing," Global News Wire, April 8, 2003; Daniel Santoro, "Investigan si un colombiano organizó los ataques a la AMIA y la Embajada," *Clarin,* March 23, 2003.

11. Noga Tarnopolsky, "Investigation Didn't Help; Maybe Civil Suit Will," *Haaretz,* February 25, 2003; Schiff, "Iranian Committee Permitted Bombing."

12. Interview with Yigal Carmon, former counterterrorist adviser to the prime minister, February 22, 2007; Francesco Relea, "Se inicia en Argentina el juicio por el atentado antijudeo de 1994," *El Pais,* September 25, 2001; "Argentina's General Prosecution Issued an Official Announcement Identifying a Lebanese National Sent on Behalf of the Hezbollah Organization as the Terrorist Responsible for the Suicide Bombing Attack at AMIA Jewish Community Center (July 1994)," Israel Intelligence Heritage and Commemoration Center (November 22, 2005), www.terrorism-info.org.il/malam_multimedia/html/final/eng/eng_n/argentina_e.htm (accessed February 20, 2008).

13. Fernando Mugica, "La Conexión Irani," *El Mundo,* June 23, 2006; Yossi Mel-

man, "FBI Again Investigating Argentina's Bombings," *Haaretz,* May 11, 2001; Larry Rohter, "Iran Blew Up Jewish Center in Argentina, Defector Says," *New York Times,* July 22, 2002; Anthony Faiola, "Menem Rejects Report He Took Iranian Payoff; Argentina's Ex-Leader Faces Renewed Scrutiny," *Washington Post,* July 23, 2002.

14. Mugica, "La Conexión Irani," 20–22; interview with Yehiam Sasson, former head of the counterterrorism staff in the Israeli Prime Minister office, February 24, 2007; Noga Tarnopolsky, "Argentina Faces a Suit Over Probe of Bombing; AMIA Families Demand Justice," *Forward,* www.forward.com (February 21, 2003); Attila Shomfalvi, "Israel, Turkey to Share Intelligence," *Ynet,* www.ynetnews .com (January 5, 2005).

15. Carmon interview; Melman, "Imad Mughniyah Still Walks Free"; Jack Kelly, "Deadly Infiltrator's Trail," *Washington Times,* September 13, 2003; Robert Baer, *See No Evil: The True Story of a Ground Soldier in CIA's War on Terrorism* (New York: Crown Publishers, 2002), 79, 99–100; Jeffrey Goldberg, "In the Party of God," *New Yorker,* October 28, 2002; Shaul Shay, *The Axis of Evil: Iran, Hezbollah, and the Palestinian Terror* (Herzliya, Israel: Interdisciplinary Center, 2003), 73; Emily Wax, "Sudan's Unbowed, Unbroken Inner Circle; Tight Web of Savvy Leaders Withstands International Criticism," *Washington Post,* May 3, 2005; "Saudi Arabia," Federation of American Scientists (March 2002), www.fas.org/ asmp/profiles/saudi_arabia.htm (accessed February 20, 2008).

16. Ethan Bronner, "In Mideast, a Renewal of Terror," *Boston Globe,* November 24, 1996; Yossi Melman, "Ramzi Nohra's Good Days," *Haaretz, Saturday Supplement,* December 1, 2000; Noam Amit and Yehuda Nuriel, "The Spy Who Loved Us," *NRG,* www.nrg.co.il (December 13, 2002); David Hirst, "Hizbullah Puts Israel in Its Sights After Bombing," *Guardian,* December 23, 1994; Daniel Sobelman, *New Rules of the Game: Israel and Hizbollah After the Withdrawal from Lebanon* (Tel Aviv: Tel Aviv University, June 2003), 14; Yossi Melman, "Opening a Window on Intelligence," *Haaretz,* July 24, 2006; Gary C. Gambill, "More Unsolved Mysteries in Lebanon," *Middle East Intelligence Bulletin* (January 2003), www.meib.org/articles/0301_11.htm (accessed February 20, 2008).

17. Gambill, "More Unsolved Mysteries"; Amit and Nuriel, "The Spy Who Loved Us"; Melman, "Ramzi Nohra's Good Days"; Nicholas Blanford, "'Double Agent' Played Deadly Role," *Daily Star,* December 9, 2002. Ramzi Nohra cooperated with Israel security forces from the early 1980s, providing information to the Lebanon border unit of the Israeli police. He also cooperated with other Israeli intelligence organizations, including the GSS. Interview with Yossi Chen, former head of the GSS Northern Command, February 18, 2007; Yossi Melman, "Nohra Was Drug Dealer Who Worked for Five Intelligence Organizations," *Haaretz,* December 8, 2002; Yossi Melman, "Drug Dealer Previously Was Israeli Agent," *Haaretz,* February 18, 2003.

18. Amit and Nuriel, "The Spy Who Loved Us"; Gambill, "More Unsolved Mysteries in Lebanon"; Blanford, "'Double Agent' Played Deadly Role."

19. Bronner, "In Mideast, a Renewal of Terror"; "Operation Grapes of Wrath—Selected Analyses from the Hebrew Press," Israel Ministry of Foreign Affairs, www.israel.org/MFA (April 21, 1996); Kevin Fedarko, "Operation Grapes of Wrath," *Time,* April 22, 1996.

20. Fedarko, "Operation Grapes of Wrath"; Daniel Ben Simon, "Grapes of Summer, Rains of Wrath," *Haaretz,* July 3, 2006; "Operation Grapes of Wrath," *Ynet,* www.ynetnews.com (January 8, 2006); "1996: Israel launches attack on Beirut," *BBC,* http://news.bbc.co.uk/onthisday/hi/dates/stories/april/11/newsid_4828000/4828386.stm (accessed February 20, 2008); "Cease-fire Understanding in Lebanon—and Remarks by Prime Minister Peres and Secretary of State Christopher," Israel Ministry of Foreign Affairs, www.israel-mfa.gov.il/MFA; "The Palestinian Arab Citizens of Israel: Status, Opportunities and Challenges for an Israeli-Palestinian Peace," Mossawa Center (June 2006), www.mossawacenter.org.

CHAPTER SEVEN NEW RIVALS, OLD RESPONSES

1. Asher Arian, "Vox Populi: Public Opinion and National Security," in Avner Yaniv, ed., *National Security and Democracy in Israel* (Boulder, Colo.: Lynne Rienner, 1993), 143–152.

2. Ronen Bergman, "The Disappearance of the Furniture Supplier," *Haaretz,* March 21, 1999; Ronen Bergman, "The Sheriff Against Mossad," *Haaretz,* Saturday Supplement, June 23, 2000; Youssef M. Ibrahim, "Key PLO Official Accused of Spying for Israel," *New York Times,* November 5, 1993; Zvi Barel, "Abu Mazen's Talking Chair," *Haaretz,* September 8, 1995; Ian Black, "Peres Blows Cover of PLO 'Mole,'" *Guardian,* November 12, 1993.

3. "Mossad Blamed as Arafat Aide Gunned Down on Paris Street," *Toronto Star,* June 9, 1992; Jonathan C. Randal, "Assassination of PLO Aide Raises Many Questions," *Washington Post,* June 10, 1992; Aaron Klein, *Striking Back: The 1972 Munich Olympics Massacre and Israel's Deadly Response* (Tel Aviv: Miskal, 2006), 11–12; "Senior PLO Official Arrested as Israeli Spy," *Mideast Mirror,* November 3, 1993; Yossi Melman, "Report: Mossad Agent in PLO Released," *Haaretz,* December 21, 2003; Bergman, "The Sheriff Against Mossad."

4. Yossi Melman, "Culture of Suspenders," *Haaretz,* August 9, 2002.

5. Yaacov Peri, *Striking First* (Tel-Aviv: Keshet, 1999), 266; Ephraim Kahana, *Historical Dictionary of Israeli Intelligence* (Lanham, Md.: Scarecrow Press, 2006), 420; Ronen Bergman and David Ratner, "Politics of War Assessments," *Haaretz,* May 11, 1997; Carmi Gillon, *Shin-Beth Between the Schisms* (Tel Aviv: Lemiskal, 2000), 192–193, 380; Uri Sagi, *Lights in the Fog* (Tel Aviv: Yedioth Ahronot, 1998), 169; Uzi Arad, "End of the Pluralism Era," *Haaretz,* September 4, 2004.

6. Gillon, *Shin-Beth Between the Schisms,* 223; "War Against the Clock: The Story of Nachshon Wachsman," *Daat,* http://daat.ac.il/daat/dapey/dapim/tfila11.doc.

7. "Special means" is a code term for putting physical pressure on an individual being interrogated. Two of the most common methods are violently shaking the

person being interrogated and seating him in a painful position. These methods and their usage are defined in the Report of Special Inquiry Commission for the Investigations of Interrogation Methods of the GSS (1987).

8. Alex Fishman and Hemi Shalev, "Rabin Ordered to Act Immediately After It Was Clear That Wachsman Had Been Held in Bir-Naballah," *Maariv*, October 16, 1994; Shimon Schiffer and Nahum Barnea, "Everything Went Wrong from the First Moment," *Yedioth Ahronot*, October 16, 1994; Aluf Ben, "Wachsman Kidnapping: From Videotape Passing to Rescue Failure," *Haaretz*, October 16, 1994; Gillon, *Shin-Beth Between the Schisms*, 217–222; interview with Peri Golan, former head of the GSS Judea district, April 7, 2007; interview with Lior Lotan, former head of the General Staff Negotiation Unit and Sayeret Matkal officer, March 22, 2007; Roni Sofer and Yossi Levy, "A Moment Before the Soldiers Broke Into the Room, the Terrorists Shot Nahshon," *Maariv*, October 16, 1994; Roni Shaked, "Four Minutes of Hell," *Yedioth Ahronot*, October 16, 1994; Moshe Zonder, *The Elite Unit of Israel* (Jerusalem: Keter, 2000), 293–304; Shalom Yerushalmi, "Voice Calling in the Desert," *NRG*, www.nrg.co.il (December 17, 2007).

9. Christopher Shea, "Why Do Suicide Bombers Do It?" *Boston Globe*, July 3, 2005; Robert A. Pape, "The Strategic Logic of Suicide Terrorism," *American Political Science Review* 97, no. 3 (August 2003): 351–354; Mia M. Bloom, *Dying to Kill: The Allure of Suicide Terrorism* (New York: Columbia University Press, 2005), 166; Simon Jeffery, "Sharon vs. Arafat," *Guardian*, December 5, 2001; interview with Peri Golan, former head of the GSS Southern Command, February 15, 2007; "Suicide Terrorism in Israeli-Palestinian Conflict, 2000–2005," Israel Intelligence Heritage and Commemoration Center, www.terrorism-info.org.il.

10. Interview with Nachman Tal, former senior officer in the GSS, March 7, 2007; interview with Yisrael Hasson, former deputy head of the GSS, December 19, 2006; interview with Yigal Levinstein, former commander of the GSS, December 26, 2006; Peri, *Striking First*, 260; Avner Yaniv, *Dilemmas of Security: Politics, Strategy, and the Israeli Experience in Lebanon* (New York: Oxford University Press, 1987), 104; Yezid Sayigh, "Palestinian Military Performance in the 1982 War," *Journal of Palestine Studies* 12, no. 4 (Summer 1983): 17–19; Nahman Tal and Anat Kurtz, "Hamas: Radical Islam in a National Struggle," Jaffee Center for Strategic Studies Memorandum No. 48, July 1997.

11. David Eshel, "Israeli Intelligence Dilemmas in Lebanon," *Defense Update*, www .defense-update.com/analysis/lebanon_war_2.htm (accessed February 15, 2008); Gillon, *Shin-Beth Between the Schisms*, 388–389; Ronen Bergman, "Moderate Legal Pressure: Interview with GSS Retiring Legal Advisor," *Haaretz*, Saturday Supplement, April 14, 2000; "Prisoners Report," *Palestinian Center for Human Rights*, www.pchrgaza.ps/files/Reports/English/pdf_spec/prisoners97.pdf (accessed February 15, 2008); "Israeli Troops Kill Hamas Activist," UPI, June 29, 1995; Alon Pinkas, "Hamas Man Died After Interrogation," *Jerusalem Post*, April 26, 1995.

12. Interview with Arie Livne, former head of the GSS Interrogations Branch, May 3, 2007; Civil Rights in Israel, 1996," Associations for Civil Rights in Israel, www.acri.org.il/Story.aspx?id=170 (accessed February 15, 2008).

13. Livne interview; Gillon, *Shin-Beth Between the Schisms*, 394–395; Yoav Limor, "Head of the GSS: The Investigators Did Not Trust Judicial System Judgment," *Yedioth Ahronot*, November 21, 1999; Roni Shaked, "Shabak Arrested a Gang Responsible for Bus Bombings," *Yedioth Ahronot*, August 24, 1995; Eliezer Hillel, "Ticking Bomb," *Ynet*, www.ynet.co.il (January 29, 2002); Tova Zimuki and Nehama Duek, "Are New Restrictions of Shakings Delayed Investigation?" *Yedioth Ahronot*, August 24, 1995; Eitan Rabin, "37 Hamas Members Arrested in Suspicion of Planning and Committing Suicide Bombings in Ramat-Gan and Jerusalem," *Haaretz*, August 24, 1995.

14. Eitan Rabin, "The Assassin Waited Near the Hotel, Shot at Shikaki, Jumped on a Motorcycle, and Escaped," *Haaretz*, October 29, 1995; Yossi Melman and Aluf Ben, "The PIJ Accuse Mossad in the Assassination of the Organization's Leader," *Haaretz*, October 29, 1995.

15. Eitan Rabin, "Yehiya Ayash, The Engineer, Died in an Explosion at the Gaza Strip," *Haaretz*, January 7, 1996; Lisa Beyer, "Death Comes Calling," *Time*, January 15, 1996; Marie W. Berry, *Targeted: Engineer of Death* (Wild Eyes Productions, 2004); interview with Yossi Chen, former head of the GSS Northern Department, January 14, 2007; Eitan Rabin, "Ayyash Was Responsible for Killing 67 Israelis and Wounding 390," *Haaretz*, January 8, 1996; Amira Hess, "Kamal Hamad, Who Delivered the Booby-Trapped Cell Phone, Is in the United States," *Haaretz*, January 8, 1996; Moshe Zonder and Nadav Zeevi, "Shabak Vengeance," *Maariv*, Saturday Supplement, August 22, 1997; Alex Fischman, "The Engineer Was Killed, Now Contractor Can Go," *Yedioth Ahronot*, Saturday Supplement, November 21, 1997; Amira Hess, "In Gaza, a Trial Has Opened for Hamad Family, Accused in Killing of the 'Engineer,'" *Haaretz*, May 10, 1999; Samuel M. Katz, *The Hunt for the Engineer: How Israeli Agents Tracked the Hamas Master Bomber* (New York: Fromm International, 1999), 251–252; Yoav Limor, "You Have Used Me to Kill the Engineer, and Now You Are Dumping Me on the Streets," *Maariv*, November 4, 1999; Joel Greenberg, "Slaying Blended Technology and Guile," *New York Times*, January 10, 1996; Uri Nir and Eitan Rabin, "Long Hunt for a Needle in a Haystack," *Haaretz*, January 7, 1996; Yossi Melman, "The Assassination at Biet La'ia Will Be Credited to K; Doubtful It Will Help Him in the Shamgar Commission," *Haaretz*, January 7, 1995; Uri Nir, "Application to Ben-Yair: Investigate if K Ordered to Assassinate Ayash out of Prestige Considerations," *Haaretz*, January 7, 1995.

16. "Hamas Attack Victim 'Stronger Than Ever,'" *Jerusalem Post*, October 5, 1997; "Report of the Commission Concerning the Events in Jordan September 1997," Jerusalem Government Press Office, February 17, 1998; Yossi Melman, "Back to the Crime Scene," *Haaretz*, September 26, 2007; Abraham Rabinovitch, "Jordan Hit Prompted Toxic Swirl of Intrigue," *Jerusalem Post*, October 2, 1997;

Julian Borger, "Mossad Own Goal Rebounds on PM," *Guardian,* October 4, 1997; Barton Gellman, "Botched Assassination by Israel Gives New Life to Hamas," *Washington Post,* October 6; Alan Cowell, "The Daring Attack That Blew Up in Israel's Face," *New York Times,* October 15, 1997; Barry Came and Stephanie Nolen, "Passport to Trouble," *Maclean's,* October 13, 1997; Karl Stark, "To Those Living in Excruciating Pain, Fentanyl Offers Hope," *Philadelphia Inquirer,* October 27, 1997; Guy Bechor, Yareah Tal, Eitan Rabin, Akiva Eldar, Reuven Shapira and Yossi Verter, "Netanyahu Secretly Visited Jordan to Broker a Deal," *Haaretz,* October 5, 1997; Julian Borger and Ian Black, "Spooking the Spooks," *Guardian,* October 13, 1997; "Canadians in Street Fight with Hamas," *Record,* September 26, 1997; Kahana, *Historical Dictionary of Israeli Intelligence,* 143; interview with M. B., former Mossad officer, November 30, 2006; Eitan Rabin, "Mossad Agents: We Thought the Operation Succeeded," *Haaretz,* October 9, 1997; Efraim Halevy, *Man in the Shadows: Inside the Middle East Crisis with a Man Who Led Mossad* (Tel Aviv: Matar, 2006), 132–141; Zeev Schiff, "In Response to the Assassination Attempt Jordan Considered to Expel Israeli Ambassador," *Haaretz,* October 5, 1997; David Makovsky, "The Antidote That Saved Relations with Jordan," *Haaretz,* October 8, 1997; Yareah Tal, "Upon Hussein's Request, Clinton Called Netanyahu to Clarify Poison Used to Attack Mashal," *Haaretz,* October 5, 1997; Stephen Handelman, "Our Man in Israel Recalled Assassins' Use of Forged Passports Angers Ottawa," *Toronto Star,* October 3, 1997.

17. Ephraim Kahana, "Reorganizing Israel's Intelligence Community," *International Journal of Intelligence and CounterIntelligence* 15, no. 3 (Fall 2002): 421–422; Kahana, *Historical Dictionary of Israeli Intelligence,* 173; Amir Oren, "Disagreement Between Aman-Mossad-Shabak on Division of Intelligence Community Budget," *Haaretz,* August 25, 2000; Yossi Melman, "Disagreement in the Committee for the Reorganization of Intelligence," *Haaretz,* June 29, 2000; interview with Dan Meridor, former chair of the Knesset Foreign Affairs and Security Committee, August 21, 2007; Yossi Melman, "Committee of Directors of the Intelligence Services," *Haaretz,* October 6, 1999; Israeli State Comptroller, *Annual Report No. 50A* (Jerusalem: State Comptroller Office and Ombudsman Office, 1999), 280; Raviv Druker and Ofer Shelah, *Boomerang* (Jerusalem: Keter, 2005), 42.

CHAPTER EIGHT **A WAR AGAINST AN ELUSIVE ENEMY**

1. Akiva Eldar, "His Real Face," *Haaretz,* June 11, 2004; Akiva Eldar, "Sharp Division in Aman," *Walla,* http://news.walla.co.il (June 13, 2004).

2. Raviv Druker and Ofer Shelah, *Boomerang* (Jerusalem: Keter, 2005), 66–67, 156–157, 160–162; Diana Bahur-Nir, "Regrettably, My Estimates of Arafat Were Correct," *Ynet,* www.ynet.co.il (June 10, 2004); Amos Harel and Avi Issacharoff, *The Seventh War* (Tel Aviv: Miskal, 2004), 84; Eldar, "His Real Face"; Druker and Shelah, *Boomerang,* 160–162; Zeev Schiff and Ehud Yaari, *Intifada* (Tel

Aviv: Shocken, 1990), 158; interview with Eitan Tal, former officer in the IDF Field Intelligence Corps, April 24, 2007.

3. Interview with Hagai Peleg, former head of Yamam, December 26, 2006; Amir Buhbut, "We're Awake at Night So You Can Sleep," *NRG,* www.nrg.co.il (May 2, 2006); interview with Yitzhak Dar, former head of the GSS Operations Branch, August 22, 2007; Noam Ofir and Roni Winkler, "Combat Helicopters' Window of Opportunity," *Israel Air Force Magazine,* October 2001; Amos Harel, Zafrir Rinat, and Yoav Stern, "Sayeret Matkal Killed Dozens of Hezbollah People in the Lebanon Valley," *Haaretz,* August 3, 2006; Amir Oren, "To Germany and Back," *Haaretz,* Saturday Supplement, January 30, 2004; interview with A. A., senior officer in the Israeli Police and former Yamam officer, January 23, 2006; Harel and Issacharoff, *The Seventh War,* 90; Amos Harel, "Former Commander of the Yamam: There Is No Significance to Sector A Territories," *Haaretz,* January 1, 2002; interview with Lior Lotan, former head of the General Staff Negotiation Unit and Sayeret Matkal officer, March 22, 2007; Druker and Shelah, *Boomerang,* 88; Ben Caspit, "Assassinating Ourselves," *NRG,* http://www.nrg .co.il (October 5, 2003).

4. Interview with Peri Golan, former head of the GSS Judea district, April 7, 2007; interview with Yigal Levinstein, former commander in the GSS, March 18, 2006; Harel and Issacharoff, *The Seventh War,* 246.

5. Moshe Givati, *Abir 21* (Jerusalem: Reut, 2003), 84–85; Naomi Levitzky, "The Intention Was to Go and Whack Somebody: A Year and a Half Ago, Moments Before the Gaza Withdrawal, Mistaaravim Unit Killed Six Fatah Hawks," *Yedioth Ahronot,* Yom Kippur Supplement, October 3, 1995; Schiff and Yaari, *Intifada,* 153–154.

6. Roni Shaked, "The Peace Reduced Shimshon," *Yedioth Ahronot,* 24 Hours Supplement, April 28, 1996; Yoav Limor, "Cherry Blooming," *NRG,* www.nrg.co.il (April 13, 2001); Yossi Yehoshua and Reuven Weiss, "The Hunter," *Yedioth Ahronot,* Saturday Supplement, April 8, 2005; Amir Buhbut, "Fighting in the [West] Bank, Looking Up North," *NRG,* www.nrg.co.il (February 11, 2005); Yifat Glik, "Thirty Seconds, Break Through!" *Yedioth Ahronot,* Saturday Supplement, September 29, 2006.

7. "Weapons Ship Mystery Deepens," *BBC,* http://news.bbc.co.uk/2/hi/middle_ east/1753233.stm (January 10, 2002); Yoav Limor, "Suddenly Shayetet Soldiers Came From Darkness," *NRG,* www.nrg.co.il (January 6, 2002); Yoni Tamler, "IDF Naval Commandos Seize PA-bound Weapons Ship," *Israel Insider,* January 6, 2002.

8. Amos Harel, "Shayetet Commander Price of Choice," *Haaretz,* July 7, 2004; Shayetet 13," Israeli Special Forces and Special Operations (Sayeret) Database, www.isayeret.com/content/units/sea/shayetet/guide.htm (accessed February 18, 2008); Amnon Lord, "Molecules Against Viruses," *Makor Rishon,* November 10, 2005; Chen Kots-Bar, "The Hug of a Brigadier," *NRG,* www.nrg.co.il (August 19, 2005).

9. Shai Lahav, "Surgical Unit," *NRG,* www.nrg.co.il (May 1, 2003); Amos Harel, "Soldier Killed in Parachuting Accident After Colliding in Air with Another Paratrooper," *Haaretz,* November 3, 2005; Glik, "Thirty Seconds, Break Through!"

10. Christopher Kondaki, "Down to the Wire: Tactics at the Start of the Next Middle Eastern War," *Defense & Foreign Affairs: Strategic Policy* (August 2001): 6; Thomas B. Hunter, "Israeli Counterterrorism and Hostage Rescue," *Journal of Counterterrorism & Security International* 6, no. 4 (Summer 2000); Omri Assenheim, "Meantime in War," *Maariv,* April 28, 2006.

11. Amos Harel, Yonatan Liss, and Roni Zinger, "Gurel Release: 'Suddenly I Heard Voices—I Realized That They Were Going to Release Me,'" *Haaretz,* July 17, 2003; Amos Harel, "Who's Open at Betunia? Dilemmas of a 'White Taxi,'" *Haaretz,* July 17, 2003; Baruch Kra and Amos Harel, "Commander of the General Staff Negotiation Team Had Important Part in the Nachshon Wachsman Failed Rescue Operation," *Haaretz,* July 17, 2003; Amos Harel, "Kidnapped Taxi Driver Released Safely in a Night Operation Near Ramallah," *Haaretz,* July 16, 2003.

12. Druker and Shelah, *Boomerang,* 152–153, 158–159; Harel and Issacharoff, *The Seventh War,* 194–195, 198–200; "'Liquidation Sale'—Israeli Media Coverage of Events in Which Palestinians Were Killed by Israeli Security Forces," *Keshev,* March 2006; Zeev Schiff, "Thwarting: From Ticking Bomb to Ticking Infrastructure," *Haaretz,* September 10, 2003.

13. Harel and Issacharoff, *The Seventh War,* 181, 184–186; Felix Frisch and Ali Waked, "Palestinians: IDF Assassinated Raed Karmi, a Senior Official in the Tanzim," *Ynet,* www.ynet.co.il (January 14, 2002); Druker and Shelah, *Boomerang,* 151–152; Amir Rappaport, "Continue as Usual," *NRG,* www.nrg.co.il (June 13, 2003).

14. Omri Assenheim and Chen Kots-Bar, "Blood Revenge," *NRG,* www.nrg.co.il (June 3, 2005).

15. Ibid.; Conal Urquhart, "Israeli Soldiers Tell About Revenge Attacks," *Guardian,* June 3, 2005); Ephrat Weiss, "Perpetrator of Terrorist Attack in Ein Ariq in Which 6 Soldiers Killed, Arrested," *Ynet,* www.ynet.co.il (September 7, 2005); Felix Frisch and Ephrat Weiss, "Inquiry: Terrorists Worked Alone and Surprised Soldiers," *Ynet,* www.ynet.co.il (February 20, 2002).

16. "Operation Defensive Shield: Special Update, March 29, 2002–April 21, 2002," Israeli Ministry of Foreign Affairs, www.mfa.gov.il (accessed February 18, 2008); Clive Jones, "'One Size Fits All': Israel, Intelligence, and the al-Aqsa Intifada," *Studies in Conflict and Terrorism* 26, no. 4 (July–August 2003): 276; Harel and Isscharoff, *The Seventh War,* 266–267, 274; Sara Bedein, "The UNRWA Refugee Camp in Jenin: A Main Hub of Terrorist Activity" Jewish Agency for Israel, www.jafi.org.il; Matt Rees, "The Battle of Jenin," *Time,* May 13, 2002.

17. "The Israel Security Agency's 2006 Report Asserts That Hamas Has Taken Over the Gaza Strip with the Support of Hezbollah and Iran," International Institute for Counterterrorism, http://www.ict.org.il/var/119/31122-Shabakreport_2006 .pdf (accessed February 18, 2008); Druker and Shelah, *Boomerang,* 257, 260–263;

Harel and Isscharoff, *The Seventh War,* 275–279; Mohammed M. Hafez and Joseph M. Hatfield, "Do Targeted Assassinations Work? A Multivariate Analysis of Israel's Controversial Tactic During the Al-Aqsa Uprising," *Studies in Conflict and Terrorism* 29, no. 4 (June 2006): 359–382; Yossi Melman, "Once the Assassinations Were the Last Resort; Today They Are Popular," *Haaretz,* March 24, 2004

18. "Under the Guise of Security: Routing the Separation Barrier to Enable the Expansion of Israeli Settlements in the West Bank," "Not All It Seems: Preventing Palestinians Access to Their Lands West of the Separation Barrier in the Tulkarm-Qalqiliya Area," *Btselem,* www.btselem.org; Matthew Taylor, "International Court Rules Against Israel's Wall," *Guardian,* July 9, 2004.

19. Oreg Myre, "The Mideast Turmoil: Tel Aviv Bombing; Body from Sea Is Identified as Figure in Attack at Club," *New York Times,* May 20, 2003; NSSC Database on Palestinian Terrorism, http://nssc.haifa.ac.il; "Victims of Palestinian Violence and Terrorism Since September 2000," Israeli Ministry of Foreign Affairs, www.mfa.gov.il.

20. Anat Zigelman, "Egged: Renew Operation of Civil Transportation Protection Unit," *Haaretz,* December 3, 2001; interview with Eran Berkowitz, former security officer in public-transport security, January 11, 2007; Anat Zigelman, "The Transportation Security Unit Began to Operate," *Haaretz,* May 27, 2002; Anat George, "Disagreement on Budgeting Delaying Multiplying Number of Security Guards," *Haaretz,* March 6, 2003.

21. "Charity Coalition," "Important Step Against Terrorism in Europe: German Court Approved State Decision to Stop Operating of Al-Aqsa Fund German Branch," and "Interpal: Helping Palestinians in Need," Israel Intelligence Heritage and Commemoration Center, www.terrorism-info.org.il (accessed February 18, 2008); "Not Yet a Dead End," *Mideast Mirror,* June 13, 2003; "Arafat Knew: Charity Money Forwarded to Terror Infrastructure," IDF, www.dover.idf.il (January 23, 2003); Matthew Levitt, "Islamic Extremism in Europe: Beyond Al-Qaeda, Hamas, and Hezbollah in Europe," Testimony Before the Joint Hearing of the House Committee on International Relations, Subcommittee on Europe and Emerging Threats, April 27, 2005; "The Financial Sources of the Hamas Terror Organization," Israel Ministry of Foreign Affairs, http://www.mfa.gov.il (July 30, 2003);

22. Yitzhak Ben-Khorin, "Professor of Terrorism," *NRG,* www.nrg.co.il (February 21, 2003); Roni Zinger, "Israelis Will Testify Against Islamic Jihad," *Haaretz,* May 18, 2005; William March, "Palestinian Cause Is Life's Common Thread," *Tampa Tribune,* June 5, 2005; Phil Long and Gail Epstein Nieves, "Professor Named in Terror Plot; 8 Are Accused as Top Leaders of Islamic Jihad," *Miami Herald,* February 21, 2003; Yossi Melman and Nathan Guttman, "Jihad Trials," *Haaretz,* May 17, 2005; Josh Gerstein, "Al-Arian: I Was Double-Crossed," *New York Sun,* January 22, 2007.

23. "Money Confiscation Operation in the West Bank Banks," "Financing and Encouraging Terrorism," Israel Intelligence Heritage and Commemoration Cen-

ter, www.terrorism-info.org.il (accessed February 18, 2008); Yair Dagan, "Terror Funding-Methods and Descriptions," *NFC,* www.nfc.co.il (February 4, 2007).

24. Ali Waked, "Final Results: Unprecedented Victory for Hamas," *Ynet,* www.ynet .co.il (January 27, 2006); Rory McCarthy, "EU Refuses to Lift Boycott on Palestinian Government," *Guardian,* April 27, 2007; Ali Waked, "Hamas Spokesmen Tried to Smuggle Hundreds of Thousands of Euros and Got Caught," *Ynet,* www.ynet.co.il (May 19, 2006); Ali Waked, "The Millionaire Who Will Unite Palestinian Factions," *Ynet,* www.ynet.co.il (June 14, 2006); Roni Sofer, "Israel to Egypt: Stop Millions Smuggling," *Ynet,* www.ynet.co.il (June 7, 2006); Moran Zelikovitch and Attila Shumfalvi, "Diskin: 11 Tons of Explosives Smuggled in Gaza Strip," *Ynet,* www.ynet.co.il (June 6, 2006); interview with Peri Golan, former GSS officer and specialist in terrorist finances, February 9, 2007.

25. Interview with Arie Livne, former head of GSS Southern Command, January 25, 2007; Druker and Shelah, *Boomerang,* 151–152, 158–161; Harel and Issacharoff, *The Seventh War,* 185–187, 193–194, 200, 211–212; Melman, "Once Assassinations Were the Last Resort"; Yael Price-Shimshi, "Popular Resistance Committee," Matah Center for Educational Technology, http://lib.cet.ac.il (accessed February 19, 2008); Avi Issacharoff, "Abu Mazen Will Meet Haled Mashal in Damascus," *Haaretz,* January 18, 2007.

CHAPTER NINE **THE SECOND LEBANON WAR AND BEYOND**

1. "Lebanon Says Israeli Plane Detonated Bomb That Killed Jihad Chief," *Lebanon Wire,* June 15, 2006; Ali Waked, "Lebanon: Senior in Islamic Jihad Killed in Bomb Explosion," *Ynet,* www.ynet.co.il (May 26, 2006); "Car Bomb Kills Islamic Jihad Leader in Lebanon," *Ya Libnan,* May 26, 2006; "Lebanon Says Israel Used Sophisticated Technology in Killing Jihad Chief," *Lebanon Wire,* June 16, 2006; Roi Nahmias, "Lebanon: New Evidence in Israeli Link to Assassinations," *Ynet,* www.ynet.co.il (June 14, 2006).

2. "Lebanon Says Islamic Jihad Killing Suspect Arrested," *Lebanon Wire,* June 10, 2006; Nicholas Blanford, "Lebanon Exposes Deadly Israeli Spy Ring," *Times,* June 15, 2006; "Discovery of Terrorist Network Working for the Israeli Intelligence Services," Lebanon Army press release (June 13, 2000); Jackie Khoury, "Israel Intelligence Network Exposed in Lebanon," *Haaretz,* June 12, 2006.

3. "Hezbollah Military Chief Assassinated," *Middle East Intelligence Bulletin,* September 1999; "Jihad Ahmad Jibril Assassinated in Beirut," *Arabic News,* May 21, 2002.

4. Asaf Gabor, "Second Phase of Prisoner Exchange Deal Failed," *MSN News,* http://news.msn.co.il (August 9, 2005); "Report: Israel Will Offer Cash Reward for Information On Ron Arad," *NFC,* www.nfc.co.il (October 30, 2004); Ofer Shelah and Yoav Limor, *Captives of Lebanon* (Tel Aviv: Miskal, 2007), 32–33; Gil Solomon, "I Went to Conduct a Drug Deal," *NRG,* http://hot.nrg.co.il (December 20, 2006); "Iranians Interrogated Tannenbaum and Sent Him in Box to Lebanon," *Ynet,* www.ynet.co.il (October 22, 2003).

5. "Israel, Hezbollah Swap Prisoners," *CNN News*, January 29, 2004; Barak Ravid, "Samir Kuntar Release Isn't Related to Ron Arad," *NRG*, www.nrg.co.il (April 23, 2005); Gabor, "Second Phase of Prisoner Exchange Deal Failed"; "Report: Israel Will Offer Cash Reward for Information on Ron Arad," *NFC*, www.nfc .co.il (October 30, 2004); Eitan Rabin, "In My Opinion, Ron Arad Is Dead," *NRG*, www.nrg.co.il (January 19, 2006).

6. Hanan Greenberg and Ali Waked, "The Attack: Officer and Soldier Killed, Soldier Kidnapped, 'Probably Alive,'" *Ynet*, www.ynet.co.il (June 25, 2006); Hanan Greenberg and Hanan Einav, "General Stern: 'Gilad Left On His Feet Against His Will,'" *Ynet*, www.ynet.co.il (June 25, 2006); Anat Bershakovsky, "Witness: 'Terrorists Tried to Climb the Guard Tower,'" *Ynet*, www.ynet.co.il (June 25, 2006); Hanan Greenberg and Ali Waked, "IDF Entered Gaza: Bridges Bombed and Electricity Cut Off," *Ynet*, www.ynet.co.il (June 28, 2006); Ali Waked and Efrat Weiss, "The Leadership Is in the Sights: Hamas Government in Israeli Jail," *Ynet*, www.ynet.co.il (June 29, 2006); Barak Ravid, "Night of Arrests: Hamas Ministers and Parliament Members Arrested; Hamas: It Will Not Help to Release Soldier," *NRG*, www.nrg.co.il (June 29, 2006); Yuval Yoaz, Amos Harel, Avi Issacharoff, Aluf Benn, and Yoav Stern, "Ministry of Justice: Israel Will Continue to Arrest Hamas Leaders," *Haaretz*, June 30, 2006; Avi Issacharoff, "Hamas Deputy Prime Minister Released From Arrest; Military Court—Not Enough Evidence," *Haaretz*, September 27, 2006.

7. Shelah and Limor, *Captives of Lebanon*, 30, 33–36; Amos Harel, "Border Crossing Left Unnoticed and 'Blind Area' Used," *Haaretz*, July 16, 2006.

8. Shai Lahav, "Surgical Unit," *NRG*, www.nrg.co.il (May 1, 2003); Amir Buhbut, Yuval Kidor and Gil Solomon, "Two Soldiers Killed in Gunplay in the North," *NRG*, www.nrg.co.il (July 19, 2006); Chen Kotz-Bar, "You Can See the Launcher Throw Ten Rockets—And Then Explode It," *Maariv*, September 12, 2007; Yoav Limor and Alon Ben-David, "Fourth Place: Egoz," *Ynet*, www.ynet .co.il (January 27, 2008); Hanan Greenberg, " Now 'Egoz' Must Continue Its Operations," *Ynet*, www.ynet.co.il (July 21, 2006); Hanan Greenberg, "The Heroes of the Second Lebanon War," *Ynet*, www.ynet.co.il (April 22, 2007); Amiram Bareket and Amos Harel "Ground Operation Began After IDF Conquered a Village Without Intending To," *Haaretz*, August 29, 2006; Amos Harel, "'Egoz' Returns to Lebanon and Sustains First Casualties," *Haaretz*, July 23, 2006; Amos Harel, "Fifth Body Recovered from Battle at Marun A-Ras; IDF Testimonies: Flaws in Planning the Force's Operation," *Haaretz*, July 23, 2006.

9. Yossi Yehoshua, "To Tell the Truth, We Expected Much More Opposition from Hezbollah," *Yedioth Ahronoth*, August 2, 2006; Amir Rappaport, "The Operation in Baalbek—For Propaganda Only," *Maariv*, September 15, 2006; Yoni Shienfeld, "The Shayetet Men in a Battle in the Middle of Tyre," *MSN News*, http://news.msn.co.il (November 20, 2007).

10. "U.N. Envoy: Lebanon Facing Critical Test," *CNN News*, August 20, 2006;

"Israel's Raid in the Bekaa Valley," *BBC*, http://news.bbc.co.uk/2/hi/middle_ east/5268870.stm (August 20, 2006); "Officer Was Killed in a Commando Action in Baalbek," *Ynet*, www.ynet.co.il (August 19, 2006).

11. Yechiel Gutman, *A Storm in the GSS* (Tel Aviv: Yedioth Ahronot, 1995), 17; interview with R., former senior officer in Mossad, January 11, 2007.

12. Tani Goldstein, "Permitted for Publication: Hezbollah Rocket Falls on Refinery," *Ynet*, www.ynet.co.il (March 22, 2007); Frances Raday, "Israel Under Rocket Attack: A Profile of Displacement and Destruction in Israel, 12 July–15 August 2006," Jacob Blaustein Institute for the Advancement of Human Rights of the American Jewish Committee, www.ajc.org (accessed February 24, 2008); "Hizbollah Rockets Displace 330,000 Israelis," *Reuters*, July 30, 2006; Julian Borger, "Lebanon War Cost Israel $1.6bn," *Guardian*, August 15, 2006; Bill Varner and Maher Chmaytelli, "UN Wins Pledges of Soldiers to Join Force in Lebanon," Bloomberg News, August 8, 2006; Commission for the Investigation of the Campaign in Lebanon, 2006, Final Report (January 2008), 70.

CHAPTER TEN FIGHTING THE TERRORISM PLAGUE

1. Paul Wilkinson, *Terrorism and the Liberal State* (London: Macmillan, 1986), 125; Peter Chalk, "The Liberal Democratic Response to Terrorism," *Terrorism and Political Violence* 7, no. 4 (1995): 10–44; Peter Chalk, *West European Terrorism and Counter-Terrorism: The Evolving Dynamic* (London: Macmillan, 1996); Peter Chalk, "The Response to Terrorism as a Threat to Liberal Democracy," *Australian Journal of Politics and History* 44, no. 3 (1998): 373–388; Ronald D. Crelinsten, "Terrorism and Political Communication: The Relationship Between the Controller and the Controlled," in Paul Wilkinson and Alasdair M. Stewart, eds., *Contemporary Research on Terrorism* (Aberdeen: Aberdeen University Press, 1987), 3–23; Ronald D. Crelinsten, "Terrorism, Counter-Terrorism and Democracy: The Assessment of National Security Threats," *Terrorism and Political Violence* 1, no. 2 (1989): 242–269; Ronald D. Crelinsten, "The Discourse and Practice of Counter-terrorism in Liberal Democracies," *Australian Journal of Politics and History* 44, no. 1 (1998): 389–413.

2. Ken G. Robertson, "Intelligence, Terrorism, and Civil Liberties," in Wilkinson and Stewart, *Contemporary Research on Terrorism*, 549–569; Audrey Kurth Cronin, "How al-Qaida Ends: The Decline and Demise of Terrorist Groups," *International Security* 31, no. 1 (Summer 2006): 31; Herb Keinon, "Civil Rights vs. Security," *Jerusalem Post*, September 10, 1999.

3. Boaz Ganor, *The Counter-Terrorism Puzzle: A Guide for Decision Makers* (New Brunswick, N.J.: Transaction Publishers, 2005), 251–265; Bruce Hoffman, *Inside Terrorism* (New York: Columbia University Press, 2006), 1–41; Alex Peter Schmid, A.J. Jongman, and Michael Stohl, *Political Terrorism: A New Guide to Actors, Authors, Concepts, Data Bases, Theories, and Literature* (New Brunswick, N.J.: Transaction Publishers, 2005), 1–32.

4. "Rafi Tetarka," Dun's 100 Israel's Largest Enterprises: 2006, http://duns100
.dundb.co.il/2007/managersh/410h.asp; Arnon Regular, "Silwan Gang: High
Compartmentalization and Strong Discipline," *Haaretz*, October 2, 2002.

5. Amit Ben Aroya, Gil Tevet, Amiram Cohen, Zafrir Rinat, Tamara Traubman,
and Yossi Melman, "Terrorist Exploded in Tel Aviv—Nobody Killed; Claim:
Security Failure in Pi Glilot Bombing," *Haaretz*, May 24, 2002; Amit Ben
Aroya, Amiram Cohen, Zafrir Rinat, and Yossi Melman, "Pi Glilot Closed Af-
ter Tanker Explosion," *Haaretz*, May 24, 2002; Yossi Melman, "Spy vs. Spy,"
Haaretz, Saturday Supplement, February 17, 2005; Amir Rappaport, "The Battle
on 'Privileged': The Battle That Stirred Up Emotions of the Negev Residents,"
Maariv, October 19, 2005.

6. Amir Rappaport, "Underground Threat," *NRG*, www.nrg.co.il (August 20,
2004); "Four Years of Violent Conflict Between Israel and Palestinians—Inter-
mediate Summary," Israel Intelligence Heritage and Commemoration Center,
www.terrorism-info.org.il (accessed February 21, 2008).

7. "Terror Against Israel in 2006—Data and Trends" and "Attempt to 'Export'
Technological Knowledge to Jenin from Gaza in Order to Produce Bomb and
Rockets Foiled," Israel Intelligence Heritage and Commemoration Center,
www.terrorism-info.org.il (accessed February 21, 2008); "Hezbollah Attempts
to Kidnap Haven't Stopped," *Ynet*, www.ynet.co.il (July 12, 2006); Barak Ravid,
Doron Nahum, and Tali Yamin-Wolkovitch, "In Israel Fear: Palestinians Kidnapped Another Israeli," *NRG*, www.nrg.co.il (June 27, 2006); Ephrat Weiss
and Ali Waked, "Eliyahu Asheri Killed; His Body Found in Ramallah," *Ynet*,
www.ynet.co.il (June 29, 2006); Bruce Hoffman, *Inside Terrorism* (New York:
Columbia University Press, 2006), 268–269; "The Israel Security Agency's 2006
Report Asserts That Hamas Has Taken Over the Gaza Strip with the Support
of Hezbollah and Iran," International Institute for Counter-Terrorism, www.ict
.org.il/var/119/31122-Shabakreport_2006.pdf (accessed May 24, 2007).

8. Tani Goldstein, "Permitted for Publication: Hezbollah Rocket Falls on Refinery," *Ynet*, www.ynet.co.il (March 22, 2007).

9. Avi Issacharoff and Yoav Stern, "Israel Confirms Hezbollah Long-Range Missile Arsenal Restored," *Haaretz*, July 24, 2007; "Time: Hezbollah Totally Rehabilitated Its Powers," *Ynet*, www.ynet.co.il (November 25, 2006).

10. Reuven Erlich, *Hezbollah* (Tel Aviv: Israel Intelligence Heritage and Commem-
oration Center, 2003); "Financing and Encouraging Palestinian Terrorism by
Iran and Its Proxies," "Large Sums of Money Transferred by Saudi Arabia to the
Palestinians Are Used for Financing Terror Organizations and Terrorist Activi-
ties," "Ismail Hania Visit in Iran," and "Suicide Bombings During the Years of
Arab-Israeli Conflict," Israel Intelligence Heritage and Commemoration Cen-
ter, www.terrorism-info.org.il (accessed February 21, 2008); Daniel L. Byman,
"Should Hezbollah Be Next?" *Foreign Affairs* 82, no. 6 (November–December
2003): 54–66; Zeev Schiff, "Hezbollah Received Intelligence Information from
Syrian-Russian Eavesdropping Stations," *Haaretz*, October 3, 2006; Lior Ben-

David, "Terrorist Organizations Fighting Against Israel," Knesset Information Center, www.knesset.gov.il/mmm/data/pdf/m01048.pdf (accessed February 21, 2008); Yoav Limor, "Suddenly Shayetet Soldiers Came From Darkness," *NRG,* www.nrg.co.il (January 6, 2002); "Seizing of the Palestinian Weapons Ship Karine A," Israel Ministry of Foreign Affairs, www.mfa.gov.il (accessed February 21, 2008); Christopher M. Blanchard, "The Islamic Traditions of Wahhabism and Salafiya," CRS Report for Congress, www.fas.org/sgp/crs/misc/RS21695.pdf (accessed February 21, 2008); Alfred B. Prados and Christopher M. Blanchard, "Saudi Arabia: Terrorist Financing Issues," CRS Report for Congress, www.ndu.edu/library/docs/crs/crs_r132499_01mar05.pdf (accessed February 21, 2008); Graham F. Fuller, "Islamist Politics in Iraq After Saddam Hussein," United States Institute of Peace, www.usip.org/pubs/specialreports/sr108.pdf (accessed February 21, 2008).

11. Jason Burke, "Al Qaeda," *Foreign Policy* 141 (June 2004): 18–26; "Al-Qaeda Claims Tunisia Attack," *BBC,* http://news.bbc.co.uk/1/hi/world/middle_east/2061071 .stm (June 23, 2002); "Deadly Attack Keeps World on Alert," *Guardian,* September 4, 2002; "Istanbul Rocked by Double Bombing," *BBC,* http://news.bbc .co.uk/1/hi/world/europe/3222608.stm (November 20, 2003); "Kenya Terror Strikes Target Israelis," *BBC,* http://news.bbc.co.uk/2/hi/africa/2522207.stm (November 28, 2002); Dexter Filkins, "Kenyans Hunting for Clues; Bombing Toll Rises to 13," *New York Times,* November 30, 2002; "Terror Bombings Hit Taba and Ras a-Satan in Sinai," Israel Ministry of Foreign Affairs, www.mfa.gov .il (accessed February 21, 2008); "Three Rockets Hit Eilat and Aqaba Harbor," *Ynet,* www.ynet.co.il (August 19, 2005); "Seven Jailed for Turkey Bombings," *BBC,* http://news.bbc.co.uk/2/hi/europe/6370117.stm (February 17, 2007).

12. "Details of April 30, 2003 Tel Aviv Suicide Bombing," Israeli Ministry of Foreign Affairs, www.mfa.gov.il (June 3, 2003); William Langley and David Bamber, "Passports to Martyrdom," *Sunday Telegraph,* May 4, 2003; Greg Myre, "The Mideast Turmoil: Tel Aviv Bombing; Body from Sea Is Identified as Figure in Attack at Club," *New York Times,* May 20, 2003.

13. Interview with Y. H., former senior officer in the Mossad Political Action and Liaison Department, December 12, 2006; Robert S. Leiken, *Bearers of Global Jihad? Immigration and National Security After 9/11* (Yorba Linda, Calif.: The Nixon Center, 2004); Efraim Halevy, *Man in the Shadows: Inside the Middle East Crisis with a Man Who Led Mossad* (Tel Aviv: Matar, 2006), 14; Ehrlich, *Hezbollah.*

14. Ganor, *The Counter-Terrorism Puzzle,* 41–46.

15. Shaul Mishal and Avraham Sela, *The Hamas Wind: Violence and Coexistence* (Tel Aviv: Miskal, 2006), 216–217; Amos Harel and Avi Issacharoff, *The Seventh War* (Tel Aviv: Miskal, 2004), 153; "'Charity Coalition': Coalition of 50 Islamic Funds Around the World, As Organization Channeling Money for Hamas Civilian Infrastructure in West Bank and Gaza," and "Financing and Encouraging Terrorism By Iran and Hezbollah in 'Territories,'" Israel Intelligence Heritage

and Commemoration Center, www.terrorism-info.org.il (accessed February 21, 2008).

16. Kimbra L. T. Krueger, "The Destabilization of Republican Regimes: The Effects Of Terrorism on Democratic Societies," *Low Intensity Conflict and Law Enforcement* 5, no. 2 (Autumn 1996): 253–277; Peter Chalk, "The Response to Terrorism as a Threat to Liberal Democracy," 376; Leonard J. Weinberg and William J. Eubank, "Terrorism and Democracy: What Recent Events Disclose," *Terrorism and Political Violence* 10, no. 1 (Spring 1998): 108–118; Scott Atran, "A Failure of Imagination (Intelligence, WMDs, and 'Virtual Jihad')," *Studies in Conflict and Terrorism* 29, no. 3 (May 2006): 286–289; Bruce Berkowitz, "Intelligence for the Homeland," *SAIS Review* 24, no. 1 (Winter–Spring 2004): 1–6; Richard K. Betts, "The New Politics of Intelligence: Will Reforms Work This Time?" *Foreign Affairs* 83, no. 5 (May–June 2004): 4; Michael C. Jensen and William H. Meckling, "Theory of The Firm: Managerial Behaviour, Agency Costs and Ownership Structure," *Journal of Financial Economics* 3, no. 4 (October 1976): 306–350; Michael C. Jensen, "Organization Theory and Methodology," *Accounting Review* 57, no. 2 (April 1983): 319–339; Kathleen M. Eisenhardt, "Agency Theory: An Assessment and Review," *The Academy of Management Review* 14, no. 1 (January 1989): 57–74; Amy B. Zegart, "September 11 and the Adaptation Failure of U.S. Intelligence Agencies," *International Security* 29, no. 4 (Spring 2005): 108–111; Eugene Bardach, "How Do They Stack Up? The 9/11 Commission Report and the Management Literature," *International Public Management Journal* 8, no. 3 (2005): 352–353; Michael Herman, *Intelligence Power in Peace and War* (Cambridge: Cambridge University Press, 1996), 307, 317–320; Shlomo Gazit, *Between Warning and Surprise: On Shaping National Intelligence Assessment in Israel* (Tel Aviv: Jaffee Center for Strategic Studies, University of Tel Aviv, 2003), 17; Knesset Foreign Affairs and Security Committee, *Report on the Committee of Inquiry Into the Intelligence System in Light of the War in Iraq* (March 2004), A:38.

17. Aluf Ben, "Israel Signed on UN Convention Against Nuclear Terror," *Haaretz,* December 12, 2006; Shlomo Shapiro, "The Communication of Mutual Security: Frameworks for European-Mediterranean Intelligence Sharing," www.nato.int/acad/fellow/99–01/shpiro.pdf (accessed February 21, 2008); Michael Herman, "Sharing Secrets," *World Today* 57, no. 12 (December 2001): 10; Stéphane Lefebvre, "The Difficulties and Dilemmas of International Intelligence Cooperation," *International Journal of Intelligence and Counterintelligence* 16, no. 4 (October–December 2003): 527–542; Richard J. Aldrich, "Transatlantic Intelligence and Security Cooperation," *International Affairs* 80, no. 4 (July 2004): 731–753; Shlomo Shapiro, "Intelligence Services and Political Transformation in the Middle East," *International Journal of Intelligence and Counterintelligence* 17, no. 4 (December 2004): 575–600; Derek S. Reveron, "Old Allies, New Friends: Intelligence-Sharing in the War on Terror," *Orbis* 50, no. 3 (Summer 2006): 453–468.

18. Ofer Shelah and Yoav Limor, *Captives of Lebanon* (Tel Aviv: Miskal, 2007), 260; "06 September 2007 Airstrike," Global Security Web site, www.globalsecurity .org/military/world/war/070906-airstrike.htm (accessed February 21, 2008); Uzi Mahnaimi, Sarah Baxter and Michael Sheridan, "Snatched: Israeli Commandos 'Nuclear' Raid," *Sunday Times,* September 23, 2007; David Golani, "Israeli Army Confirms Air Strike Over Syrian Nuclear Facilities in September 2007," *Israel Times,* October 2, 2007; Uzi Mahnaimi, Sarah Baxter, and Michael Sheridan, "Israelis 'Blew Apart Syrian Nuclear Cache,'" *Sunday Times,* September 16, 2007; Barry Rubin, "The Triumph of the 'Old Middle East,'" *Middle East Review of International Affairs,* http://meria.idc.ac.il/journal/2002/issue2/jv6n2a6.html (accessed February 21, 2008); Reuven Paz, "Middle East Islamism in the European Arena," *Middle East Review of International Affairs,* http://meria.idc.ac.il/ journal/2002/issue3/paz.pdf (accessed February 21, 2008); Daniel Benjamin, "Two Years After 9/11: A Balance Sheet," United States Institute of Peace, www .usip.org/pubs/specialreports/sr111.pdf (accessed February 21, 2008).

███████████

ABU IYAD (Salah Khalaf) (1934–1991). One of the five founders of the Fatah and for many years the organization internal security chief. He was third in the organization hierarchy.

ABU NIDAL (Sabri al-Banna) (1937–2002). Palestinian nationalist. Abu Nidal joined the Palestine Liberation Organization (PLO) in 1957 and left it in 1974 to establish Al Fatah, also called the Abu Nidal Organization, through which he participated in terrorist operations against Israel during the late 1970s and early 1980s. He was assassinated in Beirut in 2002, at the orders, some have speculated, of Iraqi leader Saddam Hussein.

AIR SQUADRON 200. Israeli Air Force fleet of five types of unmanned aerial vehicles (UAVs). These are the Searcher, a visual-intelligence UAV in service from 1992; Searcher 2, also used for guiding artillery; Skylark, used mainly in order to detect infiltration into Israel from the Mediterranean Sea; Hermes 450, an advanced UAV; and Heron, the most advanced UAV in service.

AL-AQSA INTIFADA (Second Intifada). The Al-Aqsa intifada is the name given by Palestinians to the violent series of events that erupted in the wake of Ariel Sharon's visit to the Temple Mount on September 28, 2000. It was distinguished mainly by suicide attacks against urban centers in Israel and guerrilla warfare against Israeli Defense Forces (IDF) in the occupied territories and lasted until 2005.

AL-FATAH. Palestinian nationalist movement and terrorist group established in Cairo in 1957. The five students who created the Fatah were Yasser Arafat, Khalil Al-Wazir (Abu-Jihad), Salaha Khalaf (Abu-Iyad), Khalid Al-Hassan, and Farouq Kaddoumi. They were inspired by Egyptian President Jamal Abdel Nasser's nationalization of the Suez Canal and by the FLN underground's struggle for Algeria's independence. The leader of the organization, Arafat, became the symbol of the Palestinian struggle against Israel, and the organization became the largest and most important of all Palestinian terrorist groups.

AL-SAIQA. Terrorist group. Al-Saiqa, which operated under Syrian sponsorship, was established in 1966. It gradually withered away after its leader, Zuheir Muhsein, was killed in 1979.

AMAL. Shiite organization and party, established formally in 1974. During the civil war in Lebanon Amal fought against Christian forces and later engaged in battles against Palestinian forces. Shortly after the Israeli invasion of southern Lebanon, the organization started to initiate attacks against the IDF. Today Amal is one of the two political movements in Lebanon representing the Shiite population.

AMAN. IDF Intelligence Branch, one of the three main Israeli intelligence organizations. Aman is the largest and most resource-intensive of the intelligence organizations in Israel. The most highly advanced eavesdropping and observation equipment are at its disposal. With these devices, it is able to maintain a consistent and close watch of military maneuvering and deployment, listen in on encrypted state radio frequencies, and accordingly conduct evaluations of enemy intentions.

ARAB LIBERATION FRONT. Palestinian terrorist organization established by the Iraqi Baath regime in opposition to the pro-Syrian Al-Saiqa organization. The Arab Liberation Front was headed by Dr. Abed al-Wahab al-Killani; its members were mainly from Iraq, Jordan, and Lebanon, and only a few were Palestinians.

ARAFAT, YASSER (1929–2004). Palestinian leader. Born in Cairo to Palestinian parents, he founded the first Palestine Liberation Organization (PLO) cell and soon become the leader and symbol of the Palestinian struggle against Israel. In 1993, he signed the Oslo Accords and become the chairman of the Palestinian National Authority.

ARENS, MOISHE (b. 1925). Israeli politician affiliated with the right-wing Likud Party. Arens served as a member of the Knesset in 1973–1992 and 1999–2003 and was minister of defense in 1983–1984, 1990–1992, and 1999.

ARMY OF ISLAM. Militia offshoot of Hamas. The group is based in the Gaza Strip and consists mainly of members of the Darmush clan. The Army of Islam became known in June 2006 after some of its members were involved in the kidnapping of an Israeli soldier, Gilad Shalit.

ASHURA. Shiite holiday held in remembrance of the military defeat and massacre of Hussein Bin Ali and Hassan Ibn Ali, sons of Ali and grandsons of the Prophet Muhammad, in Karbala by the sons of Muawiyah. During the course of the holiday, Shiite Moslems physically beat themselves in commemoration of the battle.

AVIGUR, SHAUL (1899–1979). Israeli political leader. Born in Poland, Avigur immigrated to Israel when he was twelve years old. He became a commander in the Haganah and was one of the founders of its intelligence branch, called Shai.

AYALON, AMI (b. 1945). Commander of the Israel Navy (1992–1995) and the head of the GSS (1996–2000). After his retirement from the military, he joined the Labor Party.

BAATH. Political movement popular in the Arab world during the 1960s and 1970s. It adheres to an ideology that blends socialist elements with secular and pan-Arabic nationalist elements. A Baathist party ruled in Iraq until 2003, and another is still in power in Syria.

BARAK, EHUD (b. 1942). Former chief commander of Sayeret Matkal (1971–1973), IDF chief of staff, and prime minister (1999–2001).

BEERI, ISSER (1901–1958). Head of the Shai, appointed in 1948 after the establishment of the IDF. He was deposed in 1949 after it was discovered that he had ordered the killing of an Arab informant in cold blood.

BEN GAL, AVIGDOR (Yanush) (b. 1936). Commander of the IDF Northern Command (1977–1981).

BLACK SEPTEMBER. Offshoot of Fatah, established in the early 1970s. It was responsible for several high-profile terrorist actions against Israeli targets, such as the attack on the Israeli delegation in the 1972 Olympic Games in Munich.

DAGAN, MEIR (b. 1945). Former IDF general and current head of Mossad.

DAR, AVRAHAM (b. 1919). Mossad operative who was sent to Egypt in 1951 in order to establish a network of informants based on the local Jewish community. The network was exposed in July 1954 after activists were caught while attempting to plant a bomb in a movie theater in Alexandria.

DAYAN, MOSHE (1915–1981). IDF chief of staff (1953–1958) and minister of defense (1967–1973). After ending his military career, he joined the Labor Party.

DAYAN, UZI (b. 1948). Commander of Sayeret Matkal (1979–1982) and IDF deputy chief of staff (1998–1999).

DEMOCRATIC FRONT FOR THE LIBERATION OF PALESTINE (DFLP). Marxist nationalist organization established in 1969 by Nayef Hawatmeh after he and some of his comrades seceded from the PFLP.

DICHTER, AVI (b. 1952), Head of the GSS (2000–2005). After his retirement, he joined the Kadima Party and currently serves as Israel's minister of internal security.

DUVDEVAN. *Mistaarvim* unit of the IDF Central Command, originally established in 1986 as a counterterrorist force on the West Bank. During its existence the unit received much praise, but it was also heavily criticized after a number of its soldiers were killed in various accidents.

EGOZ. IDF unit formed in 1995, specializing in counterguerilla warfare and microwarfare. The different terrain conditions in Lebanon and the nature of the operations carried out by Hezbollah—which, unlike Palestinian organizations, principally attacked military targets while also displaying formidable guerilla skills—dictated the type of training the unit's soldiers received. Egoz soldiers were principally instructed in camouflage, setting up ambushes, and microwarfare. After the IDF withdrawal from Lebanon in May 2000, the goals of Egoz were accordingly altered and the unit was amalgamated into the IDF counterterrorism deployment in the West Bank and Gaza Strip.

EITAN, RAFAEL (1929–2004). IDF chief of staff (1978–1983). After retiring, he established the right-wing Tzomet Party.

EITAN, RAFI (b. 1926). One of the founders of the Israeli intelligence community. He served in Aman, the GSS, and Mossad. In the latter he served as chief of the Operations Division. He was appointed head of Lakam in 1981 and deposed from his position in 1985 after his role in the Jonathan Pollard affair was discovered. In 2006 he was elected to the Knesset as the head of the Pensioner Party; currently he serves as the minister of pensioner affairs.

FATAHLAND. Israeli slang for southern Lebanon.

FIELD INTELLIGENCE CORPS. Regional battalions in the Israeli Defense Forces whose function is to collect tactical intelligence. It also includes radar units.

FIRST INTIFADA. Intifada, meaning "shaking off dirt" or "uprising" in Arabic, is the name given by Palestinians to the series of violent events that broke out in December 1987 and lasted until 1993, when the Oslo Accords were signed. This intifada was initially marked by Palestinian popular protests, which included stone throwing, mass demonstrations and rallies, and roadblocks, but quickly escalated into terrorism and guerrilla warfare.

FIRST LEBANON WAR. Military confrontation between Israel and Palestinian terrorist organizations, as well as Syria, that began on June 4, 1982, with the IDF invasion of southern Lebanon. During the war, Israeli forces reached the edge of Beirut, and Palestinian terrorist groups were forced to leave Lebanon. The war ended in June 1985 after the IDF withdrew and redeployed in the Security Zone.

GEMAYEL, BASHIR (1947–1982). Prominent Lebanese Maronite Christian leader in the late 1970s and early 1980s. On August 1982 was appointed as the president of Lebanon with the backing of Israel, but he was assassinated just a few weeks afterward.

GENERAL STAFF NEGOTIATING TEAM. IDF unit responsible for all negotiations in hostage-taking situations. The unit is headed by an officer at the rank of lieutenant general and is composed mainly of civilian specialists in psychology, negotiations, and Arab affairs.

GILLON, CARMI (b. 1950). Israeli intelligence officer appointed to head the GSS in March 1995. He resigned in February 1996 after the Shamgar Commission, which was appointed to inquire into the circumstances that led to the assassination of Prime Minister Yitzhak Rabin, found Gillon partly responsible for the failure in securing him.

GSS. *See* Shabak.

GUR, MORDECHAI "MOTTA" (1930–1995). IDF chief of staff (1974–1978). He was a minister and member of the Knesset, representing the Labor Party.

GURIEL, BORIS (1903–1983). Head of the Political Department of the Haganah and of the Political Department in the Ministry of Foreign Affairs. He was removed from office in 1951 after the creation of Mossad.

HABASH, GEORGE (1925–2008). Founder of the Popular Front for the Liberation of Palestine. Habash studied medicine in Beirut from 1944 to 1951. In the early 1950s he was active in the Youth of Vengeance, a group that advocated violent struggle against Israel according to the pan-Arabist Nasserite ideology. After the war of 1967, he turned leftward in his political thinking, established the PFLP in December 1967, and became its secretary-general.

HAGANAH. The largest and most central military Jewish organization in Palestine at the time of the British Mandate (1917–1948), Haganah ("the Defense") was established in 1920 as a nationwide organization to provide protection for the Jewish population.

HAMAS. Palestinian movement and terrorist group established formally in 1987. Hamas adheres to a combination of radical Islamist and nationalistic ideologies. In the mid-1990s, it was the first Palestinian group to use suicide attacks against Israeli targets. Since 2006, it has formed the majority party of the Palestinian National Authority.

HAMULA. In Arabic societies, an expanded family or clan consisting of hundreds or several thousands of members. For hundreds of years, it has been the single most important Palestinian social-political unit. Ottoman Empire rulers (who governed in Palestine until 1917), British Mandate officials, and prominent figures of the Jewish Yishuv all tried to identify *hamula* leaders and approach them when problems arose. Negotiation with these leaders promised immediate results.

HANDLERS. The vanguard of the human intelligence–gathering arm of the GSS. Handlers are responsible for activating collaborators and collecting real-time information in a particular geographical sector.

HAREL, ISSER (1912–2003). Israeli intelligence officer. Harel joined the Shai in 1944 and was later appointed head of the organization's Internal Department. In 1948 he was appointed head of the Shin Bet, and in 1952 he became head of Mossad. For nine years (1953–1962) he was the commissioner (high commander) of the Israeli intelligence community.

HARMELIN, YOSSEF (1922–1994). Head of the GSS (1964–1974, 1986–1988).

HEFETZ, ASSAF (b. 1944). Chief of the Israeli police (1994–1997). He joined the Border Police in 1975 and afterward was appointed chief of the Yamam.

HERZOG, CHAIM (1918–1997). Sixth president of the State of Israel. He was a former IDF general, head of Aman (1962–1965) and Israeli ambassador to the UN (1975–1979).

HOFI, YITZHAK (b. 1927). Former IDF general and head of Mossad (1974–1982).

HUMINT. Human intelligence, that is, intelligence based on human sources, as distinct from visual and signal intelligence. Interrogators and field agents are essential HUMINT workers.

HUSSEINI, HAJ AMIN AL- (1895–1974). Leader of the Palestinian National Movement until 1949. In 1921, he was appointed mufti of Jerusalem, the city's highest-ranking religious ruler, and in 1922 he became the head of the Muslim High Council of Palestine, which administered Muslim life in Palestine. He rejected any political compromise with the Jewish community.

IRANIAN REVOLUTIONARY GUARD. Special military forces established in Iran in 1979 to protect and expand the foundations of the Islamic Revolution. They are subordinated to the Iranian Defense Ministry, and their function is also to protect the regime and its leaders from any type of threat.

KAHAN COMMISSION. Investigative body established to study the massacre at the Sabra and Shatila refugee camps in 1982. Yitzhak Kahan, the president of the Israeli Supreme Court, headed the commission. One of its conclusions was that Ariel Sharon was no longer suitable to be Israel's defense minister because he refused to recognize the danger of a potential massacre of Palestinians at the hands of Lebanese Maronite Christians.

KHAMENEI, ALI (b. 1939). President of Iran (1982–1989) and Iran's supreme religious leader, widely recognized as one of the most prolific Islamic religious scholars.

KIDON. Operational unit of Mossad responsible for the organization's assassination operations (mostly of leaders of Palestinian terrorist groups), among other tasks. Each one of the unit's teams consists of between twelve and sixteen members, only two of whom are in charge of carrying out the elimination itself. The rest of the team includes security people whose role is to ensure the assassin's getaway and safety after completing his or her assignment, logistics operatives who are responsible for contact with the outside world (renting cars and hotel rooms or preparing a hideout apartment, for example), and a surveillance cell, which generally consists of the greatest number of operatives. The last are responsible for locating the assassination target, monitoring his or her daily routine, and establishing the place and time most opportune for carrying out the mission.

LEBANESE LIAISON UNIT. IDF unit responsible for providing military assistance to the South Lebanon Army and civilian aid to the population of southern Lebanon.

LEVINE, AMIRAM (b. 1946). Former commander of Sayeret Matkal and the IDF Northern Command (1994–1998). Between 1998 and 2001, he served as the deputy head of Mossad.

MAGNA CARTA. Israeli interagency agreement intended to solve the problem of duplication in the field of intelligence gathering on Palestinians and in Lebanon.

MAKLEF, MORDECHAI (1920–1978). IDF chief of staff (1952–1953).

MAPAI PARTY. Israeli political group. Mapai is an acronym of the Hebrew phrase meaning "Party of the Laborers of the Land of Israel." A Zionist and socialist party, it was established in 1930 through a union of the Achdut Ha'avoda and Hapoel Hatza'ir parties. Mapai was the central pillar of the coalition governments, and the main party in the Israeli political system until 1977. Among its leaders were David Ben-Gurion, Levi Eshkol, and Yitzhak Rabin.

MEIR, GOLDA (1898–1978). Israeli prime minister (1969–1974). For many years she was one of the leaders of the Israeli Labor Party.

MILITARY INTERVENTION UNIT. In a hostage-rescue situation, a military intervention unit is responsible for "freezing" the situation until the takeover unit arrives. When the lives of hostages are in danger, the intervention unit may carry out the rescue operation.

MISTAARVIM. Made up of two Hebrew words meaning "to assault" and "to blend in" or "become Arab," *mistaaravim* is the name given to military and police units whose soldiers use their good command of the Palestinian dialect and Middle Eastern appearance in order to assimilate into the Arab population. After going undercover, they gather information and engage in special operations.

MOFAZ, SHAUL (b. 1948). IDF chief of staff (1998–2002). Immediately after ending his military carrier, he joined the Likud Party and became minister of defense (2003–2006). Today he is affiliated with the Kadima Party and serves as the minister of transportation.

MORDECHAI, YITZHAK (b. 1944). Israeli general, now retired; commander of the IDF Northern Command (1991–1994) and minister of defense (1996–1999).

MOSSAD (Institute for Intelligence and Special Operations). One of the three main Israeli intelligence organizations. Mossad's activities are conducted mostly outside of Israeli territory. Its main role is to gather civilian, political, and military intelligence and to engage in clandestine operations outside Israel. In the last decade, it has also devoted extensive efforts to collecting information on the subject of nonconventional weaponry.

NETANYAHU, JONATHAN (Yoni) (1946–1976). Chief commander of Sayeret Matkal from 1975–1976. During the Entebbe rescue operation he was severely injured and died shortly afterward.

NEVIOT. Mossad branch that specializes in wiretapping.

NILI. Jewish underground movement operated in Palestine and assisted the British military forces during World War I, mainly by providing intelligence on the status of the Ottoman Army.

PALESTINIAN ISLAMIC JIHAD (PIJ). Palestinian terrorist group formed during the late 1970s in the Gaza Strip. It adheres to a combination of radical Islamist and nationalist ideologies. It joined Hamas during the mid-1990s in the initiation of suicide attacks against Israeli targets and is considered by many to be the most militant of all Palestinian groups.

PALESTINE LIBERATION FRONT. Palestinian nationalist and terrorist organization established in 1977. The organization operated with the support of Saddam Hussein's regime in Iraq and conducted a number of terrorist attacks, the most famous of which was the hijacking of the *Achille Lauro*, an Italian cruise ship, in 1985. U.S. forces captured its leader, Abu Abbas, during the 2003 invasion of Iraq. In the course of the Al-Aqsa intifada, it committed several acts of terrorism. The organization now has a limited presence in the West Bank.

PALMACH. The semiregular military forces of the Haganah in Palestine from 1941 to 1948. Palmach (the Hebrew acronym for Plugot Mahatz, "striking forces") was established on May 15, 1941, to establish a military body that would protect the population in the event that the Germans invaded the country. As a semiregular militia, Palmach had a unique military culture that put an emphasis on socialist values and had a less formal hierarchy and discipline than conventional military forces. In 1948, with the establishment of the Israeli army, Prime Minister David Ben-Gurion ordered Palmach to disband.

PELED, YOSSI (b. 1941). Israeli general (now retired) and commander of the IDF Northern Command from 1986 to 1991.

PERES, SHIMON (b. 1923). Israeli statesman and politician, until recently affiliated with the Labor Party. Peres served as Israeli prime minister twice (1984–1986, 1995–1996) and was elected president in 2007.

PERI, YAAKOV (b. 1944). Head of the GSS between 1988 and 1995.

POPULAR FRONT FOR THE LIBERATION OF PALESTINE (PFLP). Palestinian terrorist group established in 1967 in Beirut by Dr. George Habash. It adheres to a combination of nationalist and Marxist ideologies. Its golden era was the 1970s, when it focused on hostage-taking operations.

POPULAR FRONT FOR THE LIBERATION OF PALESTINE-GENERAL COMMAND (PFLP-GC). Palestinian terrorist group established by Ahmed Jibril and his supporters in 1968 after splitting off from the PFLP. The group relied over the years on the massive help of the Syrian regime, which allows it to continue to commit terrorist acts to this day. Throughout the years, the PFLP-GC opposed any kind of peace negotiations with Israel and harshly criticized Fatah on the matter of the peace process.

POPULAR RESISTANCE COMMITTEES. Islamic militia established after the outbreak of the Al-Aqsa Intifada. It operates in the Rafah area of the Gaza Strip. This militia is composed of members of the Abu Samhadana *hamula* (clan), the strongest in Rafah.

QAWUQJI, FAWZI AL- (1890–1976). Syrian army officer who participated in the Syrian rebellion against the French in 1932. In 1948 he was appointed commander of the Arab Salvation Army.

RON, ALIK (b. 1957). Commander of Yamam from 1988 to 1992, former commander of Shaldag, and head of the Israeli Police Northern Command between from 1997 to 2001.

SAYERET GIVATI. Reconnaissance unit of the Givati Brigade. Its main mission is gathering tactical intelligence. Deployed in the Southern Command, it concentrates most of its activities on the Gaza Strip.

SAYERET GOLANI. Reconnaissance unit of the Golani Brigade. Its main mission is gathering tactical intelligence. Established in 1948, it is the only reconnaissance unit whose soldiers receive extensive counterterrorist training, since it is also considered an intervention unit in the Northern Command.

SAYERET MAGLAN. IDF commando unit established in the mid-1980s as an elite antitank force. Soldiers in this unit specialize in using sophisticated rockets against enemy armored corps. In the second half of the 1990s, Maglan soldiers also began to operate in the capacity of an elite antiterrorist unit in southern Lebanon, and later additionally fought against Palestinians during the Al-Aqsa intifada.

SAYERET MATKAL. The General Staff Reconnaissance Unit, an IDF special unit subordinated to Aman. Although the unit's main function is to infiltrate territories of neighboring countries in order to gather intelligence, it has also been involved in numerous counterterrorism operations.

SAYERET NAHAL. Reconnaissance unit of the Nahal Brigade. Its main mission is gathering tactical intelligence by means of reconnaissance missions. Deployed in the Central Command, it concentrates on fighting terrorist groups in the West Bank.

SAYERET PARATROOPERS. Reconnaissance unit of the Paratroopers Brigade. Its main mission is gathering tactical intelligence. It is considered one of the top Israeli commando units and until the 1970s, along with the Sayeret Matkal, the top antiterrorist unit.

SAYERET SHALDAG. Commando unit of the Israel Air Force. Established in 1974, its main mission is to mark ground targets for aircraft by means of position-pinpointing equipment. However, over the years the unit also functioned as an antiterrorist commando unit, and its soldiers participated in various operations in the West Bank during the Al-Aqsa intifada.

SAYERET YAEL. Special unit of the IDF Combat Engineering Corps. It specializes in explosives, engineering reconnaissance, crossing water obstacles, and breaching buildings. It was formed after the Israeli army's failure to break into the house where Hamas terrorists held kidnapped IDF soldier Nachshon Wachsman in 1994.

SECOND LEBANON WAR. Military confrontation between Israel and Hezbollah that erupted after the latter attacked an IDF patrol and kidnapped two Israeli soldiers near the Israel-Lebanon border on July 12, 2006. The Israeli response included the air bombardment of Hezbollah bases all over Lebanon including Beirut, as well as ground attacks. Hezbollah fighters fired approximately 3,900 rockets on northern Israel during the war. Hostilities ended on August 14, 2006, after the UN Security Council adopted resolution 1701 declaring that its peacekeeping force in southern Lebanon would be expanded.

SECURITY ZONE. Area in southern Lebanon under the control of Israel and the South Lebanon Army in the years 1985–2000. This strip of land was established as a security zone after the redeployment of IDF forces in 1985 to southern Lebanon as the last step of the First Lebanon War. The area borders were identified by their colors: The southern border with Israel was known as the Purple Line, and its northern border in Lebanon was called the Red Line.

SEPARATION FENCE. Barrier built between Israel and the Palestinian territories. Construction commenced in 2002 and continues to this day. The fence is equipped with surveillance cameras and is guarded by units of the Border Police. Even though the fence is widely considered a success by Israelis, it has been the object of much criticism by the international community, which argues that it harms the Palestinian citizens' right of freedom of movement.

SHABAK. Known also as the Shin Bet until the late 1960s, Shabak (a Hebrew acronym for the General Security Service [GSS]) is one of the three main Israeli intelligence organizations. It specializes in gathering intelligence in Israel and the occupied territories about elements attempting to subvert state institutions or harm its citizens through acts of terrorism.

SHAI. Intelligence branch of the Haganah.

SHALOM, AVRAHAM (b. 1928). Former head of the GSS who retired after his involvement in the Bus 300 affair was revealed.

SHAYETET 13 (Flotilla 13). Commando unit of the Israeli Navy, established in 1949. It is activated primarily in special marine operations, which include infiltration into enemy area from the sea. During the Al-Aqsa intifada, it participated in various operations in the West Bank.

SHILOAH, REUVEN (1909–1959). Israeli intelligence pioneer. Before the establishment of the State of Israel, he served in the Shai and was one of the organization's more successful operatives. After 1948, he became Prime Minister David Ben-Gurion's advisor for intelligence affairs and initiated several structural reforms in the Israeli intelligence community. He founded Mossad and headed it organization from 1949 to 1952.

SHIMSHON UNIT. IDF Southern Command *mistaaravim* unit that operated in Gaza between 1988 and 1994. The unit was formed and designed to use *mistaaravim* tactics when fighting terrorists in the first intifada, and it concentrated on the arrests of suspects of various terrorist activities. During the six years of its existence it achieved significant success. However, the unit sometimes employed highly controversial methods, such as unwarranted shooting, which marred its reputation and for which a number of unit commanders were put on trial.

SHOMRON, DAN (1937–2008). IDF chief of staff (1987–1991).

SIGINT. Signal intelligence, based on the detection of electronic signals (telephone calls, fax transmissions, email, and the like).

SILWAN CELL. Terrorist network affiliated with Hamas that operated in 2001 and 2002. Members of the group were Palestinians from East Jerusalem as well as Israeli citizens. They used their freedom of movement to commit two suicide attacks and five other bombings.

SOUTH LEBANON ARMY (SLA). Militia established under Israeli auspices in the late 1970s. It was dismantled after the withdrawal of the IDF from Lebanon in 2000. In the beginning, it included mainly Druze and Christian Lebanese from the Major Haddad militia. After the Israeli invasion of Lebanon, the SLA expanded its manpower and the Shiites became the largest group of soldiers. The SLA had two chief commanders: Major Saad Haddad from its founding until 1984, and Antoine Lahad between the years 1984 and 2000.

SPECIAL DUTIES OFFICERS. Aman HUMINT officers, trained either as handlers of agents or as interrogators.

STAGE PLAN. Resolution adopted at the twelfth session of the Palestine National Council on June 8, 1974. The program stated that Palestinians agreed to settle in any part of Palestine that Israel relinquished and would struggle to liberate the rest of the occupied territories in stages, either peacefully or by military means. The resolution also affirmed that Palestinians would not tolerate any Arab country's control of Palestinian territories and would strive to create an independent state.

SYRIAN SOCIAL NATIONALIST PARTY (SSNP). Lebanese political party established in 1932. The SSNP ideology revolves around the principle of a "Greater Syria," which is to include Syria, Lebanon, various areas of Turkey, Israel, and other countries. The party participated in the Lebanese civil war and engaged in terrorist activities against Israeli forces when the IDF invaded Lebanon.

TACTICAL INTELLIGENCE. Intelligence required for planning and conducting tactical operations.

TAKEOVER UNITS. In hostage-taking situations, a detachment whose tasks are to overcome terrorists and rescue hostages. Israel currently employs three takeover units: Sayeret Matkal, Yamam, and Shayetet 13.

TANZIM. Palestinian terrorist organization affiliated with Fatah. Marwan Barghouti, who headed the organization until his arrest in 2002, established Tanzim in 1994. From the beginning of the Al-Aqsa Intifada, Tanzim joined in the fighting against Israel, and its members committed numerous acts of terrorism, including suicide bombings.

UNJT 154. Aman unit established in 1948 as Intelligence Service 10. It dealt with the activation of agents outside the borders of Israel. During the years 1963–1964, the unit was disbanded and its functions were delegated to Mossad at the order of Meir Amit, who headed both agencies at the same time.

UNIT 504. The HUMINT unit of Israeli military intelligence. Most of its members are officers who serve in the (salaried) standing army. Intelligence gathering is performed mostly by means of recruiting collaborators in the border areas. In the past, members of Unit 504 would extend their operations to the four countries that border Israel: Syria, Lebanon, Jordan, and Egypt. However, over the years, the unit—now known as Unit 6154—became increasingly specific to the Lebanon area.

UNIT 8200. Israeli counterpart to the American National Security Agency (NSA), subordinated to Aman. It was previously known as Unit 848.

UNIT 9900. Aman unit that collects visual intelligence (VISINT) by means of satellites. Currently, three Israeli satellites are active: Ofeq 5, a military satellite that carries advanced photographic equipment; Eros 1, a commercial satellite that can detect objects smaller than six feet; and Eros 2, also a commercial satellite.

VARASH. Intelligence council whose name is the acronym of the Hebrew phrase meaning Secret Services Heads Committee. It consists of the heads of Mossad, Aman,

GSS, and the military secretary of the government. Sometimes it also includes representatives from the National Security Council and the Ministry of Foreign Affairs. It meets at least once a month in order to coordinate among the different intelligence organizations.

VISINT. Visual intelligence, based on the gathering of visual data by satellites, pilotless aircraft (UAVs), and advanced photographing equipment.

WAHHABISM. Islamic reformist movement that emerged some two hundred years ago with the aim of ridding Islamic societies of cultural practices and interpretations that had been acquired over the centuries. Most Wahhabists live in Saudi Arabia.

WAR OF 1967 (Six-Day War). Military confrontation between Israel and Jordan, Syria, and Egypt. It broke out on June 5, 1967, with a surprise Israel Air Force attack on Syrian and Egyptian military airports. During the war, which lasted six days, Israel conquered the Sinai Peninsula (including the Gaza Strip), the West Bank, and the Golan Heights.

WEIZMANN, CHAIM (1874–1952). President of the World Zionist Organization (1920–1929, 1935–1946) and first president of the State of Israel (1948–1952).

YARIV, AHARON (1920–1994). Former general in the IDF and head of Aman between 1964 and 1973. After his retirement, he joined the Labor Party.

YATOM, DANI (b. 1945). IDF general and head of Mossad (1996–1998) after his retirement from the military. Today he is a member of the Knesset representing the Labor Party.

X COMMITTEE. Israeli government committee responsible for authorizing targets for assassination. The foreign media coined its name. The committee was established in 1972 and consisted of Prime Minister Golda Meir, Minister of Defense Moshe Dayan, Foreign Minister Abba Evan, Minister of Education Yigal Allon, and Minister Without Portfolio Israel Galili. During its meetings, Mossad head Zvi Zamir would present the evidence incriminating the terrorist activist marked for assassination, and members of the commission would decide whether to approve it.

ZAMIR, ZVI. (b. 1925). Former IDF general and head of Mossad from 1978 to 1982.

SOURCES

Alexander, Yonah. *Palestinian Secular Terrorism: Profiles of Fatah, Popular Front for the Liberation of Palestine, Popular Front for the Liberation of Palestine-General Command, and the Democratic Front for the Liberation of Palestine*. Ardsley, N.Y.: Transnational Publishers, 2003.

Anti-Defamation League. "Democratic Front for the Liberation of Palestine." www.adl.org.

Argaman, Yosef. *It Was Top Secret*. Tel Aviv: Ministry of Defense, 1990.

——. *Shadows War*. Tel Aviv: Ministry of Defense, 2007.

Assenhaim, Omri. "Shimshon's Choice." *NRG*, www.nrg.co.il.

Asser, Martin. "Ahmed Jibril and the PFLP-GC." *BBC,* http://news.bbc.co.uk.

Baumgarten, Helga. "The Three Faces/Phases of Palestinian Nationalism, 1948–2005." *Journal of Palestine Studies* 34, no. 4 (Summer 2005): 32.

Bergman, Ronen. "'Keshet' Unit in Mossad Provides Electronics and Logistics." *Haaretz,* November 12, 1998.

Bronner, Ethan. "In Mideast, A Renewal of Terror." *Boston Globe,* November 24, 1996.

Buhbut, Amir. "Fighting in the [West] Bank, Looking Up North." *NRG*, www.nrg.co.il.

Commission of Inquiry Into the Events at the Refugee Camps in Beirut. *Final Report.* Jerusalem: State of Israel, 1983.

Dinor, Ben-Zion, ed. *The Book of Hagana History.* Tel Aviv: Maarahot, 1964.

Eldar, Mike. *Flotilla 13: The Story of Israel's Naval Commandos.* Tel Aviv: Maariv, 1993.

Eshel, David. "The Israel–Lebanon Border Enigma." *IBRU Boundary and Security Bulletin* (Winter 2000–2001): 72–83.

Farsoun, Samith K., and Christina F. Zacharia. *Palestine and the Palestinians.* Boulder, Colo.: Westview Press, 1997.

Federation of American Scientists. "AMAN—Military Intelligence," "Iranian Revolutionary Guard Corps," "The Islamic Traditions of Wahhabism and Salafiyya." www.fas.org.

Frisch, Felix. "Bomb Unit." *NRG*, www.nrg.co.il.

Gelber, Yoav. *Growing a Fleur-de-Lis: The Intelligence Services of the Jewish Yishuv in Palestine 1918–1947.* Tel Aviv: Ministry of Defense, 1992.

Gillon, Carmi. *Shin-Beth Between the Schisms.* Tel Aviv: Lemiskal, 2000.

Granot, Oded. "Intelligence Corps." In *IDF and Its Corps: Encyclopedia of Army and Security*, ed. A. Kfir and Y. Erez, 5:22–23. Tel Aviv: Revivim, 1981.

Greenberg, Hanan, and Ali Waked. "Who Are You, Jamal Abu Samhadana?" *Ynet*, www.ynet.co.il.

Haber, Eitan, and Michael Bar-Zohar. *The Quest for the Red Prince.* London: Weidenfeld and Nicolson, 1983.

Halamish, Yehoshua, and Eliezer Rotenshtreich. "Iraq Behind a Terrorist Organization," *Yedioth Ahronoth*, April 8, 1980.

Harel, Amos. "Only for Those Who Are Serious!" *Haaretz*, May 19, 2006.

——. "'Shaldag' Unit—New Home for Generals." *Haaretz*, July 18, 2003.

——. "Shayetet Commander Price of Choice." *Haaretz*, July 7, 2004.

Harel, Amos, and Amir Barakat. "The Operation Began After IDF Forces Unintentionally Conquered the Village." *Haaretz*, August 29, 2006.

Hunter, Thomas B. "Israeli Counterterrorism and Hostage Rescue." *Journal of Counterterrorism & Security International* 6, no. 4 (Summer 2000).

Inquiry Commission Into the Military Campaign Held in Lebanon in Summer 2006. *Full Report.* Jerusalem: State of Israel, 2008.

"Intifada Al-Aqsa." *MSN*, http://news.msn.co.il.

Israel State Comptroller. *Critique Report of Israel's Security Fence.* Jerusalem: State Comptroller Office and Ombudsman Office, 2002.

Israeli Defense Forces. "Field Intelligence Corps." www1.idf.il.

Israeli Ministry of Defense. "Area of the Seam." www.securityfence.mod.gov.il.

Israeli Ministry of Foreign Affairs. "The Palestinian Liberation Front Headed by Abu al-Abbas (Residing in Iraq), as a Tool of the Iraqi Regime for Carrying Out Terrorist Attacks against Israel." www.mfa.gov.il.

Israeli Parliament (Knesset). "The Peace of Lebanon War," "Six Days War," "Workers Party of Eretz Yisrael (Mapai)." www.knesset.gov.il.

Issacharoff, Avi. "Abu Mazen Will Meet Haled Mashal in Damascus." *Haaretz*, January 18, 2007.

Kafala, Tarik. "The Iraqi Baath Party." *BBC*, http://news.bbc.co.uk.

Kanaana, Sharif. "Survival Strategies of Arabs in Israel." *MERIP Reports* 41 (1975): 6–7.

Klein, Aaron. *Striking Back: The 1972 Munich Olympics Massacre and Israel's Deadly Response.* Tel Aviv: Miskal, 2006.

Kra, Baruch, and Amos Harel. "Commander of General Staff Negotiation Team Had Important Part in Nachshon Wachsman Failed Rescue Operation." *Haaretz*, July 17, 2003.

Lahav, Shai. "Surgical Unit." *NRG*, www.nrg.co.il.

Lavie, Aviv. "The Darkest Corner in Israel." *Haaretz*, December 1, 2003.

"Lebanon Political Parties—Amal Movement." *Lebanon Wire*, www.lebanonwire.com.

Limor, Yoav. "Cherry Blooming." *NRG*, www.nrg.co.il.

Limor, Yoav, and Alon Ben-David. "In the First Place: Sayeret Golani." *Ynet*, www.ynet .co.il.

——. "Seventh Place: Sayeret Givati." *Ynet*, www.ynet.co.il.

——. "Sixth Place: Sayeret Nahal." *Ynet*, www.ynet.co.il.

Maiberg, Ron. *Code Name: Bayonet.* Dragoman Films Distribution, 2006.

Melman, Yossi. "All His Life in a Tight-Lipped Department." *Haaretz*, January 7, 1999.

——. "Golda Didn't Give an Order." *Haaretz*, February 18, 2006.

——. *Israel: Foreign Intelligence and Security Services Survey.* Tel Aviv: Zmora-Bitan, 1982.

——. "Mossad Continues Internal Investigation In Order to Find Out Reasons for Operational Failure." *Haaretz*, March 1, 1998.

——. "Mossad Needs New Workers, But Is Afraid of Double Agents." *Haaretz*, August 4, 2000.

——. "There Are Precedents to Karpinsky's Claims." *Haaretz*, July 4, 2004.

——. "Week of Fighting Against Drug Smuggling." *Haaretz*, December 25, 1996.

Mishal, Shaul, and Avraham Sela. *The Hamas Wind: Violence and Coexistence.* Tel Aviv: Miskal, 2006.

Mossad. "HaMossad leModi'in u le Tafkidim Meyuhadim." www.mossad.gov.il.

National Memorial Institute for the Prevention of Terrorism. "Palestinian Islamic Jihad (PIJ)," "Popular Front for the Liberation of Palestine (PFLP)," "Sabri Al-Banna," "Tanzim." http://tkb.org.

NATO Glossary of Terms and Definitions. www.nato.int/docu/stanag/aap006/aap-6–2007 .pdf.

Palmach. "Summary." www.palmach.org.il.

Permanent Observer Mission of Palestine to the United Nations. "Political Program Adopted at the 12th Session of the Palestine National Council." www.un.int/ palestine/PLO/docone.html.

Regular, Arnon. "Silwan Gang: High Compartmentalization and Strong Discipline." *Haaretz*, October 2, 2002.

Rofeh, Sharon. "Lebanese Liaison Unit Dismantled." *Ynet*, www.ynet.co.il.

Sayaret Paratroopers. "Battle Heritage." www.gal-ed.org.il.

Schiff, Zeev, and Ehud Yaari. *Intifada.* Tel Aviv: Shocken, 1990.

Shalev, Arie. *The Intifada: Causes and Effects.* Tel Aviv: Papyrus, 1990.

Shalom, Danny. "Battle Squadron." *Hazofe,* February 3, 2008.

Tamir, Moshe. *The War Without a Name.* Tel Aviv: Ministry of Defense Publishers, 2006.

"What Is Ashura?" *BBC,* http://news.bbc.co.uk.

Winkler, Roni. "Broadcasting from the Field." *Israel Air Force Magazine* 141 (October 2001).

Yaacobi, Yotam. "SLA Soldiers Still Here." *Nana,* http://news.nana10.co.il.

Yaari, Ehud. "Behind the Terror." *Atlantic Monthly,* June 1987.

Yehoshua, Yossi. "To Tell the Truth, We Expected Much More Opposition from Hezbollah." *Yedioth Ahronoth,* August 2, 2006.

Zipori, Shlomi. *Justice in Disguise.* Tel Aviv: Agam, 2004.

Zonder, Moshe. *The Elite Unit of Israel.* Jerusalem: Keter, 2000.

Page numbers in italics refer to figures and tables.

A'bayat, Hussein Muhammad Salim, 119
Abbas, Mahmoud (Abu Mazen), 95
abductions, as counterterrorist tactic:
  abduction of senior Hezbollah members,
  85, 87–88, 132; ineffectiveness of policy, 85,
  87–88, 93, 133–34; and second intifada, 113;
  and Second Lebanon War, 132
abductions, as terrorist act, 140; Arad
  abduction (1986), 83–85; Goldwasser
  and Regev abduction (2006), 131; Gurel
  abduction (2003), 116–17; Wachsman
  abduction (1994), 9–10, 97–101. *See also*
  hostage rescue operations
Abu Hassan, Musa Ibn Jouma, 53
Abu Jihad, 78–81
Abu Marzuk, Mussa, 106
Abu Nidal group, *6*, 67
Abu Rodaina, Nabil, 99
Abu Samhadana, Jamal (Abu 'Atiya'), 120
Abu Shanab, Isma'il Hassan, 119
Abu Zahary, Sammy, 126
Action Directe (France), 38
Adwan, Kamal, 44–45
Agranat Commission, 146
Ahmad, Samir, 42
Air France hijacking of 1976, 54–62
airport attacks, 36, 38–39, 41, 43
Akawi, Lutfi al-, 27
Alon, Jo, 41
Amal, 70, 83
Aman, *4, 5*, 71; and abduction of Hezbollah

members, 85; and assassinations, 27, 118;
  and conflicting assessments, 73–74, 97,
  111–13; countering the financing of ter-
  rorism, 124; and division of authority, 97,
  109–10; intended function of, 20, 71; and
  jurisdictional rivalry, 21, 71–74; and Oslo
  Accords, 96–97; training for, 111–12
AMIA. *See* Argentine Israelite Mutual As-
  sociation (AMIA) building attack of 1994
Amin, Ibrahim al-, 71
Amin, Idi, 56, 59
al-Aqsa Charitable Foundation, 125
al-Aqsa intifada. *See* intifada, second
Arab Bank, 126
Arab League, 18
Arab Liberation Front, 32, 62
Arab Salvation Army, 17–18
Arab–Israeli War of 1967, 30–32
Arad, Ron, 83–85, 87–88, 93, 130
Arafat, Mussa, 104
Arafat, Yasser: control of PLO, 32; Fatah
  recruitment following 1967 war, 31–32;
  and Karameh raid of 1968, 33; and Oslo
  Accords, 96–97; and second intifada, 111;
  and suicide attacks, 101; and Wachsman
  abduction, 99
Arava Brigade, 32–33
Arbel, Dan, 45
Arbel, Yehuda, 32
Arditi, Mickey, 50
Arens, Moshe, 72, 74

Argaman, Shachar, 100

Argentina, 86, 88–90

Argentine Israelite Mutual Association (AMIA) building attack of 1994, 88–90

Argov, Shlomo, 68

Arian, Sami al-, 125–26

Army of Islam, 126, 130

Arnan, Avraham, 37

artillery strikes on Israel, 67, 92–93, *139;* and global terrorism, 142; increasing use of, 139–40; lack of effective response to, 141; and Second Lebanon War, 131–34, 140

artillery strikes on southern Lebanon, 87, 92–93

Ashkenazi, Gabi, 117

Assad, Hafez al-, 34

Assaf, Ze'ev, 63

assassinations, as counterterrorist tactic: assassination of Black September members (Basiso assassination), 95–96; assassination of Fatah members, 41, 43–45, 119; assassination of Hamas members, 104–9; assassination of Hezbollah members and relatives, 86, 90–92, 129, 140; assassination of PFLP members, 39–40, 61–62, 129; assassination of PIJ members, 119–20, 128–29; assassination of PLO members, 40–46, 78–81; Ayash "The Engineer" assassination, 104–6; and collapse of ceasefire with Palestinian Authority, 118; "focused prevention" as euphemism for, 117; Haddad assassination, 61–62; Hafez as first assassination target, 26–28; Hamza assassination, 128–29; ineffectiveness of assassinations/raids in decreasing Palestinian violence, 41–46, 80, 110, 122, 126, 144; Jihad assassination as retaliation for "Mothers Bus" hijacking, 78–81; Kanafani assassination as retaliation for Lod massacre, 39–40; Mashal assassination attempt as retaliation for Machane Yehuda Market attack, 106–9; motives for, 80; Mughniyah (Fuad) assassination, 90–92; Mughniyah (Imad) assassination, 140; Musawi assassination, 86; Operation Spring of Youth, 44–45; Operation Wrath of God as retaliation for Munich Olympics attack, 40–46; Palestinian retaliatory operations in response to, 41–45, 86; and policy recommendations, 144; questionable connections between targets and terrorist acts, 43–45; and Rabin's frustration with suicide attacks, 103–6; reprisal actions against Palestinian police, 120–21; as retaliation for second intifada, 117–22; selection of targets, 118–20; and Shahar Unit, 19–20; Shikaki assassination, 104; and Unit 101, 23–25. *See also* retaliatory raids

assassinations, as terrorist act: attempt on Golda Meir, 41, 43; attempt on King Hussein of Jordan, 33; and retaliation for Operation Wrath of God, 41; Shlomo Argov (Israeli ambassador to the UK), 68; Wasfi Tel (Jordanian prime minister), 34

Athens airport attack of 1973, 43

aviation security, 36, 39, 46

Avigur, Shaul, 14

Aviram, Ishay, 83

Avital, Shai, 64

Awal, Ali Abed al-, 79

Ayalon, Ami, 103

Ayash, Yehiya "The Engineer," 103–6

Azoulai, Avner, 69

Balawi, Hakam, 94

Bangkok embassy attack of 1972, 43

Banna, Marwan al-, 68

Barak, Ehud, 56–58, 79, 100, 109–10

Barak, Hanan, 131

Barak, Natan, 118

Barghouti, Marwan, 113

Bar-Lev, Omer, 58, 61, 64

Basiso, Ataf, 95–96

Basque underground, 38

Battikhi, General, 108

Baum, Shlomo, 24
Beeri, Isser, 20
Begin, Menachem, 67, 72
Beinisch, Dorit, 99
Belgium, and financing of terrorism, 124, 125
Ben-Avraham, Amos, 64, 85
Benayoun, Haim, 77
Ben-Eliezer, Benjamin, 118
Ben-Gal, Avigdor, 63
Ben-Gurion, David, 20–21, 25
Bennett, Steve, 107
Ben-Shimol, David, 100
Ben-Yair, Michael, 102–3
Ben-Yair, Miriam, 78
Berro, Ibrahim Hussein, 88–89
Betser, Muki, 50, 58, 60
Biton, Barry, 107
Black September (1970), 34
Black September organization, 6, 34;
    Basiso assassination, 95–96; Munich
    Olympics attack, 40; and Operation
    Wrath of God, 41, 46; Sabena Airlines
    hijacking of 1972, 36–38
"Blood Bus" attack of 1978, 66–67
Border Police, 51, 114, 148. See also Yamam
Borowitz, Ida, 60
Böse, Wilfried, 54–56
Bouchiki, Ahmed, 45
Bouvier, Antonio Degas, 55
British Mandate, 14–17, 19
Buckley, William, 90
bus attacks: "Blood Bus" attack of 1978,
    66–67; Bus 300 affair, 75–77; Herzliya
    Hebrew school bus attack of 1968, 32;
    Maale Akrabim road attack of 1954, 25;
    and public transit security, 124
Bush, George W., 90

Canada, and Mashal assassination attempt,
    106–9
Carlos the Jackal, 55
Carmon, Yigal, 91
Center for Political Research, 4, 110

Central Agency for Intelligence and Secu-
    rity Problems, 21
Central Institute for Intelligence and
    Security, 21. See also Mossad
Chambers, Erica, 46
charitable institutions, 73, 81–82, 124–26, 145
Chir, Hussein Abad al-, 43
CIA, 33, 90
Circassians, 22
Clinton, Bill, 108
Cohen, Baruch, 41, 42
Cohen, Victor, 48
Committee of Inquiry Into the Intel-
    ligence System in Light of the War in
    Iraq, 146
Communist Party, 22
counterterrorism: countering the financ-
    ing of terrorism, 124–27; emergence of
    doctrine (1920s to 1950s), 14–29; and
    Great Arab Revolt of 1936, 14–17; and
    military innovation/adaptation, 7–11; in
    the 1940s, 18–21; overview of intelligence
    community, 4; overview of models, 2;
    overview of thwarting forces, 5; policy
    (and violations of policy) on not sur-
    rendering to demands of terrorists, 36, 84,
    93, 133; policy recommendations, 143–49;
    policy responses to hijackings, 35–38; and
    public pressure, 8–11, 80, 92–93, 133–34,
    136; reasons for lack of success of war
    model, 6–7, 135–37. See also abductions,
    as counterterrorist tactic; artillery strikes
    on southern Lebanon; assassinations, as
    counterterrorist tactic; criminal justice
    model; defensive model; elite units;
    hostage rescue operations; intelligence
    organizations; interagency competition;
    interrogation of suspects; Israel Defense
    Forces; reconciliatory model; war model
criminal justice model, 1; defined/
    described, 2; lack of attention to, 136; and
    policy recommendations, 51, 148. See also
    police force

crisis management stage of defensive
model, 144–45

Dabash, Bashir Khalil, 120
Dagan, Meir, 3, 34–35
Damuni, Jamal Salim, 119
Danin, Ezra, 15
Dar, Avraham, 27
Dayan, Moshe, 24, 27, 37, 48–51
Dayan, Moti, 118
Dayan, Uzi, 64
de Cuellar, Perez, 84
defensive model, 1; and aviation security,
36, 39, 46; buffer zone between West Bank
and Israeli territory (Separation Fence),
122–24; and buffer zone in Lebanon, 83;
countering the financing of terrorism,
124–27; defined/described, 2; effectiveness
of, 10, 122–23, 135; and embassy security,
43; first Israeli semidefensive model,
32–34; and hostage-taking, 65; as last
resort, 136; Palestinian enmity toward
Israel due to settlements east of the
Separation Fence, 123; policy recommendations for three stages, 144–45; and
public perception of policymakers, 8;
public transit security, 124; security guards
at entrances to businesses, 123–24; wall
around Jerusalem, 123
democratic dilemma, 1, 3
Democratic Front for the Liberation of
Palestine (DFLP), 6, 32, 47–51
Denmark, and financing of terrorism, 125
deterrence, 5–6; effective measures (see defensive model); ineffectiveness of abductions, 85, 87–88, 93, 133–34; ineffectiveness
of artillery strikes on southern Lebanon,
93; ineffectiveness of assassinations/raids,
25, 41–46, 80, 110, 122, 126, 144
DFLP. See Democratic Front for the
Liberation of Palestine
Dib, Ali Hassan, 129
Dichter, Avi, 111

Din, Mahdi Shams al-, 71
Din Veheshbon operation, 87, 92
Dirani, Mustafa, 83, 87, 129
Druze, 22
Duvdevan special forces, 5, 80, 113; and first
intifada, 114; and Gurel abduction, 117;
and policy recommendations, 148

Efrat, Yonah, 52
Egoz Unit, 5, 113, 114, 132
Egypt: assassination of Egyptian intelligence agent Hafez, 26–28; and fedayeen,
22; and origins of PLO, 32; smuggling
from, 138; war of 1967, 30–32
Eitan, Rafael, 63–64
El Al hijacking of 1968, 36, 61
El Reda, Samuel Salman, 88
elections, and war model, 92–93
elite units, 24–25; Arava Brigade, 32–33;
competition among, 9–10, 59, 64–65,
113–17, 137; Duvdevan, 5, 80, 113, 114,
117, 148; Egoz Unit, 5, 113, 114, 132; and
first intifada, 114; Kfir (900) Brigade,
148; lack of policy on jurisdiction in
hostage situations, 78; lack of training for
hostage rescue, 51, 53, 63; lives of soldiers
endangered for questionable operations, 85, 93, 132–34; mismatch between
training and operation assignments, 10,
113–16, 137, 148; organizational culture
of, 24; policy recommendations, 146–49;
and problems of military innovation/
adaptation, 10; Rimon Unit, 5, 34–35; and
second intifada, 111–17; Shahar Unit of
Palmach, 19–20; Shayetet 13, 5, 113–15, 132,
141; Shimshon, 5, 80–81, 114; special forces
in the occupied territories, 80–81; and terrorists' improved capabilities in the 2000s,
131–33; training, 24, 148; Unit 101, 23–25;
Yamas, 5, 80, 114, 148. See also abductions,
as counterterrorist tactic; assassinations,
as counterterrorist tactic; hostage rescue
operations; Mossad; paratroopers; Sayeret

Matkal; Yamam; *and other headings begin-
ning with* Sayeret
embassy attacks, 43, 86
embassy security, 43
"The Engineer." *See* Ayash, Yehiya
Entebbe Airport hostage situation (1976),
53–62, 162n17
Eshkol, Levi, 30
espionage. *See* intelligence organizations
ETA, 38
Europe: and financing of terrorism, 124–25;
Mossad intelligence gathering in, 35, 143;
Operation Wrath of God, 41–46; terrorist
groups, 38, 142–43

Fadlallah, Sheikh Mohammed Hussein, 70
Fallahian, Ali, 88
Fatah, *6;* assassination of Fatah leaders,
41, 43–45, 119; and Black September, 34;
establishment in Lebanon, 66; expulsion
from Jordan, 33–34; and first Lebanon
war, 67–70; and Karameh raid of 1968,
32–33; and PLO, 32; recruitment following 1967 war, 31–32; terrorist acts, 30,
66–67, 75–77
fedayeen, 22–29
Fein, Baruch, 50
fence, as defense against suicide attacks,
122–24
financing of terrorism, 124–27, 141, 145
France: and assassination of Basiso, 95–96;
and financing of terrorism, 124; and
hijackings, 53–62; and Operation Wrath
of God, 43; terrorist groups, 38
Friendship Family, 70

Ganor, Boaz, 3
Gathering and Prevention (intelligence
organization), 72
Gaza Strip, 75–82; control of Palestinian
population in the occupied territories
following 1967 war, 31–32; decline of
terrorism in the early 1970s, 35; and first

intifada, 81–82; and Oslo Accords, 96; and
Rimon Unit, 34–35; and Shimshon special
forces, 80–81; smuggling over Egyptian
border, 138; terrorist acts in, 34–35, 75–77,
98–99, 101
Gemayel, Amine, 69
Gemayel, Bashir, 69
General Security Service (GSS), *4;* and
assassinations, 104–6, 117–18; and aviation
security, 36, 39; and Bus 300 affair, 75–77;
conflicting assessments, 73–74, 97, 111–13;
countering the financing of terrorism, 124;
and division of authority, 97, 109–10; and
first intifada, 8–9, 81; HUMINT network
in the occupied territories following 1967
war, 31, 34; intended function of, 71; legal
restrictions on activities, 76; Metulla District, 73; and Oslo Accords, 96–97; policy
recommendations, 146, 148; and rivalry
over Lebanon, 71–74; and rivalry over
thwarting terrorists attacks, 109–10; and
second intifada, 111–17, 126; and Separation Fence as defense against suicide attacks, 122–24; and Sharon, 111; and suicide
attacks, 102; and Wachsman abduction,
99. *See also* interrogation of suspects
Germany, 38, 40, 54–55
Ghul, Adnan Mahmud Jaber al-, 120
Gideonim, *5*
Gilad, Amos, 111
Gillon, Carmi, 73, 99, 102–3
Givati. *See* Sayeret Givati
Global Coalition against Terrorism, 90
Gluska, Eyal, 64
Golani. *See* Sayeret Golani
Goldwasser, Ehud, 131
Grapes of Wrath understandings, 93
Great Arab Revolt of 1936, 14–17
Greece, Athens airport attack of 1973, 43
Grissom, Adam, 7–8, 9
Gruber, Shlomo, 25
GSS. *See* General Security Service
Gur, Motta, 48–51

Gurel, Eliyahu, 116–17
Guri, Yehudit, 62
Guriel, Boris, 20

Habash, George, 32, 61
Haddad, Wadie, 61–62
Hafez, Mustafa, 26–28
Haganah, 14–17
Haj, Dawoud, 120
Hajaj, Ahmed, 117
Haled, Leilah, 55
Halevy, Ephraim, 108
Halevy, Ilan, 75
Halil, Shirin, 117
Hallaq, Ahmed, 90–92
Hamad, Kamal, 104–5
Hamad, Osama, 104–5
Hamas, 6; assassination of Hamas leaders, 104–9, 119–20; and charitable institutions, 81–82, 124–25; economic embargo on Hamas government, 126; financing of terrorism, 124; and Hezbollah, 82; origins of, 81–82; Pi Glilot oil and gas depot attack, 138; and Rabin, 103–4; and Second Lebanon War, 130; suicide attacks, 101, 105, 106; and Wachsman abduction, 97–101
Hamshari, Mahmud, 43
hamulas, 15
Hamza, Abu, 128–29
Hanif, Asif Mohammed, 142–43
Haniya, Ismail, 126
Haran, Danny and Einat, 130
Hardan, Iyad Mahmud Naif, 119
Harel, Isser, 20, 21
Haridi, Amro al-, 28
Harizat, Abdel Samed, 102
Harkabi, Yehoshafat, 27
Harmelin, Yossef, 73
Hassan, Crown Prince of Jordan, 108
Hatib, Sheikh Nimer al-, 19–20
Hawatmeh, Nayef, 32
Hefetz, Assaf, 51, 64
Herzog, Chaim, 19, 21

Hezbollah, 87–88, 129, 140; abduction of senior members, 85, 87–88, 132; adoption of abductions as tactic, 93; assassination of senior members and their relatives, 86, 90–91, 129, 140; Buenos Aires bombing of 1994, 88–90; charitable institutions, 73; conflicting assessments about, 73–74; and defensive model, 83; described, 70–71; escalation of tensions in the 1990s, 85–87, 92–93; and financing of terrorism, 141; and Hamas, 82; and Iran, 70, 86; and jurisdictional rivalry among intelligence organizations, 71–74; and Operation Grapes of Wrath (1996), 92–93; origins of, 70; prisoner exchanges, 84, 93, 129–30; and Second Lebanon War, 116, 130–34, 140; "sleeper" cells, 90; suicide attacks, 101
hijackings: bus hijackings, 75–78; and hostage rescue, 53–62, 75–78; impact on Israeli policy, 35–38; and Jordan, 33; and Sayeret Matkal, 36–38, 53–62; security measures, 36, 39, 46; "Skyjack Sunday," 61. See also Entebbe Airport hostage situation
Hirsch, Yitzhak, 54
histaarev, 19, 80
Hofi, Yitzhak, 57
Horev, Amos, 51
Horev Commission, 51, 116
Horowitz, Michael, 8
hostage rescue operations: Bus 300 affair (1984), 75–77; capabilities of Yamam passed over, 10, 64, 76, 117; and competition among elite units, 9–10, 64–65, 97; and criminal justice model, 51; and defensive model, 65; Entebbe Airport (1976), 53–62, 162n17; and establishment of Yamam, 51; Gurel rescue (2003), 117; lack of training for, 51, 53, 63; Ma'alot school hostage crisis (1974), 47–51; Misgav Am kibbutz (1980), 62–65; "Mothers Bus" affair (1988), 77–78; and Munich Olympics of 1972, 40; policy recommendations, 51, 144–45; public pressure on policymakers, 133; and Sabena

Airlines hijacking of 1972, 37–38; Savoy Hotel incident of 1975, 51–53; terrorists' advantages in siege situations, 53; training for, 36, 51, 53; Wachsman case (1994), 9–10, 97–101. *See also* abductions, as terrorist act

human intelligence (HUMINT): and Aman, 112; and first intifada, 81; and Great Arab Revolt of 1936, 15; GSS network in the occupied territories following 1967 war, 31; and Hamas, 82; and jurisdictional rivalry, 71–72; and second intifada, 112; and Shai, 14; and suicide attacks, 102

Hussein, King of Jordan, 33–34, 107–9

Hussein, Saddam, 141

Husseini, Abdel-Kader al-, 17

Husseini, Haj Amin al-, 15

IDF. *See* Israel Defense Forces

innovation. *See* military innovation/ adaptation

institutionalization, as hindrance in counterterrorism, 7

intelligence organizations, *4;* in Argentina, 89–90; early organizations, 14–29; effect of pressure at the top, 8–9; and first Magna Carta, 96–97; formation of new organizations upon Israeli independence, 20–21; institutionalization as hindrance for, 7; intelligence capabilities undermined by interagency rivalries, 72–74; intelligence capabilities undermined by retaliatory assassinations, 42; international cooperation/noncooperation, 90, 147; and peace process, 94–96; policy recommendations, 146–49; and problems with terrorism as top priority, 137; rifts caused by Mossad assassinations, 96. *See also* Aman; General Security Service; human intelligence; interagency competition; interrogation of suspects; Mossad; Political Department of the Ministry of Foreign Affairs; Sayeret Matkal; Shin Bet; signal intelligence; visual intelligence

interagency competition: attempts to mitigate, 20–21, 72–73, 96–97, 109–10; and conflicting assessments, 73–74, 97, 110, 111–13; and early organizations, 15, 20–21; first Magna Carta, 96–97; jurisdictional rivalry among intelligence organizations, 21, 71–74; and prestigious operations, 9–10, 59, 64–65, 97, 113–17; reasons for, 71; reasons for policymakers' preference for GSS, 111–12; and responsibility for thwarting attacks, 109–10; and scarce resources, 9, 71, 137; and second intifada, 111–17; second Magna Carta, 109–10; state comptroller's assessment of issues, 109–10; unwillingness to cooperate and share knowledge/information, 9, 11, 15, 72, 97, 110

Internal Security Services, 20. *See also* Shin Bet

interrogation of suspects: death of detainees, 102; effect of pressure at the top of intelligence organizations, 8–9; and first intifada, 8–9; and jurisdictional rivalry between Aman and GSS, 72; legal issues, 102–3; methods described, 172n7; and suicide attacks, 102–3; and Wachsman abduction, 99

intifada, first, 8–9, 81–82, 94, 114

intifada, second (al-Aqsa intifada), 111–27; assassinations in response to, 117–22; conflicting assessments about, 111–13; and improved terrorist capabilities, 138–40; and interagency competition, 111–17; and Iran, 141; Operation Defensive Shield, 121–22; and Separation Fence as defense against suicide attacks, 122–24

IRA. *See* Irish Republican Army

Iran: and Buenos Aires bombing of 1994, 88, 89; and financing of terrorism, 141, 145; and Hezbollah, 70, 86; and origins of suicide tactic, 101; and second intifada, 141

Iraq, 32

Irish Republican Army (IRA), 38

Islamic Jihad, international, 85–86, 124. *See also* Palestinian Islamic Jihad

Israel: control over Palestinians following independence, 21–23; emergence of counterterrorism doctrine in the pre-state and early post-state period (1920s to 1950s), 14–29; formation of intelligence organizations upon independence, 20–21; Grapes of Wrath understandings, 93; international condemnation for retaliatory raids, 25, 93; Madrid summit of 1991, 94; Oslo Accords, 82, 95–97, 101–2, 109; overview of intelligence community, *4;* overview of thwarting forces, *5;* and problems with terrorism as top priority, 135, 137; Second Lebanon War, 116, 130–34; Sinai War (1956), 28; UN Partition Resolution, 17–20; violations of policy on not surrendering to demands of terrorists, 133; war of 1967, 30–32. *See also* counterterrorism; Gaza Strip; intelligence organizations; national security organizations; occupied territories; policymakers; public; terrorist acts; West Bank; Yishuv

Israel Defense Forces (IDF), *4, 5;* and Din Veheshbon operation in Lebanon, 87; first counterterrorism force (*see* Unit 101); and first Lebanon war, 67–70; institutionalization as hindrance for, 7; and Israeli independence, 20; Operation Defensive Shield, 120–22; Operation Grapes of Wrath (1996), 92–93; policy recommendations, 146–49; and second intifada, 112–17, 120–22; and Second Lebanon War, 130–34; and war of 1967, 31–32. *See also* Aman; assassinations, as counterterrorist tactic; elite units; Israeli Air Force; Israeli Navy; retaliatory raids; Sayeret Matkal; Shin Bet

Israeli Air Force (IAF), *4,* 112; Arad abduction (1986), 83–85

Israeli Navy, *4,* 115

Israeli police. *See* police force

Italy, 38, 43

Iyad, Abu, 42

Jabarin, Sufian, 103

Japanese Red Army, 38–39

Jibril, Ahmed, 129

Jibril, Jihad, 129

Jibril prisoner exchange, 84, 93

Jihad, Abu, 78–81

Jihad, Umm, 79

Jijazi, Mohammed, 88

Jordan: artillery strikes from, 142; attacks on Jordanian politicians, 33–34; as base for 1960s attacks, 30, 32–33; and hijackings, 61; Karameh raid of 1968, 32–33; and Mashal assassination attempt, 106–9; mass arrests of PLO activists and expulsion of PLO headquarters, 33–34

Kadosh, Yaakov, 47

Kahan Commission, 70

Kalmanovich, Shabtai, 84

Kanafani, Ghassan, 39–40

Kano, Khader, 42

Karine A, 114–15, 141

Karmi, Raed, 118, 119

Kasfi, Jawad, 85

Ka'ush, Kamal, 62

Kendall, Sean, 107

Kfir (900) Brigade, 148

Khalil, Mohammad (Sheikh Khalil), 120

Khamenei, Ali, 88

kidnapping. *See* abductions, as counterterrorist tactic; abductions, as terrorist act

Kimche, David, 69

Klingberg, Marcus, 84

Kolberg, Ziv, 64

Kubaysi, Basil al-, 43–44

Kuhlmann, Brigitte, 54–55

Kuntar, Samir, 130

Lakam, *4*

Lebanon, 66–74; and Arad abduction

(1986), 83–85; artillery strikes from, 67, 92–93, 131–34, *139,* 139–41; assassination of Bashir Gemayel, 69; conflicting assessments about, 73–74; as destination for Palestinian organizations expelled from Jordan, 34; Din Veheshbon operation (1993), 87; Fatah military forces in (1970s), 66; first Lebanon war, 67–70; Grapes of Wrath understandings, 93; and Hamas, 82; and Hamza assassination, 128–29; and Iran, 70; and jurisdictional rivalry among intelligence organizations, 71–74; Operation Grapes of Wrath (1996), 92–93; Phalange massacre at Sabra and Shatilla refugee camps, 69–70; rise of Hezbollah, 70–71; Second Lebanon War, 116, 130–34, 140; "security zone" in southern Lebanon as buffer, 83; and Syria, 68; and terrorist attacks of the 1970s, 66–67. *See also* Hezbollah
letter bombs, 42–43
Levi, Kochava, 52
Levine, Amiram, 48, 49, 50, 57
Levy, Moshe, 69, 76
Lipkin-Shahak, Amnon, 3
Livne, Zvi, 49
Lod Airport massacre (1972), 39
Lotan, Lior, 100–101
Lubrani, Uri, 72, 84

Maale Akrabim road attack (1954), 25
Ma'alot school hostage crisis (1974), 47–51
Machane Yehuda Market suicide attack (1997), 106
Madrid summit of 1991, 94
Magna Carta, first, 96–97
Magna Carta, second, 109–10
Maimon, David, 35
Maimoni, Jean-Jacques, 60
Majzoub, Mahmoud al-, 128–29
Majzoub, Nidal al-, 128
Makadmeh, Ibrahim, 119
Maklef, Mordechai, 23–24

Maronite Christians, 68–70
Mashal, Khaled, 106
media: and Bus 300 affair, 76; and Entebbe Airport hostage situation, 61; and policy recommendations, 145; and Shai's intelligence activities, 16; television as "theater of terror," 35
Meir, Golda, 41, 43, 48–51
Menem, Carlos, 89–90
Metulla District, 73
Meyari, Ali el-, 55
MI6, 33
Mike's Place suicide attack (2003), 142–43
military, 5, 7–11. *See also* elite units; Israel Defense Forces
Ministry of Defense, *4*
Ministry of Foreign Affairs, *4,* 20
Misgav Am kibbutz hostage situation (1980), 62–65
missile attacks. *See* artillery strikes on Israel; artillery strikes on southern Lebanon
mistaaravim, 19
Mofaz, Shaul, 99–100, 117
Mohtashamipour, Ali-Akbar, 70
Mordechai, Narkiss, 48
Mordechai, Yitzhak, 73, 76, 77, 108
Moreno, Emanuel, 133
Mossad, *4;* and Entebbe Airport hostage situation, 57; and first Lebanon war, 68–70; intelligence capabilities undermined by retaliatory assassinations, 42; intended function of, 71; investigation of Argentina embassy attack of 1992, 86; investigation of Argentina suicide attack of 1994, 89–90; and jurisdictional rivalry over Lebanon, 71–74; and Maronite Christians, 68–70; and Operation Wrath of God, 42–46; origins of, 20, 21; and Oslo Accords, 95–97; and rivalry over thwarting terrorists attacks, 109–10; worldwide intelligence gathering, 35, 143. *See also* assassinations, as counterterrorist tactic

"Mothers Bus" affair (1988), 77–78
Mubarak, Hosni, 98–99
Mughniyah, Fuad, 90–91
Mughniyah, Imad, 86, 90–91, 140–41
al-Muhajiron group, 142
Munich Olympics attack of 1972, 40; questionable connections between assassination targets and Munich, 43–45
Murr, Elias, 128
Musawi, Abbas, 86
Muslim Brotherhood, 81

Nagl, John, 9
Nahal. See Sayeret Nahal
Najjar, Mohammed Yusef, 44–45
Nasrallah, Hassan, 130, 132
Nasser, Kamal, 44–45
Nasser, Wael Talib Mohammed, 120
national security organizations, 4–5; counterterrorist focus of policymakers as window of opportunity for, 10–11; organizations of the 1920s to 1950s, 14–29 (see also Haganah; Shai); problems with terrorism as top priority, 135, 137. See also elite units; intelligence organizations; interagency competition; Israel Defense Forces
Nativ, 4
Netanyahu, Binyamin, 3, 92, 106–8
Netanyahu, Iddo, 60
Netanyahu, Yoni, 59, 162n17
Netherlands, and financing of terrorism, 125
Netiv Meir School, 47–51
Night of the Pitchforks, 86
Nili, 14
Noah's Ark operation, 114–15
Nohra, Mofid, 91–92
Nohra, Ramzi, 91, 171n17

Obeid, Abdel Karim, 85
Obeid, Keis, 130
occupied territories: buffer zone between West Bank and Israeli territory (Separation Fence), 122–24; control of Palestinian population following 1967 war, 31–32; GSS network in the occupied territories following 1967 war, 31; and Oslo Accords, 96; Palestinian enmity toward Israel due to settlements west of the Separation Fence, 123; special forces in, 80–81; and suicide attacks, 101–3. See also Gaza Strip; intifada, first; intifada, second; West Bank
Okamoto, Kozo, 38, 39
Okudaira, Takeshi, 38–39
Operation Defensive Shield, 120–22
Operation Grapes of Wrath, 92–93
Operation Sharp and Smooth, 132
Operation Spring of Youth, 44–45
Operation Wrath of God, 40–46
Oranim Plan, 67
Oslo Accords, 82, 95–97, 101–2, 109
Oudeh, Shams, 99

Palestine Liberation Organization (PLO), 6; Arafat's assumption of control over, 32; assassination of members, 40–46, 78–81; expulsion from Jordan, 33–34; and first intifada, 81; and first Israeli semidefensive model, 32–34; and Madrid summit of 1991, 94; origins of, 32; and Oslo Accords, 82, 95–97, 101–2, 109; as umbrella organization, 32. See also terrorist acts
Palestinian Authority: and division of authority among intelligence organizations, 96–97; economic embargo on Hamas government, 126; and Israeli assassination policy, 118; and second intifada, 111; and suicide attacks, 101
Palestinian Islamic Jihad (PIJ), 6, 85–86; assassination of PIJ leaders, 119–20, 128–29; and financing of terrorism, 125; and Rabin, 103–4; suicide attacks, 101
Palestinian Liberation Front, 6, 32
Palestinian National Front in the occupied territories, 6

Palestinian terrorist groups. *See* terrorist groups, Palestinian

Palestinians: and Black September (1970), 34; change in conflict from territorial dispute to ideological/theological dispute, 149; control of Palestinian population in the occupied territories following 1967 war, 31–32; election boycotts, 93; Great Arab Revolt of 1936, 14–17; grievances ignored, 46; need for health and welfare services, 145; Palestinian enmity toward Israel due to settlements east of the Separation Fence, 123; Phalange massacre at Sabra and Shatilla refugee camps, 69–70; refugees and the early years of Israeli statehood, 21–29; and UN Partition Resolution, 17–20

Palmach, 19, 24, 34

paratroopers, 5, 23; Karameh raid of 1968, 32–33; and Qibya village raid, 25; and second intifada, 113; and Unit 101, 25. *See also* Sayeret Matkal

Passover Massacre (2002), 120

Peled, Ruby, 52

Peled, Yossi, 73

Peleg, Hagai, 112

Peres, Shimon, 58, 92–93, 104

Peretz, Meir, 62, 64

PFLP. *See* Popular Front for the Liberation of Palestine

Phalange (Lebanese Kataeb Party), 69–70

Pi Glitot oil and gas depot attack, 138

Pico, Giandomenico, 84

PIJ. *See* Palestinian Islamic Jihad

PLO. *See* Palestine Liberation Organization

police force, 5; establishment of Yamam as hostage rescue unit, 51; excluded from decision making, 136; and first intifada, 114; and policy recommendations, 148; and second intifada, 112. *See also* Yamam

policy recommendations, 143–49

policymakers: capabilities of Yamam passed over by, 53, 64–65; close ties with armed forces, 136; and conflicting assessments by intelligence organizations, 73–74, 97, 111–13; and military innovation/adaptation, 8–11; perceptions of elite units, 65; preference for GSS, 111–12; problems with terrorism as top priority, 135, 137; and public perceptions of defensive model, 8; public pressure in hostage situations, 133; and scarce resources, 9; war model as result of election pressure, 92–93; war model as result of public pressure on, 8, 10–11, 80, 85, 110

Political Department of the Ministry of Foreign Affairs, 20

Popular Front for the Liberation of Palestine (PFLP), *6*, 32; airport attacks, 38–39; assassination of PFLP leaders, 61–62, 119; hijackings, 36, 55, 61; Israeli assassination of leaders, 129; and Operation Wrath of God, 41

Popular Resistance Committees, 126, 130

Poraz, Nir, 100–101

Posen, Barry, 8

prevention stage of defensive model, 144. *See also* defensive model

prisoner exchanges, 84, 93, 108–9, 129–30

psychological impact of terrorism, 8, 10, 135, 140; and policy recommendations, 144, 145

public: perception of defensive model, 8; and policy recommendations, 144, 145; pressure on policymakers in hostage situations, 133; public perception of Shamir during first intifada, 94; and Second Lebanon War, 132; and television as "theater of terror," 35; war model as result of election pressure on politicians, 92–93; war model as result of public pressure on policymakers, 8, 10–11, 80, 85, 110, 133–34

Qablan, Jamal, 75

al-Qaeda, 141–42

Qana village shelling (1996), 93

Qawasmeh, Abdullah Abd al-Kader Husni al-, 119
Qawuqji, Fawzi al-, 18
Qibya village raid, 25
Quba, Khalil al- (Abu Yusuf), 120

Rabbani, Mohsen, 86, 88
Rabin, Yitzhak: and Arad abduction, 84; assassination of, 105–6; and division of authority among intelligence organizations, 97; and "Mothers Bus" affair, 77; and reconciliatory model, 94; return to war model, 103–6; and Savoy Hotel incident of 1975, 52; and suicide attacks, 102; and Wachsman abduction, 97–99
Rafa, Mahmoud Kassem, 129
Rafsanjani, Hashemi, 88
Rahim, Ziad, 48, 50–51
Ram, Victor, 78
Ramat Hakovesh kibbutz, 30
Ran, 15
Rantisi, Abd al-'Aziz 'ali 'Abd al-Hafiz a-, 119
Rechamim, Mordechai, 36
reconciliatory model, 1; defined/described, 2; ignored, 46; and policy recommendations, 144; and Rabin, 94
reconstruction stage of defensive model, 144–45
Red Army Faction (Germany), 38, 54–55
Red Brigades (Italy), 38
Regev, Eldad, 131
research methodology, 12–13, 154n13
Resistance of the Believers, 83
retaliatory raids, 25–26, 68; and first Lebanon war, 67–70; ineffectiveness in decreasing Palestinian violence, 25, 42–46; Karameh raid of 1968, 32–33; Qibya village raid, 25; questionable connections between targets and terrorist acts, 43–45. *See also* abductions, as counterterrorist tactic; assassinations, as counterterrorist tactic

ricin, 107
Rimawi, Ramez, 117
Rimon Unit, 5, 34–35
Rome airport attack of 1973, 43
Ron, Alik, 77
Rosan, Nawaf al-, 67–68
Rosen, Stephen, 10
Ross, Dennis, 99

Sa'adah, Umar, 119
Saadon, Ilan, 82
Sabena Airlines hijacking of 1972, 36–38
Sagi, Yehoshua, 69
Sahar, Yehezkel, 21
Said, Hussein, 68
Said, Jamal, 84
Saida, Shadi, 120
Al Saiqa, 6
Salafi jihad, 141
Salameh, Ali Hassan, 34, 45–46
Saleh, Ali Hussein, 129
Samueli, Mustafa, 23
Sanchez, Ilich Ramirez, 55
Sasportas, Avi, 82
Savoy Hotel hostage incident of 1975, 51
Sayaret Yael, 120–21
Sayeret Givati, 5, 23, 113
Sayeret Golani, 5, 59, 63, 113
Sayeret Maglan, 5, 43, 81–82, 113, 115–16, 132
Sayeret Matkal ("The Unit"), 5, 37–38; abduction of senior Hezbollah members, 85, 87–88, 132; and Bus 300 affair, 76; and competition among elite units, 9–10, 59, 64–65, 97; creation of, 37; and Entebbe Airport hostage situation, 57–62, 162n17; expansion of duties, 38; and Gurel abduction, 117; and Jihad assassination, 78–81; lack of training for hostage rescue, 51, 53; and Ma'alot school hostage crisis, 48–51; and Misgav Am kibbutz hostage situation, 63–64; and organizational culture, 64–65; and policy recommendations,

148; and Sabena Airlines hijacking of
1972, 36–38; Sayeret Matkal and Shaldag
operation of September 2007, 148–49; and
second intifada, 113; and Second Lebanon
War, 132–33; training and original man-
date, 37–38; and Wachsman abduction,
9–10, 99–101
Sayeret Nahal, 5, 113
Sayeret Shakad, 5
Sayeret Shaldag, 5, 113, 132, 148
Schneorson, Levi Yitzhak, 14
Second Lebanon War, 116, 130–34, 140, 148
Separation Fence, 122–24
September 11, 2001, 90, 143
Shacham, Mishal, 23
Shahar Unit, 19–20
Shai, 14–20
Shakher, Nasser Issa, 103
Shaldag. See Sayeret Shaldag
Shalit, Gilad, 126, 131
Shalom, Avraham, 76
Shamir, Yitzhak, 76–77, 80, 94
Shani, Esti, 62
Shani, Sami, 62
Sharif, Omar Khan, 142–43
Sharon, Ariel: and first Lebanon war, 67,
69–70; and Qibya village raid, 25; and
raid on fedayeen Samueli's house, 23; and
Rimon Unit, 34–35; and second intifada,
111, 112–13, 117–18; and shaping of Israeli
war model counterterrorism doctrine,
24, 29
Shavit Shabtai, 3
Shayetet 13, 5, 113–15, 132, 141
Shehadah, Salah Mustafa, 119
Shigenobu, Fusako, 39
Shiite Muslims, 72, 88, 141. See also Amal;
Hezbollah
Shikaki, Fathi, 104
Shiloah, Reuven, 20–21
Shimshon special forces, 5, 80–81, 114
Shin Bet, 16, 20–23
Shomron, Dan, 58, 59, 60, 77

Shukeiri, Ahmad, 32
a-Shuli, Mahmud, 119
signal intelligence (SIGINT), 17, 37, 71, 95
Simpson, Colin, 68
Sinai War (1956), 28
Six Day War of 1967, 30–32
"Skyjack Sunday," 61
Slotzker, Pavel, 131
smuggling, 126, 138
South Africa, and financing of terrorism,
124
South Lebanon Army (SLA), 84
suicide attacks, 101–3, 110, 139, 140; assas-
sinations in response to, 104–9; Buenos
Aires bombing of 1994, 88–90; and
election pressure on Peres, 92; by non-
Palestinians, 142–43; origins of tactic,
101; and public transit security, 124; and
Rabin's return to war model, 103–5; and
security guards at entrances to businesses,
123–24; Separation Fence as defense
against, 122–24
Sunni Muslims, 141. See also Hamas
Supreme Arab Committee, 17–18, 21
Switzerland, and financing of terrorism, 124
Syria: and Black September, 34; and
financing of terrorism, 141; Grapes of
Wrath understandings, 93; and Lebanon,
68; and Palestinian Liberation Front, 32;
Sayeret Matkal and Shaldag operation of
September 2007, 148–49
Syrian Social Nationalist Party, 69

Talaldin, Carlos Alberto, 88, 89
Talalka, Suleiman al-, 27–28
Tannenbaum, Elchanan, 129–30
Tatarka, Rafi, 137–38
Tel, Wasfi, 34
television as "theater of terror," 35. See also
media
"terror monkeys," 51
Terrorism and the Liberal State (Wilkin-
son), 1, 3

terrorist acts: 1950s, 23–26; 1960s, 30, 32–38; 1970s, 35–62, 66–67; 1980s, 62–65, 75–78, 83–85; 1990s, 85–90, 94, 97–106; 2000s, 116–17, 120–22, 130–31, 137–39, 142–43; attacks on Jewish targets outside of Israel, 141; financing of, 124–27, 141, 145; first wave of global terrorism in the 1970s, 38–40; and Great Arab Revolt of 1936, 14–17; percentage of different types, *139;* as psychological threat more than major threat to national security, 8, 10, 135, 144; state support for, 145; threats from non-Palestinian terrorists, 142; and UN Partition Resolution, 17–18. *See also* abductions, as terrorist act; artillery strikes on Israel; assassinations, as terrorist act; bus attacks; counterterrorism; embassy attacks; hijackings; hostage rescue operations; intifada, first; intifada, second; suicide attacks

terrorist groups, non-Palestinian, 38–39; Amal, 70, 83; global jihadist movement, 141–42; and hijackings, 54–55; international terrorist network, 90; al-Muhajiron group, 142. *See also* Hezbollah

terrorist groups, Palestinian: evolution of tactics, 7; fedayeen, 22–29; and first intifada, 81–82; foreign sponsors, 32; improved capabilities in the 2000s, 131–33, 138–40; international nature of terrorist organizations, 72; Jordan as base for (1960s), 30; limitations of, 135; overview, *6;* PLO as umbrella organization for, 32; use of media, 35. *See also* Arab Liberation Front; Black September organization; Democratic Front for the Liberation of Palestine; Fatah; Hamas; Palestine Liberation Organization; Palestinian Islamic Jihad; Palestinian Liberation Front; Popular Front for the Liberation of Palestine

Thabit, Thabit Ahmad, 119

Tiomkin, Moshe, 53

Toma, Miguel Angel, 90

torture. *See* interrogation of suspects

Touma, Maher, 91

Tzafrir, Eldad, 63

Uganda. *See* Entebbe Airport hostage situation

UN Partition Resolution, 17–20

The Unit. *See* Sayeret Matkal

Unit 101, *5,* 23–26

Unit for the Protection of Public Transport, 124

United Kingdom, 42–43, 68, 142–43

United States, 108, 125–26, 146; CIA, 33, 90

Vaknin, Yitzhak, 47–48

Varash (Committee of the Heads of Services), 20–21

Vardi, Rehaviah, 27

Velayati, Ali Akbar, 88

visual intelligence (VISINT), 66, 71

Wachsman, Nachshon, 9–10, 97–101

war model, 1; defined/described, *2;* and Din Veheshbon operation in Lebanon, 87; high cost of, 134; ineffectiveness of abductions, 85, 87–88, 93, 133–34; ineffectiveness of artillery strikes on southern Lebanon, 93; ineffectiveness of retaliatory assassinations/raids, 25, 42–46, 80, 110, 122, 126, 144; intelligence capabilities undermined by retaliatory assassinations, 42; as Israel's most common approach to terrorism, 3, 135; lives of soldiers endangered for questionable operations, 85, 93, 132–34; and Rabin's frustration with suicide attacks, 103–5; reasons for lack of success, 6–7, 135–37; as response to election pressure, 92–93; as response to public pressure, 8, 10–11, 80, 133–34, 136; and Sharon, 24, 29. *See also* abductions, as counterterrorist tactic; assassinations, as counterterrorist tactic; retaliatory raids

Wazir, Khalil al-, 78–81

Weizman, Ezer, 63
Weizmann, Chaim, 14
West Bank, 75–82; Ayash "The Engineer" as father of suicide attacks in, 104; buffer zone between West Bank and Israeli territory (Separation Fence), 122–24; control of Palestinian population in the occupied territories following 1967 war, 31–32; and Duvdevan, 80; and Egoz Unit, 114; Fatah recruitment following 1967 war, 31–32; and financing of terrorism, 126; and first intifada, 81–82; Operation Defensive Shield, 120–22; and Oslo Accords, 96; reprisal actions against Palestinian police, 120–21; and second intifada, 114–17, 120–22; terrorist acts in, 101, 120–22
Wilkinson, Paul, 1, 3
Winograd Commission, 134
World and Islam Studies Enterprise (WISE), 125

X Commission, 118

Yaari, Yedidya, 115
Yadin, Yigael, 67
Yaghmour, Jihad, 99
Ya'iri, Uzi, 53
Yamam, 5; and Bus 300 affair, 75–76; capabilities passed over by policymakers, 53, 64–65; and competition among elite units, 10, 64–65, 97; establishment of, 51; left out of hostage rescues, 10, 64, 76, 117; and "Mothers Bus" affair, 77–78; and policy recommendations, 148–49; and second intifada, 112; training, 51; and Wachsman abduction, 10, 99–101
Yamas special forces, 5, 80, 114, 148
Yaron, Amos, 69
Yassin, Adnan, 94–96
Yassin, Sheikh Ahmed, 98, 108, 119
Yasuda, Yasuyuki, 38
Yatom, Dani, 106, 109
Yatom, Ehud, 75–77, 100
Yishuv, 14–21

Zahar, Mahmoud A-, 126
Zamir, Zvi, 61
Zblodovsky, Yisrael, 16
Zegart, Amy, 7
Zeituni, Etgar, 118
Zerah, Silvan, 49
Zibri, Abu-Ali Mustafa a-, 119
Zorea, Giora, 50
Zuckerman, Erez, 115
Zwaiter, Abdel, 40–41, 43